From the Margins to the Center

**Recent Titles in the
Praeger Series in Political Communication**
Robert E. Denton, Jr., *General Editor*

The 1992 Presidential Campaign: A Communication Perspective
Edited by Robert E. Denton, Jr.

The 1992 Presidential Debates in Focus
Edited by Diana B. Carlin and Mitchell S. McKinney

Public Relations Inquiry as Rhetorical Criticism: Case Studies of Corporate Discourse and Social Influence
Edited by William N. Elwood

Bits, Bytes, and Big Brother: Federal Information Control in the Technological Age
Shannon E. Martin

Warriors' Words: A Consideration of Language and Leadership
Keith Spencer Felton

Electronic Magazines: Soft News Programs on Network Television
William C. Spragens

Political Campaign Communication: Principles and Practices, Third Edition
Judith S. Trent and Robert V. Friedenberg

Candidate Images in Presidential Elections
Edited by Kenneth L. Hacker

Earthtalk: Communication Empowerment for Environmental Action
Edited by Star A. Muir and Thomas L. Veenendall

The Clinton Presidency: Images, Issues, and Communication Strategies
Edited by Robert E. Denton, Jr., and Rachel L. Holloway

Politics, Media, and Modern Democracy: An International Study of Innovations in Electoral Campaigning and Their Consequences
Edited by David L. Swanson and Paolo Mancini

In Contempt of Congress: Postwar Press Coverage on Capitol Hill
Mark J. Rozell

From the Margins to the Center

CONTEMPORARY WOMEN AND POLITICAL COMMUNICATION

Patricia A. Sullivan
and Lynn H. Turner

Praeger Series in Political Communication

Westport, Connecticut
London

Library of Congress Cataloging-in-Publication Data

Sullivan, Patricia Ann.
    From the margins to the center : contemporary women and political communication / Patricia A. Sullivan and Lynn H. Turner.
        p. cm.—(Praeger series in political communication, ISSN 1062-5623)
    Includes bibliographical references and index.
    ISBN 0-275-94993-1 (alk. paper)
    1. Women in public life—United States. 2. Communication in politics—United States. 3. Communication—Sex differences.
    4. Women—Language. I. Turner, Lynn H. II. Title. III. Series.
    HQ1391.U5S85   1996
    320'.082—dc20   96-20707

British Library Cataloguing in Publication Data is available.

Copyright © 1996 by Patricia A. Sullivan and Lynn H. Turner

All rights reserved. No portion of this book may be reproduced, by any process or technique, without the express written consent of the publisher.

Library of Congress Catalog Card Number: 96-20707
ISBN: 0-275-94993-1
ISSN: 1062-5623

First published in 1996

Praeger Publishers, 88 Post Road West, Westport, CT 06881
An imprint of Greenwood Publishing Group, Inc.

Printed in the United States of America

The paper used in this book complies with the Permanent Paper Standard issued by the National Information Standards Organization (Z39.48-1984).

10 9 8 7 6 5 4 3 2 1

Copyright Acknowledgment

The authors and publisher are grateful for permission to reproduce portions of the following copyrighted material:

The lines from "Culture and Anarchy," from *The Fact of a Doorframe: Poems Selected and New, 1950–1984* by Adrienne Rich. Copyright © 1984 by Adrienne Rich. Copyright © 1975, 1978 by W. W. Norton & Company, Inc. Copyright © 1981 by Adrienne Rich. Reprinted by permission of the author and W. W. Norton & Company, Inc.

For Our Families—

Ray, Eathel, Joe

Ted, Sabrina, Roberta, Jerry

Contents

Illustrations	ix
Series Foreword *by Robert E. Denton, Jr.*	xi
Acknowledgments	xv
Introduction	xvii
1. Politics, Power, and Gender	1
2. Gender, Moral Boundaries, and Political Communication	29
3. Denying Politics: The Strange Case of Lani Guinier	53
4. Power and Politics: A Case Study of Hillary Rodham Clinton	69
5. Re-Visioning Moral Boundaries: A Case Study of Janet Reno	95
6. Re-Visioning Political Communication	113
References	127
Index	145

Illustrations

Lani Guinier	54
Hillary Rodham Clinton and Senator Bob Dole discussing health care reform, February 1993	70
Hillary Rodham Clinton speaking on health care reform	72
Hillary Rodham Clinton overseeing preparations for the Clintons' first state dinner, February 1993	83
Janet Reno	94
Caricatures of Janet Reno	109

Series Foreword

Those of us from the discipline of communication studies have long believed that communication is prior to all other fields of inquiry. In several other forums I have argued that the essence of politics is "talk" or human interaction.[1] Such interaction may be formal or informal, verbal or nonverbal, public or private but it is always persuasive, forcing us consciously or subconsciously to interpret, to evaluate, and to act. Communication is the vehicle for human action.

From this perspective, it is not surprising that Aristotle recognized the natural kinship of politics and communication in his writings *Politics and Rhetoric*. In the former, he establishes that humans are "political beings [who] alone of all the animals [are] furnished with the faculty of language."[2] And in the latter, he begins his systematic analysis of discourse by proclaiming that "rhetorical study, in its strict sense, is concerned with modes of persuasion."[3] Thus, it was recognized over 2,300 years ago that politics and communication go hand in hand because they are essential parts of human nature.

Back in 1981, Dan Nimmo and Keith Sanders proclaimed that political communication was an emerging field.[4] Although its origin, as noted, dates back centuries, a "self-consciously cross-disciplinary" focus began in the late 1950s. Thousands of books and articles later, colleges and universities offer a variety of graduate and undergraduate coursework in the area in such diverse departments as communication, mass communication, journalism, political science, and sociology.[5] In Nimmo and Sanders's early assessment, the "key areas of inquiry" included rhetorical analysis, propaganda analysis, attitude change studies, voting studies, government and the news media, functional and systems analyses, technological changes, media technologies, campaign techniques, and research techniques.[6] In a survey of the state of the field in 1984, the same authors and Lynda Kaid found additional, more specific areas of concern such as the presidency, political polls, public opinion, debates, and advertising to name a few.[7] Since the first study, they also noted a shift away from the rather strict behavioral approach.

Five years later, Dan Nimmo and David Swanson argued that "political communication has developed some identity as a more or less distinct domain of scholarly work."[8] The scope and concerns of the area have further expanded to include critical theories and cultural studies. While there is no precise definition, method, or disciplinary home of the area of inquiry, its primary domain is the role, processes, and effects of communication within the context of politics broadly defined.

The editors of *Political Communication Yearbook: 1984* noted that "more things are happening in the study, teaching, and practice of political communication than can be captured within the space limitations of the relatively few publications available."[9] In addition, they argued that the backgrounds of "those involved in the field [are] so varied and pluralist in outlook and approach, . . . it [is] a mistake to adhere slavishly to any set format in shaping the content."[10] And more recently, Nimmo and Swanson called for "ways of overcoming the unhappy consequences of fragmentation within a framework that respects, encourages, and benefits from diverse scholarly commitments, agendas, and approaches."[11]

In agreement with these assessments of the area and with gentle encouragement, Praeger established the Praeger Series in Political Communication. The series is open to all qualitative and quantitative methodologies as well as contemporary and historical studies. The key to characterizing the studies in the series is the focus on communication variables or activities within a political context or dimension. As of this writing, nearly forty volumes have been published and there are numerous impressive works forthcoming. Scholars from the disciplines of communication, history, journalism, political science, and sociology have participated in the series.

I am, without shame or modesty, a fan of the series. The joy of serving as its editor is in participating in the dialogue of the field of political communication and in reading the contributors' works. I invite you to join me.

Robert E. Denton, Jr.

NOTES

1. See Robert E. Denton, Jr., *The Symbolic Dimensions of the American Presidency* (Prospect Heights, IL: Waveland Press, 1982); Robert E. Denton, Jr., and Gary

Woodward, *Political Communication in America* (New York: Praeger, 1985; 2nd ed., 1990) Robert E. Denton, Jr., and Dan Hahn, *Presidential Communication* (New York: Praeger, 1986); and Robert E. Denton, Jr., *The Primetime Presidency of Ronald Reagan* (New York: Praeger, 1988).

2. Aristotle, *The Politics of Aristotle*, trans. Ernest Baker (New York: Oxford University Press, 1970), p. 5.

3. Aristotle, *Rhetoric*, trans. Rhys Roberts (New York: The Modern Library, 1954), p. 22.

4. Dan Nimmo and Keith Sanders, "Introduction: The Emergence of Political Communications as a Field," in *Handbook of Political Communication*, ed. Dan Nimmo and Keith Sanders (Beverly Hills, CA: Sage, 1981), pp. 11–36.

5. Ibid., p. 15.

6. Ibid., pp. 17–27.

7. Keith Sanders, Lynda Kaid, and Dan Nimmo, eds., *Political Communication Yearbook: 1984* (Carbondale: Southern Illinois University, 1985), pp. 283–308.

8. Dan Nimmo and David Swanson, "The Field of Political Communication: Beyond the Voter Persuasion Paradigm," in *New Directions in Political Communication*, ed. David Swanson and Dan Nimmo (Beverly Hills, CA: Sage, 1990), p. 8.

9. Sanders, Kaid, and Nimmo, *Political Communication Yearbook: 1984*, p. xiv.

10. Ibid.

11. Nimmo and Swanson, "The Field of Political Communication," p. 11.

Acknowledgments

Collaboration on this book brought us together as friends and colleagues; as we completed it, we felt a bit sad. Of course, we know we'll work together on other projects centering on communication and gender issues.

From the Margins to the Center: Contemporary Women and Political Communication consumed much of our time over the past two years. As we struggled with articulating the role that rhetoric can play in re-visioning politics, we appreciated our family and friends. Ray, Ted, and Sabrina supported us in many ways during research trips to each others' homes. Our parents, Eathel, Joe, Roberta, and Jerry, sacrificed time with us as we defined and redefined the rhetorical approaches highlighted in this book.

Pat also wishes to thank her dear friend Carole Levin for encouraging her to pursue this study as well as many others. Trish Weenolsen has offered warm support over many years. Steve Goldzwig has waited patiently for Pat to finish this book and return to a number of their coauthored essays. Lynn Spangler provided ongoing encouragement for this study. Pat was inspired by her nieces, Rachel and Kate, to examine factors that deny women access to political discourse. SUNY–New Paltz assisted this project in a number of ways. Rob Miraldi, chair of the Communication and Media Department, encouraged Pat to apply for a course release to facilitate completion of this project. A. David Kline, Dean of Liberal Arts, and William Vasse, Vice- President for Academic Affairs, approved this course release. A Research and Creative Projects Grant from SUNY–New Paltz made it possible to reproduce photos to accompany the book's case studies.

Lynn also wishes to thank the College of Communication at Marquette

University, which underwrote some of the expenses of this book both through research grants and through indirect support, such as copying and secretarial assistance. Elizabeth Harding, a graduate research assistant, provided excellent assistance for two years. The McNair Program at Marquette University offered research support in the form of two wonderful summer research assistants, Khadijah Ali-Coleman and Daniel Zarate, as well as travel funding to present sections of this book at conferences. Rich West, Lynn's colleague, deserves thanks for his patience as he waited for her to finish this project, enabling her to devote time to their work together.

Introduction

Scientists.... tell us that bifurcations or evolutionary branchings in chemical and biological systems involve a large element of chance. But as the evolutionary theorist Erwin Laszlo points out, bifurcations in human social systems also involve a large element of choice. Humans, he points out, "have the ability to act consciously, and collectively," exercising foresight to "choose their own evolutionary path." And he adds that in our "crucial epoch" we "cannot leave the selection of the next step in the evolution of human society to chance. We must plan for it, consciously and purposefully." . . .

Initially this may seem an impossibly difficult task. But as we have seen, our views of reality—of what is possible and desirable—are a product of history.

—Riane Eisler, *The Chalice and the Blade*
(1988, pp. 186–187)

Sometimes in a brief woman-to-woman glance across a committee room, we look at one another with unmistakable frustration, sometimes amazement. We wonder whether we'll ever be the kind of players we should be. We wonder whether we'll ever change the system so that every kind of voice is heard, no matter whether it comes in bass or soprano. But then another day comes and one of us notches up some small victory—an amendment added to a bill maybe, or just a strong op-ed in a newspaper on a critical issue. And we take a collective deep breath and think that we have a fighting chance . . . and we know we will keep on fighting.

—Marjorie Margolies-Mezvinsky, *A Woman's Place . . . The Freshmen Women Who Changed the Face of Congress* (1994, p. 87)

We began this book with the belief that, as Sandra Lipsitz Bem (1993) argues, we view the world through distorting lenses (or assumptions). One of these assumptions posits that men and women are polar opposites. Although we agree with Bem that this is a distortion, a social construction, or as Eisler might say, an historical artifact, this lens permeates social institutions and both women and men are affected by it. One of the outcomes of this assumption of polarity has been to divide the world into two spheres—public and private—and assign men dominion over the public and women authority in the private realm. Further, we are affected at the level of belief systems which may cause us to interpret women's behavior differently from men's. Additionally, our own behavioral choices may also be influenced by social expectations regarding what is appropriate to our sex. Thus, social life is very different for men and women. As a result, we began our investigation of women in public leadership roles with the belief that women can offer something unique to the political landscape.

Senator Barbara Boxer (Democrat-California) comments on this "unique" perspective in her (1994) book *Strangers in the Senate: Politics and the New Revolution of Women in America*. Boxer states that there are clear differences between women and men and that for her these differences were starkly illustrated by a debate in the Senate Judiciary Committee concerning anti-stalking legislation which Boxer sponsored. The two women members of this Senate subcommittee were Senators Dianne Feinstein (Democrat-California) and Carol Moseley-Braun (Democrat-Illinois). Both of these women had themselves been stalked. Senator Feinstein brought her personal story to the discussion in the Judiciary Committee. It is this personal perspective with issues and events that women can bring to the public debate. Boxer concludes, "[t]oo many women are stalked. Too many women are beaten. Too many women are raped. Too many women are harassed. And women in the Senate will make sure these problems receive new and much-needed attention" (p. 230). In this book, we are interested in the ways that women bring their unique perspectives to public discourse. We set out to discover how women are *redefining* the public leadership realm through their communication—both in their expressions of different experiences and in their choices of communication styles and strategies.

In our efforts to discover how women are re-visioning public life as well as accommodating to the constraints placed upon them in the public domain, we drew extensively on ideas advanced by Bem in her 1993 book *The Lenses of Gender: Transforming the Debate on Sexual Inequality* and the framework suggested by Joan C. Tronto (1993) in her book *Moral Boundaries: A Political Argument for an Ethic of Care*. We believe it is particularly instructive to examine women's political communication through the combined matrix of Bem's lenses of gender and Tronto's moral boundaries. Bem's lenses provide us with a context for investigating discrimination against women in the public sphere. The lenses form underlying, foundational assumptions in Western culture that shape people's conceptions of social reality. And, as Bem points out, "they also shape the more material things—like unequal pay and inadequate day care—that constitute social reality itself" (p. 2). Tronto's work specifies how looking through Bem's lenses creates moral boundaries which place women as outsiders in the political arena. Tronto argues that women's voices are muffled and their arguments rendered ineffective by the presence of these boundaries, yet the boundaries cannot be removed entirely because we need some separation between moral and political arguments, as well as between public and private life. Thus, what needs to occur is a redrawing or a re-visioning of these moral boundaries in an effort to hear women's voices as well as the other voices outside the boundaries. By the same token, Bem suggests that we need to look *at* rather than *through* the lenses of gender that she identifies, in an effort to see more clearly.

In the first two chapters of this book, we lay the groundwork for our study of contemporary women political communicators. To do this, in Chapter 1 we explicate Bem's three lenses of gender: (1) men and women are polar opposites, (2) men are inherently the dominant and superior sex, and (3) both 1 and 2 are "natural." The outcome of looking through these lenses is that women are denied a hearing in the public realm and the public and private domains remain bifurcated. In this chapter we also provide our definitions of "political communication" and "political women" as well as our rationale for selecting the women we profile in the case studies in subsequent chapters. In Chapter 2 we discuss Tronto's three moral boundaries: (1) the boundary between morality and politics (suggesting that these two ideas are distinct and unrelated to each other), (2) the moral point of view boundary (the notion that moral judgments are made from a disinterested stance), and (3) the boundary between public and private life. We suggest that Bem's and Tronto's ideas inform each other and work together to form a framework for our investigations. Also in Chapter 2, we discuss three strategies that political women use to confront the boundaries and challenge the lenses of gender. These strategies include (1) denying, (2) confronting and accommodating, and (3) re-visioning.

We define the denying strategy as an expression of faith in a rationalist paradigm. Deniers believe that they will be successful if they follow the rules set out by the system. Thus, deniers fail to acknowledge that they are constrained by boundaries. Confronting and accommodating is another strategy that is invested in a rationalist paradigm. Rather than simply following the rules, however, confronting and accommodating requires the rhetor to finesse the system by striking the appropriate balance between confronting the boundaries and accommodating to them. In this strategy the rhetor is aware that she is constrained but believes that she can surmount the boundaries through her careful and strategic communication. The final strategy we discuss, re-visioning, is an effort to, in Tronto's terms, "redraw" the boundaries. Re-visioning strategically places care as central in the political process and in political decision-making. A rhetor using re-visioning challenges the boundaries by illustrating the relationship between politics and morality, the personal and the public, and by contextualizing political discourse.

In Chapters 3, 4, and 5 we provide case studies of three contemporary women who, especially in each particular case we focus on, exemplify each of the three strategies. In Chapter 3 we discuss Lani Guinier and her discourse (or lack of it) from the time President Clinton announced her nomination for Assistant Attorney General for Civil Rights in April 1993, until he withdrew her name from consideration in June 1993. We argue that Guinier's cooperation with the White House's orders for her silence reflects a strategy of denial. We believe Guinier has moved to a different strategy since June 1993, but during the short period that she was a nominee, she operated as a denier. In this chapter we elucidate how Guinier's strategy, combined with media representations of her and her ideas, cost the nation a chance to hear a voice from the margins. We pay particular attention to how the media used Guinier's dual status as a woman and an African American to further marginalize her.

Chapter 4 profiles Hillary Rodham Clinton and her testimony to the House and Senate subcommittees about the Clinton health care plan. We assert that Rodham Clinton used a strategy of confrontation and accommodation whereby she alternately showed she had "mastered" the rules of rational discourse while indicating that she was also a traditional woman—a mom, a wife, and a daughter. While we noted a change in Guinier's discourse after the case we explicated, we argue that Rodham Clinton has been consistent in her strategy choice throughout her tenure as First Lady. In this chapter we also point out how the media coverage of Rodham Clinton has both responded to and possibly shaped her rhetorical choice.

We focus on Attorney General Janet Reno in Chapter 5. The specific case we examine is her discourse after the fire at the Branch Davidian complex in Waco, Texas in April 1993. We argue that Reno approached this discourse with a strategy aimed at re-visioning the moral boundaries that Tronto delineates. Reno spoke as both a private person and a public figure. She contextualized her decision-making and she went beyond justifying the decision to move past a "morality first" or "politics first" stance. Instead, she indicated that morality and politics are intertwined. In this case study, as with the other two, we address the ways the media responded to Reno. We argue that her re-visioning strategy was positively received in the media but as a woman, Reno was not completely immune from mediated attempts to maintain the boundaries and the lenses of gender. Although Reno received positive reviews for her handling of the questions surrounding Waco, she was also caricatured in the media as a masculine old maid with no fashion sense.

In our final chapter we confront some of the implications and limitations of our analysis. First, we note that, although this book concentrates on women's voices, it is possible for men to choose a strategy of re-visioning. And, as our case studies testify, not all women situate care centrally in their rhetoric or try to redraw the boundaries that exclude voices from a public hearing. Although we have examined contemporary political women throughout the book and focused on their unique contributions to the public dialogue, we do not wish to conclude with the idea that the differences between women and men are unbridgeable or that they should continue to be primary in the way we see the world. Therefore, in this last chapter we caution against making difference paramount. The stronger the voices of difference, the more we are likely to hear the rhetoric of divisiveness that is the antithesis of re-visioning.

This book does not represent the first call for a transformation of political discourse and public policy that places conceptions of care and nurturance—values usually associated with women—centrally. Tronto's and Bem's work as well as Julia T. Wood's (1994) book, *Who Cares? Women, Care, and Culture*, make the same point. Helen M. Sterk and Lynn H. Turner (1994) argue along similar lines by stating, "[a] key challenge to communication and gender scholars is how to reconcile (gender-based) difference with (human) similarity" (p. 216). In accomplishing this re-visioning or reconciliation, we need to place equal value on community and diversity. In a speech delivered recently at the Speech Communication Association's annual convention, David Zarefsky (1995) spoke cogently about the need for renewing "our commitment to American community" (p. 2). Zarefsky argues for a dialectic between community and diversity saying, "[p]ursuing either [community or diversity] alone is destructive. We need not the logical consistency of making a choice but the rhetorical accommodation of embracing both. The tension between goals should not be resolved but managed" (p. 6). We assert that one way to manage this tension and promote greater community, without obscuring differences, is through re-visioning strategies that redraw the moral boundaries and look *at* the lenses of gender.

Interestingly, the definition of care and compassion may itself be a contested site. The *Chicago Tribune* recently published a front page story headlined "The Politics of Compassion." In this article, Democratic and Republican views of compassion were presented and they differed sharply. "The Democratic argument typically goes like this: Republicans with their budget cuts are heartless and cruel to the poor, the elderly and children. Republican rhetoric stands in sharp contrast: Democrats have built a huge social welfare structure that America can no longer afford and, in the process have created a culture of dependence and irresponsibility" (Neikirk, 1995, p. A1). As we point out in Chapter 6, re-visioning does not mean that Democrats and Republicans will stop disagreeing, even over the meaning of compassion. What may change is the discussion and decision-making surrounding such controversies. In Chapter 6 we discuss some of the ways public discourse may change as a result of re-visioning.

Finally, in Chapter 6 we observe that our own rhetorical choices bear examination also. We acknowledge that the women who are the subjects of our case studies are privileged speakers in many ways, despite the fact that they are constrained by boundaries and stereotypes of women. Therefore, we point to future studies which can examine the perspectives of women who do not have access to good educational opportunities, relative wealth, and traditional power. We agree with Karen A. Foss and Sonja K. Foss (1991) that public address itself could be re-visioned to make space for "the eloquence of women's lives." Foss and Foss argue that letter writing and newsletters, gardening, quilting, shopping, and other ritual communication activities in women's lives deserve attention and study. We do not disagree with this argument but we also believe that the values that undergird political institutions must shift before a large audience will be able to hear the articulation of these alternative visions of influence.

Finally, we hope this book demonstrates the utility of the framework we have created, from combining Bem's and Tronto's work, for examining the rhetorical choices contemporary women are making in political discourse. Our applications of this frame to the three cases illustrate a range of options and focus on the promise that re-visioning offers as a way of opening rhetorical space for voices on the margins.

1

Politics, Power, and Gender

light welling, searching the shadows

Matilda Joslyn Gage; Harriet Tubman;
Ida B. Wells-Barnett; Maria Mitchell;
Anna Howard Shaw; Sojourner Truth;
Elizabeth Cady Stanton; Harriet Hosmer;
Clara Barton; Harriet Beecher Stowe;
Ida Husted Harper; Ernestine Rose

and all those without names
because of their short and ill-environed lives
—Adrienne Rich, "Culture and Anarchy"
(1984, p. 278) in the *Fact of a Doorframe*

Women dwell on the margins of political discourse and a number of scholars have documented factors in Western culture that consign them there. As Susan Moller Okin observes, "[i]t must be recognized at once that the great tradition of political philosophy consists, generally speaking, of writings by men, for men, and about men" (1979, p. 5). This state of affairs results from "our Aristotelian hangover" (Stiehm, 1983, p. 31) because "Aristotle's theory of the household" as outlined in the *Politics* (1961) proposes that the "adult male rules 'naturally' over the slave, who is without the faculty of deliberation, the child who has it in a yet immature form, and the woman whose capacity 'remains inconclusive'" (Stiehm, 1983, p. 32). Additionally, Elizabeth V. Spelman (1983) indicates that Aristotle's definitions of rational and irrational elements of the soul undergird his argument "that women are naturally subordinate to men" (p. 21). These beliefs reinforce contemporary practices that push women away from the center of political discourse.

In this chapter we provide an overview of belief structures in Western culture that place women on the margins of the political world. We also discuss our definitions for "political communication" and "political women." These definitions inform this book as well as provide a rationale for our selection of particular women for analysis. Finally, we provide a summary of research on women as political communicators and situate our work in terms of that context.

BELIEF STRUCTURES IN WESTERN CULTURE

In Western culture fundamental belief structures have framed women and men and limited their human possibilities (Bem, 1993). Although these belief structures are human creations, Sandra Lipsitz Bem argues that human beings forget they created these structures and instead view them as naturally occurring. In the *Lenses of Gender: Transforming the Debate on Sexual Inequality* (1993), Bem summarizes taken-for-granted beliefs about "natural" differences between women and men that inform Western cultural experience—including Western political cultural experience. Through much of the nineteenth century, these "natural" differences were articulated as religious beliefs. Later in the nineteenth century, and even in our own time, scientists have argued for natural differences on biological grounds.

Because these beliefs seemed so natural, Bem claims that until the first wave of feminism in the nineteenth century, U.S. citizens did not see any inconsistency between statements concerning equality included in the country's foundational documents, such as the Constitution and the Declaration of Independence, and the denial of equal rights for women. Jean Bethke Elshtain (1995) comments on this paradox by stating that although women and slaves were omitted from the formal definition of equality, "the general principle [of equality] named both a partial and imperfect reality and a continuing aspiration" (p. 68). Thus, Elshtain maintains, people were able to balance the ideal of equality with the real state of the country, which denied equality to some of its citizens.

This state of affairs changed with the first wave of feminism in the nineteenth century, which brought about fundamental political equality for women, and the second wave of feminism, initiated in the 1960s, which identified sexual discrimination issues. During the second wave of feminism, for example, many citizens became aware of pay inequities in the workplace.

We argue, in accord with Bem, that although the first and second waves of feminism encouraged important changes for women and men in terms of gender roles, much work remains to be done. First- and second-wave feminists sought equal access for women trying to enter institutions—including political institutions—created by men. These feminists did not question the shapes of the institutions themselves. More recently, some researchers, ourselves among them, have committed themselves to exposing those assumptions about sex and gender that Bem points out insidiously permeate our institutions, our discourse, and our psyches. Through this subtle process, these assumptions color our cultural life, perpetuating and recreating male power over generations.[1] Bem refers to these assumptions as the "lenses of gender" and we join her in encouraging U.S. citizens to look *at* rather than *through* them. When people examine their assumptions and look *at* the lenses, they will recognize that the next step for feminism is a cultural analysis examining the complex subtleties of power and care expressed by both women and men (see, for example Foss and Griffin, 1995; Sterk, 1995; Wood 1992, 1994). Institutional stasis and embedded cultural values need continued examination, however, if women and men are to move forward together, transforming political power structures.

We suggest this continued examination focus on the three "lenses of gender"—androcentrism, gender polarization, and biological essentialism—that Bem asserts reproduce male power in a systematic fashion.[2] The three lenses, taken for granted as gendered life scripts by many U.S. citizens, function insidiously, steering women and men to embrace particular roles.[3] We agree with Bem that institutional structures must be questioned and transformed in order to change the ground for the debate over sexual equality. Looking "at" rather than "through" the three lenses of gender provides a starting point for examining the foundations of political institutions and the discourses that legitimate them.

Androcentrism

The lens of androcentrism, or "male-centeredness," goes beyond the assumption of male superiority (Bem, 1993). In U.S. society the lens of androcentrism functions subtly as a taken-for-granted, unspoken norm that casts all female experiences as "other" (as in "other" than what is normal). In sum, the lens of androcentrism frames male experience as the norm and female experience as a deviation from the norm. Many aspects of culture function to keep this lens in place. Language, for example, maintains androcentrism by highlighting men and male experience as normative. For instance, a senior at Virginia Military Institute, preparing to put first-year cadets through their paces, made the following statement reflecting taken-for-granted assumptions about the male as standard. He said of the regimen at the military institute that "it builds character, and brings out the man" (Allen, 1995, p. B6). This speaker clearly believed that the standard human person is male.

Marjorie Margolies-Mezvinsky (1994) provides additional examples of cultural mechanisms that foster this lens in her book, *A Woman's Place . . . The Freshmen Women Who Changed the Face of Congress*. Margolies-Mezvinsky cites Karan English as stating that men in Congress refer to each other as "congressmen" or "the Honorable" or "my esteemed colleague" while congresswomen are called by their first names. Further, the book recounts stories of congresswomen who were stopped by security guards, asked to leave members only sections, and completely ignored by others on the Hill who simply assumed that they could not be members of Congress. Here men are the expected, the standard, while women are deviations, either unnoticed or gawked at as "other."

Vice-President Bush revealed his taken-for-granted, androcentric biases during the 1984 vice-presidential debate with Geraldine Ferraro when he failed to honor the form of address chosen by Ferraro for the debate. She asked to be addressed as "congresswoman." Although all involved agreed to this form of address prior to the debate, Bush addressed Ferraro as "Mrs." Ferraro, of course, kept her own name when she married John Zaccaro. Bush's failure to honor the form of address selected by Ferraro implied that he could not conceive of a female identity independent of its connection with a male identity (see Sullivan, 1989).

Although Bem lauds second-wave feminist writers such as Kate Millett (1969) and Adrienne Rich (1976) for highlighting the significance of male power as patriarchal power, she suggests that the concept of androcentrism adds a further dimension to understanding male dominance in U.S. society. The concept of androcentrism "goes beyond telling *who* is in power to tell *how* their power is culturally and psychologically reproduced" (Bem, 1993, pp. 40–41). In other words, the concept of androcentrism encourages us to look at the deep structures of power and their salience over time.

The development of androcentrism in Western U.S. society (and more specifically its manifestations in development of the law) can be traced to its roots in Judeo-Christian theology, ancient Greek philosophy, and Freudian psychoanalytic theory.[4] The history of woman as "other" in Judeo-Christian tradition, as delineated by Bem and John Phillips (1984), is grounded in the significance of Eve as "everywoman." Eve, who succumbed to temptation in the Garden of Eden, is the "other" or "transgressor" against society's norms, as every woman after her becomes. Eve's crimes, according to Phillips, included unbridled sexuality, disobedience, and vanity. Phillips argues for the importance of the story of Eve by saying "her story, along with other stories, other images, other ideas, shapes a Western ideology of women. Through the developing history of this theme, continually reworked and retold not only in theology but also in art, music, literature, law, and social custom, the nature and destiny of Woman in the Western world is disclosed" (p. xiii). Riane Eisler (1988) argues, in the *Chalice and the Blade* that Eve's identification with evil and deviance was a means of discrediting the Goddess and discouraging Goddess worship. Eisler's explanation of the political motives possessed by the authors of the creation story argues forcefully against the assumption of naturalness that grounds this lens of androcentrism.

Rosemary Radford Reuther (1983) provides a fuller picture of the emergence of woman as "other" in the Judeo-Christian tradition. She notes that "two primary myths" in Western culture have "scapegoated women as the primordial cause of evil" (p. 65). From Hesiod's *Work and Days* came the story of Pandora—the Greek version of the "fall." Prometheus stole fire from the gods and presented it to the human world. Zeus decided to punish "mankind" for receiving such a powerful gift from Prometheus and sent another gift in the form of Pandora, "endowed with all female graces but filled within with 'falsehood, treacherous thoughts, and a thievish nature'" (p. 166). In the popular Greek myth, Pandora opens the box and releases all trouble upon "mankind." As Reuther observes, "For Hesiod, Pandora stands for woman herself as a bane upon males, without whom they would live a happy and blessed existence" (p. 166).[5] Pandora, then, is the Greek version of the Judeo-Christian Eve, but, as Reuther notes, "The Hebrew myth of Eve has had much greater cultural impact than that of Pandora, since Christian theology has understood it to be divine revelation" (p. 166).[6]

Bem identifies another significant misogynistic legacy from ancient Greek philosophy. Plato and Aristotle envisioned a social hierarchy that cast women as inherently lower (along with slaves) in the social hierarchy. Although Okin (1979) notes that Aristotle and Plato differed greatly in their philosophies, both reached the same conclusion about the role of women in society. Okin traces Plato's ideas about women through *The Phaedrus*, *The Republic*, and *The Laws* and concludes that a woman ultimately emerges as the possession of a man. Aristotle, according to Okin, "determines that woman is inferior by considering the functions she performs and the relevant qualities that she manifests in Athenian society" (p. 93). Of course, as Okin observes, Aristotle did not take into account that women played particular roles in the Athenian *polis* because they were dominated by men. Instead, Aristotle presents the roles of women (and slaves) as representing a natural hierarchy.

Dale Spender (1989), in the title of her book, the *Writing or the Sex? Or Why You Don't Need to Read Women's Writing to Know It's No Good*, concurs that hierarchy based on sex is seen as natural. The book title speaks for itself as she argues that "eminent literary men" view writing as a male activity and claim "they would like to appoint a woman [to a faculty position] but there simply isn't one who is qualified—who comes up to standard [the male standard]" (p. 36). By neatly omitting any context, the argument about men's superiority can be justified as "natural." Women are defined, a priori, as inferior.

Furthermore, the belief in hierarchy informed the Enlightenment thought that framed the U.S. Constitution and the constitutions of all modern democracies. Although the belief in hierarchy might seem incompatible with the Enlightenment belief concerning individual natural and inalienable rights, the intellectual founders of modern democracies believed those rights could be denied to the "others" (i.e., women, blacks, whites who did not own property) (Bem, pp. 54–55)[7] while being maintained for themselves. Finally, the roots of androcentrism can be traced to Freud's assertion that even the child recognizes that the female body is inferior to the male body. Freud can be credited with a particularly clever intellectual stroke in naturalizing the idea of woman as "other." As Bem notes, by making this distinction come from the child's perspective rather than the theorist's, Freud made the androcentric lens seem natural and inevitable. In sum, theological, philosophical, and psychological androcentric influences framed woman as "other" in societies shaped by Western thought.

A number of scholars have addressed the significance of androcentrism for "the politics of naming" and communication. Hélène Cixous (1981) says any "political reflection" begins with "reflections on language" and the awareness that men have had the power to name reality. When we pose the question, "What is it?" and ask for a reply, "we are already caught in masculine interrogation." "Masculine interrogation" or a masculine naming of the world "orders the constitution of meaning" (p. 45). As Dale Spender notes in *Man Made Language* (1980), citing Edward Sapir (1970) and Benjamin Whorf (1976), naming is a value-laden political process rather than "a neutral or random process" (p. 163). Those who have the power in society have the power to name—to privilege their definitions of reality. Spender agrees with Bem, saying that in Western societies privileged white males have had the power to name and "influence reality" (p. 165). Additionally, they have the power to "influence reality" on an ongoing basis because "when one group holds a monopoly on naming, its bias is embedded in the names it supplies and these 'new' names help to maintain and strengthen its initial bias" (p. 164).[8] As Casey Miller and Kate Swift (1977) argued almost twenty years ago, until very recently the people who made language their "special province" (and who exerted the most influence on language) were male. When these men wrote about language or developed new vocabulary, their perspective was male. When they thought about women it was in terms of their relationship to men—as wives, daughters, lovers. Language clearly reflects these perspectives and perpetuates these biases.

In her analysis of the English language, Spender (1980) discusses the politics of naming in religion and notes: "When one has the power to name, it appears that one can structure almost any reality without undue interference from the evidence" (p. 176). For example, Spender cites Elaine Pagels (1976) and Mary Daly (1973, 1974, 1975, 1978) on the significance of naming God as *exclusively* masculine (p. 166). According to Daly, woman is cast as "other"—as the negative—when the primary category is seen as the category "male." These researchers concur that women are defined into the category "other" when the power to name and define is exclusively men's.

The politics of naming, controlling, and framing reality will emerge as particularly important in our study of women as political communicators. Due to the influences of Judeo-Christian theology, ancient Greek philosophy, and psychoanalytic theory on Western culture (including U.S. culture) public institutions, including political institutions, became "homes" or "natural" niches for privileged males. For citizens viewing these institutions through the taken-for-granted lens of androcentrism, women seem "out of place." The lens of androcentrism provides the basis for the development of the second lens of gender polarization.

Gender Polarization

When male-centeredness is the norm, it becomes a method for organizing social life within a culture (Bem, 1993). As we look *through* the lens of gender polarization, we assume that women and men "naturally" adopt opposite sets of gender roles. The lens of gender polarization (the legacy of ancient philosophical thought, Judeo-Christian theology, and psychoanalytic theorizing) limits human potential in two ways.

First, this lens provides completely different "scripts" for males and females, reifying their opposition to one another. A second limitation is the definition of any deviation from the scripts as wrong religiously, biologically, and psychologically. When these two limits are combined, their effect constructs a link between sex and gender that reifies the opposition between males and females and between masculinity and femininity. Certainly, all the Western cultural influences that shaped the androcentric lens shaped the gender polarization lens.

In her analysis of the gender polarization lens, Bem traces gender polarization to late-nineteenth- and early-twentieth-century social scientists and physicians who argued that children "naturally" adopt particular gender roles or scripts.[9] A number of movements in psychology and psychiatry have specifically conceptualized a natural connection between physiological and psychological attributes. Kohlberg's (1969) cognitive development theory, for example, postulates deviancy for failure to appropriately make this connection.

Bem cites the work of two scholars, Helen Thompson Woolley and Leta Stetter Hollingworth who, in 1903, as experimental psychology was emerging as a discipline, published a study outlining findings from their lab studies of female-male difference. They argued that their tests indicated that women and men were equal in many capabilities including: intelligence, motor skills, and sensory and affective processes. Lewis Terman, the creator of the Stanford-Binet IQ Test, was impressed with the findings of Woolley and Hollingworth, but was determined to develop a test to demonstrate his belief that women and men differ in their mental capabilities. Terman and his coauthor, Catharine Cox Miles (1936), constructed a Masculinity-Femininity test that took as its starting point taken-for-granted, "natural" assumptions about the components of femininity and masculinity. The test offered "either-or" options, thereby precluding any possibility that a test taker could emerge with both a masculine and a feminine orientation. Of course, it never occurred to Terman and Miles that they were measuring a test taker's "adherence to the cultural norms of masculinity and femininity that were operative in twentieth-century America" (Bem, p. 104). Through their research, Terman and Miles added scientific legitimacy to deeply embedded Western cultural assumptions—all the androcentric assumptions discussed previously—about gender. Other tests following the Terman and Miles model were developed and in 1980, the American Psychiatric Association's Diagnostic Statistical Manual included a new category—"gender identity disorders" (p. 106).

The psychological research, then, was framed by researchers' assumptions concerning gender polarization. These assumptions about masculinity and femininity informed Lawrence Kohlberg's research in the 1960s and 1970s. Kohlberg argued that children recognize patterns of masculinity and femininity and actively seek to internalize those patterns. For Kohlberg, children "naturally" sought to conform to these patterns. Of course, as Bem points out, Kohlberg's assumptions about gender blinded him to the possibility that children are compelled by *culture* rather than *nature* to embrace these particular patterns.[10] When we view particular patterns as "natural" rather than as the products of culture, the world is neatly divided perceptually along the lines of "gender schematicity."

Gender schematicity is the internalizing of the gender polarization in the culture, the learned readiness to see reality as carved naturally into polarized sex and gender categories, not carved—whether naturally or unnaturally—into some other set of categories. It is the imposition of a gender-based classification on social reality, the sorting of persons, attributes, behaviors, and other things on the basis of the polarized definitions of masculinity and femininity that prevail in the culture, rather than on the basis of other dimensions that could serve equally well. (Bem, p. 125)

In 1909, Clara E. Haase, a student at Milwaukee Downer Women's College, expressed the gender polarization lens in her senior essay entitled "Ideal Education for Girls." She wrote, "It were far better not to class girls with boys while receiving their education, the most important reason being that they are so entirely different and therefore should be taught diversely" (p. 10). More recently, Shannon Faulkner's two-and-one-half-year struggle to gain admission to the Citadel, a military institution in South Carolina, speaks to the continued effect gender polarization exerts on U.S. culture. When Faulkner left the Citadel at the end of the initial "hell week," the *New York Times*, for example, covered her departure as center-column, front-page news. The headline (Manegold, 1995, p. A1.), "Female Cadet Quits the Citadel, Citing Stress of Her Legal Battle," was accompanied by a close-up photo of Faulkner looking distressed and wiping sweat from her brow. Although 35 cadets dropped out of the Citadel during "hell week," only Faulkner's story was "news" because it fit an "old symbolic mold"[11] of polarized gender roles. According to this mold, Faulkner was expected to fail and her failure proved that women just don't belong in the military.

Another article in the *Times*, on page eight (not front-page news), gaged responses to Faulkner's failure. A number of individuals interviewed about Faulkner's situation sympathized with her and decried the conduct of the male cadets who mocked her presence on the campus. An equal number of respondents, however, blamed Faulkner for her failure. One young woman interviewed said: "This just leaves the impression of female hysteria, of women saying, 'Give me this, and they can't take it.' I'm tired of women like her representing my gender" (Rimer, 1995, p. A8). A male interviewed said, "she deserved to be there, but she was out of shape" (Rimer, 1995, p. A8).[12] In this news story, more complexity was introduced than the gender polarization lens usually allows because the quoted speakers indicate that men and women could conceivably be similar (i.e., both could attend the Citadel). Yet, their comments support the androcentric lens by suggesting that Faulkner's success depends on her becoming more like a man (the normative human)— less hysterical, more fit. Gender polarization is also subtly reinforced in the suggestion that women can attend the Citadel, for example, only by changing their natural ways and becoming more "manly"—more like their polar opposites.

Immediately following Faulkner's experiences at the Citadel, came a story in the *Times* covering the Virginia Women's Institute for Leadership established at Mary Baldwin College. Rather than admitting women to the prestigious, all-male Virginia Military Institute, the State of Virginia created the Institute for Women (an arrangement sanctioned by the United States Court of Appeals for the Fourth Circuit). As Deborah L. Brake, a staff counsel at the National Women's Law Center said, "the whole design of the program is based on gender stereotypes: Women need more confidence-building. Women have a self-esteem issue. These very stereotypes are the ones that have come back to haunt women in the workplace" (quoted in Allen, 1995, p. B6). The plan for separate military academies, of course, suggests that women and men are fundamentally different and should receive different training and opportunities. The options for women result in no-win situations or double binds (Jamieson, 1995). Here the bind becomes segregation based on differences or integration based on loss of identity.

Faulkner's experience joined her with women in political roles who have faced opposition when they entered a world defined by men. In the autobiographical narrative Ferraro wrote following the 1984 campaign, she expressed her frustration in confronting the androcentric political world and its polarized gender roles. She said she expected the final question she received from a reporter during the vice-presidential debate:

Congresswoman Ferraro, you have had little or no experience in military matters and you might some day find yourself Commander in Chief of the armed forces. How can you convince the American people and the potential enemy that you would know what to do to protect the nation's security, and do you think in any way that the Soviets might be tempted to try to take advantage of you simply because you are a woman? (quoted in Ferraro, 1985, p. 261)

Because she understood the constraints she faced as a woman entering a male-defined world, Ferraro had anticipated the question and said she would do whatever was necessary to defend the country, but she also highlighted the reporter's androcentric assumption by addressing his logic. She said that someone doesn't need to be "black in order to despise racism" or "female in order to be terribly offended by sexism" (pp. 261–262). Of course, no reporter asked George Bush to assure the audience that he could "act like a man," and his closing statement during the debate featured his military experience. He could safely assume that many members of the audience would believe that he, as a male with military experience, was more suited than Ferraro to serve as vice president of the United States.[13]

These assumptions, grounded in gender polarity, allow women to be defined as out of place when they enter areas traditionally dominated by men. Because men and women are presumed polar opposites, their activities and spheres of influence should also be separate. This creates isolation for path breakers like Shannon Faulkner and Ferraro who attempt to integrate the female and male domains. Recently, Ferraro was interviewed about Faulkner's situation at the Citadel and said: "Shannon Faulkner had nobody at all. She had a much tougher job than I did—to be in a situation where the great majority dislike you and think you're taking away something that is theirs exclusively" (quoted in Rimer, 1995, p. A8). Representative Patricia Schroeder (Democrat-Colorado) also has recounted her experiences when she was elected to Congress and treated as though she "just didn't belong." She said when she was elected to Congress "learning the ropes" on the House floor was "a snap compared with arranging child care for two young children" (Schroeder, 1989, p. 57) Furthermore, she said when she traveled with her children on a plane, she "was amazed to find that my colleagues simply 'didn't see us'" (p. 57).[14] Keeping the lens of gender polarity firmly in place requires disconfirming those who challenge it.

Hillary Rodham Clinton, in her efforts to redefine the role of First Lady, has been a highly visible force in questioning androcentric assumptions and polarized gender roles. In Chapter 4 of this book we provide an extended analysis of Rodham Clinton's approach to political communication. An issue of *Time* early in 1995, included an illustration that spoke to Rodham Clinton's struggles. She was depicted as the "Makeover Candidate of the Week: Having declared herself 'naive and dumb,' Hillary Clinton struggles to reinvent herself in a more popular First Lady mode" (p. 9). In the illustration, Rodham Clinton was a chameleon—she had transformed herself into Barbara Bush (complete with white hair, synthetic pearls, and a "frumpy," royal blue dress). As Frank Rich (1995) remarked in a column for the *New York Times*, Rodham Clinton is in a "no-win" situation.

Mrs. Clinton can't win for losing. When she exercises her clout in private, she's Lady Macbeth, or perhaps, as post-inauguration rumors had it, a lamp-throwing lesbian. If she does so in public, she's a "bitch." In less than three years she has also been the Yuppie Wife from Hell, Florence Nightingale, the ditzy prophet of the Politics of Meaning, the $100,000 con artist, a Superwoman effortlessly fielding her roles as mother and wife on top of health-care duties, and stealth candidate for President in 2,000. (p. E17)

Faulkner, Ferraro, Schroeder, and Rodham Clinton are in company with many other women who have faced "traps" or "double binds" in attempting to enter an androcentric world defined by gender-polarized roles. Kathleen Hall Jamieson (1995) links the development of "double binds" to Western cultural influences that have cast women as "other" and explains the significance of the "double bind," a term coined by psychologist Gregory Bateson. As women attempt to enter a world defined in male terms and polarized along gender lines, they encounter the "double bind," "a strategy perennially used by those with power against those without" (Jamieson, 1995, p. 5). In practical terms, when a woman encounters a double bind situation, she is damned regardless of the communication choices she makes. Because gender roles are polarized and the world is framed in "either-or" terms, appropriate choices do not exist for women. Women are damned if they choose to emulate male-identified communication patterns when attempting to assume roles traditionally associated with men. On the other hand, women are damned if they use communication patterns traditionally associated with women when they enter the androcentric world.[15] Rodham Clinton's chameleon-like qualities represent her efforts to respond "appropriately." Regardless of her choices, however, as Margaret Carlson (1995) observes, Rodham Clinton will fall short of public expectations, because "[w]hile men have a wide latitude in how they behave in public, women still have to tread a tightrope" (p. 36).

The lenses of androcentrism and gender polarization, then, operate insidiously, as unexamined cultural assumptions that limit human potential. Although Bem acknowledges the power of androcentrism and polarization as lenses that frame gender expectations in U.S. culture, she claims that the lens of biological essentialism is the one that provides legitimacy for the other two lenses. When individuals attempt to draw attention to issues of sexual inequality, and encourage others to look *at* rather than look *through* the lenses of gender, they confront the power of the lens of biological essentialism.

Biological Essentialism

For Bem (1993), the lens of biological essentialism enables the lenses of androcentrism and gender polarization to stand unchallenged in U.S. culture. When we view gender identities through the lens of biological essentialism, these identities seem "natural." The lens of biological essentialism, in denying the role that culture plays in shaping gender identities, "has secularized God's grand creation by substituting its scientific equivalent: evolution's grand creation" (p. 2). Although Bem recognizes the biological differences between women and men, she argues that these differences possess no independent meaning. Their meaning is only derived through cultural interpretation, and this meaning is subject to historical variations.

In many countries scientists legitimize social inequity through biological essentialism.[16] For example, scientists in the United States justified the enslavement of Africans by suggesting that they were "naturally" suited to lives of slavery. Although few people are aware of the sterilization and immigration laws passed in the U.S. during the early 1900s,

Bem points out that they were based on the assumption that American intelligence levels would fall if "defective strains" were introduced (Bem, p. 7).[17]

The roots of the biological essentialist lens can be traced by mapping the efforts of scientists, particularly social scientists, to support many nineteenth-century beliefs with evidence making them seem "natural" and inevitable. The last half of the nineteenth and early-twentieth centuries in the United States were marked by the emergence of social movements (i.e., the first wave of the feminist movement, abolitionism) and a wave of new immigrants. Bem says an examination of scientific theories from this period illustrates "how science is intertwined with cultural ideology" (p. 9). For example, Edward Clarke (1873) used the concept of "vital energy" to "naturalize" nineteenth-century cultural beliefs about women's roles (the beliefs challenged by the women's movement). The concept of "vital energy" suggested a hydraulic model of energy. This model posits that energy exists in a finite amount and once energy is deployed in one direction, it is depleted and cannot be deployed elsewhere.

In his book *Sex in Education*, Clarke argued that education might sap too much energy from a woman's reproductive system and therefore interfere with her "natural" role in society—that of child bearer and rearer. Herbert Spencer (1852, 1873, 1876) applied Charles Darwin's ideas concerning evolution and "survival of the fittest" in promoting a conservative social agenda. Spencer argued that biology was destiny and that men and women were "naturally" ordained to fulfill particular roles in society. As a social Darwinist, Spencer suggested that because women were "naturally" more charitable than men, they should be denied the right to vote. He said their charitable instincts might encourage them to provide assistance to the weak in society, thereby denying progress as the "naturally" more fit in society survive.

Sociobiologists in the 1970s also made arguments concerning "natural" sex differences and the universality of a social organization based on male superiority. In mapping theories that explain the social world, sociobiologists concentrate on "evolutionary and genetic factors, rather than cultural or historical factors, because they rightly see any purely environmental explanation as inadequate" (Bem, p. 19). For sociobiologists, the universals they observe in the social world are the result of only biology, not culture.

As an example of 1970s sociobiological reasoning, Bem notes the work of Edward O. Wilson, who suggested that gender roles evolved "naturally" over time. For Wilson, the key to understanding evolution was the recognition that the natural selection process was genetic. The survival of the fittest translated into survival of the "best" genes. For the "best" genes to survive, biology dictates that women and men take different approaches to sexual reproduction that translate into different approaches to nurturing and rearing their offspring. Wilson reasoned that biology dictated aggressive behavior for men and passive behavior for women because "one male can fertilize many females but a female can be fertilized by only one male" (Wilson, 1975, p. 124). Thus, women need passivity to wait and discover the male with the best genes and the one most likely to stay with them after insemination. Men, however, need to be aggressive and indiscriminate because their evolutionary success is based on quantity.

Other sociobiologists extended Wilson's ideas and were able to generate biologically based rationales for female and male behavior patterns (i.e., rape is a "natural" response for men and "toying" with male affections is "natural" for women as they seek the "best" partner). Some political leaders have twisted this biological principle into convoluted knots to substantiate their viewpoints. North Carolina state Representative Henry Aldridge opposed funding for abortions in the case of rape saying that when women are "truly raped, the juices don't flow; the body functions don't work and they don't get pregnant" (quoted in Goodman, 1995, p. A10).

A number of scholars have critiqued sociobiological theories and pointed out that they emerged in the 1970s in the midst of second-wave feminism. The work of several feminist scientists (i.e., Bleier, 1984, 1986; Harding, 1986; Keller, 1985; Rose, 1983) argues that sociobiological research legitimates a political ideology that maintains hegemony while its practitioners deny that it is anything other than neutral, objective research. For example, Ruth Bleier (1986) notes: "I believe that the heightened interest in biological sex differences either to explain or justify the myriad forms of gender asymmetries is not unrelated to the social-political context of the 1970s and 1980s, when the women's movement has forced into public scrutiny and policy questions of inequalities in employment and education and in legal and social status" (p. 147). In sum, feminist critics of sociobiological theories claim they were developed to justify sexual inequality and legitimate the status quo in terms of gender roles.

From this discussion of theories grounded in biological essentialism, it becomes apparent why Bem sees this lens as the most critical one in her goal to transform the entire debate on the inequality between the sexes. When cultural assumptions about gender (the assumptions encoded in the lenses of androcentrism and gender polarization) are "naturalized" and presented under the cloak of science or "objective" fact, they emerge as immutable. Stephen Jay Gould (1981) agrees and presents a strong case that "quantitative data are as subject to cultural constraint as any other aspect of science" and should "have no special claim upon truth" (p. 27). Patricia J. Williams (1991) discusses what she refers to as the "ruse" of neutral writing and its ideological implications. She writes: "[a]nd the object of such ruse is to empower still further; to empower beyond the self, by appealing to neutral, shared, even universal understandings" (p. 92). These universal understandings presented under the cloak of scientific objectivity include the belief that biology is destiny.

Recent statements by Newt Gingrich, Speaker of the United States House of Representatives, indicate that taken-for-granted assumptions about biological essentialism are alive in our culture. Representative Patricia Schroeder, a senior member of the House Armed Services Committee, called the attention of members to the following statements Gingrich made while teaching a history course at Reinhardt College. Gingrich, speaking of female qualifications to serve in the military said: "Females have biological problems staying in a ditch for 30 days because they get infections, and don't have upper body strength" (quoted in Seelye, 1995, p. A20). He also stated that men are "naturally" equipped to serve in ditches because they "are basically little piglets; drop them in the ditch, they roll around in it" (quoted in Seelye, 1995, p. A20). Furthermore, Gingrich went on to say that women may be biologically more suited than men to fill particular roles in the military. He noted that if serving in the military "means being on an Aegis cruiser managing the computer controls for 12 ships and their rockets, a female again may be dramatically better than a male who gets very, very frustrated sitting in a chair all the time because males are biologically driven to go out and hunt giraffes" (Seelye, 1995, p. A20).

Ellen Goodman (1995) awarded Gingrich "The Double Standard-Bearer prize" in her annual "Equal Rites Award" column for those comments on women and men in the military. She also singled out Senator Trent Lott, the Republican majority whip, for the "Gender Spaciness" award for the following comment made in the context of a discussion about gender differences in right and left brain-sidedness: "I think that we're the party of Mars, but we would like to have the Venus side of American society in our party, too" (p. A10). In addition to being spacey, the quote suggests essential brain differences between men and women.

A recent cover of *Spy* magazine featuring a digitally altered photo of Hillary Rodham Clinton also reflects cultural assumptions concerning biologically essential gender roles. A photo of Rodham Clinton's head is attached to a hermaphroditic body. The body is wearing a black dress (the pose is an emulation of the famous photo of Marilyn Monroe standing over an exhaust grate in New York city with her dress unfurled and blowing in the wind) and white jockey shorts that obviously contain male genitals. The story trumpeted on the cover of the magazine supposedly gives the "real truth" about Rodham Clinton's financial dealings in Whitewater. "Where that shady $100,000 came from and what it bought: HILLARY'S BIG SECRET" (*Spy*, October 1995). The cover photo suggests that the First Lady is powerful due to the fact that she is actually male or at least half male. The illustration is rich in interpretive possibilities—all of them pointing in the direction of cultural assumptions connected with biological essentialism. One implication might be that Rodham Clinton is actually male because only a male (driven by testosterone) could have wielded the power that Rodham Clinton wielded in Whitewater.

Another interpretation might suggest that "radical feminists" (or Feminazis in Rush Limbaugh's lexicon) aren't actually female. Of course, both these interpretations suggest that Rodham Clinton is a freak—the ultimate "other." The illustration, then, supports conventional cultural assumptions concerning gender by posing the question, "What is it [this Hillary Rodham Clinton creature]?" When the hermaphroditic Rodham Clinton emerges as a freak in the illustration, the underlying message is both that her ideas are "radical" and may be disregarded by those who understand the "true" biological natures of women and men, and that essential womanhood is not controverted by Rodham Clinton's example, because she is *not* a woman.

Gingrich's and Lott's statements and the cover of *Spy* reveal the saliency of the lens of biological essentialism. Bleier (1986), in decrying theorizing that reduces our understanding of human behaviors to biology, echoes Bem in arguing that our cultural expectations limit human potential. Together, the lenses of biological essentialism, gender polarization, and androcentrism function to restrict human possibilities.

Although cultural assumptions embedded in the lenses of gender have discouraged women from assuming public leadership roles, women have become powerful political communicators in spite of these obstacles. Our work focuses upon rhetorical strategies political women have developed to encourage their audiences to look *at* rather than *through* the lenses of gender. We now provide definitions as a starting point for our analysis, offer a rationale for selecting particular women as case studies, and situate this book in terms of other research on women as political communicators.

DEFINITIONS

Two terms must be defined for the purposes of this study of rhetorical strategies utilized by women as political communicators. First, we define "political communication" broadly for the purposes of our analysis. Our approach to political communication corresponds with a suggestion made by David Swanson and Dan Nimmo (1990) that "the study of political communication would do well to move away from context-based conceptions of itself, particularly the unicentric campaign touchstone" (p. 11). Although we value the study of campaign communication, we are more generally interested in examining patterns of communication for women in public leadership positions. We base this interest on two beliefs. First, women who already have positions of leadership may be less constrained and more able to speak in their own authentic voice. Second, these women are in positions potentially to exert more influence than candidates are able to exercise. As our next chapter establishing the framework for analysis demonstrates, women have been discouraged from participating in public life while they are supported for contributions in private life. Our concern revolves around *how* women function in political leadership roles usually reserved for men, once they overcome the obstacles and actually assume a measure of public power. Specifically, we are concerned with *how* women are *redefining* the public leadership realm through their communication.

Some feminist scholars might see our concentration on the public realm of leadership as accepting the androcentric assumption that politics is practiced in public life. Sociologists such as Jill Bystydzienski (1992) argue that politics is not enacted exclusively in the realm of public life and feminist scholars have struggled to identify alternative venues for the enactment of politics. We support the efforts of feminists (for example, Bystydzienski, 1987; Vickers, 1987) who are examining how women exercise political power through kinship networks and local neighborhood organizations. We also recognize that due to the way we framed our study, women exercising community-based political power, nonhierarchical power (Foss and Griffin, 1995; Noddings, 1984, 1989; Ruddick, 1989; Wood 1992, 1994), or unintrusive power (Rakow, 1992) were not included in our analysis. While we respect and acknowledge the importance of examining these types of power, our project concentrates on transformation in the public realm of politics. We believe the values that undergird political structures and institutions must change before a large audience will be able to hear voices articulating alternative definitions of power.[18]

Just as we define political communication broadly for the purposes of our study, we rely upon a broad definition of "political women." A woman of politics is one performing a highly visible leadership role and speaking out on or demonstrating an awareness of gender issues. Although we define public leadership broadly, in this study we do concentrate on women committed to looking *at* rather than *through* the lenses of gender. For our purposes, this means that the discourse of the women we analyze embodies a definition of politics as "empowerment." We accept a feminist definition of empowerment as articulated by Bystydzienski (1992).

As used by feminists, empowerment is taken to mean a process by which oppressed persons gain some control over their lives by taking part with others in developing activities and structures that allow people increased involvement in matters which affect them directly. This process involves the use of power, but not "power over" others or power as competence which is generated and shared by the disenfranchised as they begin to shape the content and structure of their daily existence and to participate in a movement for social change. (p. 3)

Thus, although we define political communication and political leadership broadly, we do limit our analysis to women who demonstrate, through their rhetoric, an awareness of gender issues.

RATIONALE FOR SELECTION OF WOMEN FOR STUDY

Media coverage of Campaign 1992 heralded "the year of the woman," and a writer for *Time* said: "It is now thinkable that someday women candidates for public office will be simply taken for granted" (Smolowe, 1992, p. 34). In the wake of the Hill-Thomas hearings and voter disenchantment with "politics as usual," women became highly visible candidates during the 1992 election season (Smolowe, 1992, p. 34). Although the election of President Bill Clinton and his expressed commitment to appointing more women and people of color to positions in his administration stimulated our interest in pursuing this book, we are skeptical of the actual ground gained by women in political leadership roles. President Clinton has appointed women to highly visible posts in his administration (i.e., Janet Reno as U.S. Attorney General, Hazel O'Leary as Director of the Department of Energy, Carol Browner as Director of the Environmental Protection Agency, and Jocelyn Elders as Surgeon General), but his support for these women has varied. He also abandoned the nominations of Zoë Baird and Kimba Wood to serve as U.S. Attorney General and Lani Guinier as Assistant Attorney General for Civil Rights.

Additionally, although women seem to be more visible in political roles, we cannot overlook the fact that "more visible" is a relative term. "The year of the woman" was marked by a "watershed" change in the U.S. Senate. When the Senate was called to order in January 1993, seven (out of 100) of the seats were occupied by women. Clearly, however, male influence continues to dominate the Senate. A study conducted by the Inter-Parliamentary Union, released in 1995, found: "Of 106 nations with freely elected parliaments, the United States ranks 43rd with 10.9 percent of national seats held by women, a lower figure than that of Russia and many Eastern European and Latin American countries. Canada ranks 21st with 18 percent of seats held by women" (reported in Crossette, 1995, p. A10). Spender (1989) notes that "[w]omen who want to contribute equally with men in conversation have to be committed and courageous" (p. 19), and we assume an even greater commitment is required of the women who enter the political realm defined by men.

We have selected highly visible "committed and courageous" women who assumed leadership roles in conjunction with President Clinton's election and "the year of the woman." In this book we examine the constraints they have faced as political communicators and their rhetorical responses to those constraints. The rhetoric of the women included in this study suggests they are concerned with the issues of empowerment identified by Bystydzienski (1992), and, in particular, they seem to struggle with definitions of power. We also made a conscious effort to consider issues of diversity in selecting our case studies. Because our case studies feature women associated in one way or another with the Clinton administration, we do not analyze the discourse of women associated with the Republican party. If our study included a broader scope of women as political communicators, Senator Nancy Kassebaum (Republican-Kansas), for example, would qualify as a highly visible leader who demonstrates an awareness of gender issues (including issues associated with empowerment).[19]

Highly visible political women represent the three rhetorical strategies outlined in Chapter 2. Lani Guinier (Chapter 3), Hillary Rodham Clinton (Chapter 4), and Janet Reno (Chapter 5) enact three different rhetorical patterns utilized by political women as they address the inherent constraints of their situations (i.e., the lenses of gender that frame woman as "other" in political life). In each chapter, we examine the special role media play in legitimating the lenses of gender. Our analysis follows in the steps of other studies that have examined women as political communicators.

RESEARCH ON WOMEN AND POLITICAL COMMUNICATION

Previous research on women and political communication provides a backdrop for our study. Scholars in communication, political science, and women's studies have examined the challenges women face when they enter political life, and their responses to those challenges. Research by political scientists on women as political communicators tends to concentrate on the practical difficulties women face and the differences they make in government when they enter politics. Susan J. Carroll (1994) identified "reasons related to the political opportunity structure" (p. 119) that hindered women in their efforts to enter politics. Carroll's study concentrated on measures women needed to take to enhance their electability.

The Center for the American Woman and Politics (CAWP) at the Eagleton Institute of Politics, Rutgers University, has published studies tracing the election of women to positions at all levels of government. These studies delineate "how women are doing" in terms of numbers, but also explore whether women "make a difference [influence policy or political processes]" when they are elected or appointed to political office. Susan J. Carroll, Deborah Dodson, and Ruth Mandel (1991) note that "women are present in sufficient numbers at various levels of office in various locales to expect that if, in fact, women are likely to have a distinctive impact on public policy or the political process, that impact might begin to be evident" (p. 2). One CAWP research project examined the influence women are having in state legislatures. Telephone interviews of representative samples of women and men legislators indicated: "While the gender gap in policy attitudes among state lawmakers suggests that women and men bring different perspectives to their work in the legislatures, attitudes alone cannot reshape the legislative agenda" (Carroll, Dodson, and Mandel, 1991, p. 7). CAWP (Dodson, 1991a, 1991b) also published a number of case studies suggesting that women are "making a difference" in a variety of political contexts. A recent study of the 103rd Congress highlighted "women's distinctive contributions to the policy-making process in Congress" (Dodson, Carroll, Mandel, Kleeman, Schreiber, and Liebowitz, 1995, p. 25) Jamieson (1995) identifies the problems and double binds women face when they enter political life, but agrees with the CAWP studies that women are making a difference and are able to demonstrate "how to break the ties that bind" (p. 214).

Although the CAWP studies and Jamieson's work suggest that women are gaining greater access and exerting more influence in the political world, other studies are less optimistic. In a review essay in *Feminist Studies*, Joan Tronto (1991) examines a number of books (Bookman and Morgen, 1988; Cott, 1987; Harrison, 1988; Klein, 1984; Mansbridge, 1986; Rupp and Taylor, 1987) on women and political communication that are less than optimistic about the actualization of feminist goals in politics. Tronto suggests that while these books "consider a wide range of women's political experiences and strategies from the 1910s to the 1980s" in assessing successes and failures, the authors overlook "certain overarching biases in U.S. political life that will inevitably make the goals of the feminist movement difficult to achieve" (p. 86). In the review essay, Tronto proposes that these biases must be addressed and implies that political frameworks must change.

The most prominent of these biases are, first, that the U.S. political system responds most easily to issues raised by those in the middle- or upper-middle class; second, that Americans see the world through individualistic glasses so that any analysis that grows out of a nonindividualistic framework will encounter special difficulties. (p. 86)

Tronto thus argues that women must transform political frameworks rather than accept androcentric political frameworks.

A number of researchers also highlighted the "gender gaps" that surface when women question androcentric political frameworks. Pamela Johnston Conover (1988) outlines types of gender gaps. One gender gap (which has narrowed and is receiving minimal research attention) encompasses differences between women and men in voter participation. Another gender gap refers to differences in voting choices between women and men. A number of studies indicate that over the past few years women have been more likely than men to vote for Democratic candidates (Klein, 1985; Wirls, 1986).

In the communication literature, researchers mainly concern themselves with three areas: (1) political advertising and images of political women that are reflected in the media, (2) analyses of news coverage given to women politicians and candidates, and (3) characteristics of women's political rhetoric, especially as it differs from men's. For example, in the first category, David Procter, Roger Aden, and Phyllis Japp (1988) analyzed the television advertising in the 1986 Nebraska gubernatorial campaign, where two women ran against each other. Procter and his colleagues suggest that Kay Orr's successful campaign was the result of her ability to portray herself as both competent and forceful as well as compassionate and warm in her television ads.

Judith S. Trent and Teresa Chandler Sabourin (1993) echoed these conclusions in their study which analyzed, the content of negative television advertisement spots used by women who ran for Congress or state governorships in 1982, 1983, 1984, and 1986. They concluded that women use negative ads as frequently as men, but when they do so they are under some constraints that men generally can avoid. Being negative violates gender expectations and places women in a precarious position relative to voters who expect them to be "nice." On the other hand, women have to take care to avoid creating the impression that they fit gender expectations for women too completely. Thus, women have to make an effort to "blend aspects of the female stereotype with more traditional candidate attributes (i.e., masculine qualities) to show that they are not *too* nurturing" (p. 262). The results of the Trent and Sabourin and Procter, Aden, and Japp studies argue that women have to project a careful blend of masculinity and femininity in their political advertising to be successful. Yet, Lynda Lee Kaid, Sandra L. Myers, Val Pipps, and Jan Hunter (1984) found, in their study of televised political advertising, that women candidates were more successful than their male counterparts when they were pictured in stereotypical male settings—a construction site and a farm. The authors suggest that this may have been the case because viewers were impressed that a woman was able to perform well in male environments. This reversal of expectations may have led viewers to evaluate the female as "inordinately successful" (p. 51).

Other authors (e.g., Kahn, 1993; Kahn and Goldenberg, 1991) investigate the coverage that women candidates receive in the news media, usually concluding that the media cover male and female candidates differently. Women receive less news coverage, and what coverage they do receive focuses more on their viability as candidates than on their positions on issues. For example, Kim Fridkin Kahn (1993) discovered that despite the fact that women actually discuss the issues more frequently than men in their campaigns, the media fail to report these concerns. Rather, she found that the media consistently give more coverage to male candidates on the issues. Further, although women candidates stress their leadership qualities in their campaign ads, the media generally ignore this and focus instead on stereotypical descriptions for female candidates.

Finally, a group of researchers has been concerned with political women as rhetors. Mary Boor Tonn (1992) profiles Mary Harris "Mother" Jones, a turn-of-the-century labor union agitator. Boor Tonn argues that "Mother" Jones's rhetorical style was unique and successful in that it was dramatic, narrative, and rooted in shared experiences. "Mother" Jones, according to Boor Tonn, was able to transcend public/private dichotomies by weaving "a potent personal message designed to build empathy and rapport among isolated individuals, convincing them that their oppression was politically motivated rather than personally based, and as such required a political solution" (p. 284). In another essay, Boor Tonn (1996) proposes that "Mother" Jones succeeded rhetorically by "correlating maternal purposes with her specific goals as an agitator for coal miners" (p. 3). Patricia Sullivan (1993) argues elsewhere that Patricia Schroeder, Representative from Colorado, overtly claims her decision-making process is contextual. Schroeder "objects to politicians who speak in abstract terms about family values and says those values must be contextualized" (Sullivan, p. 539). Sullivan asserts that Schroeder, in enacting contextualized decision-making, provides a feminized value system for framing political rhetoric.

In her introduction to the second volume of her two-part study on the rhetoric of early feminists, Karlyn Kohrs Campbell (1989) speaks to the special problems early women rhetors had and how they dealt with them.

[W]omen speakers relied on personal experience coupled with examples to recreate the processes by which they had arrived at conclusions; they invited women in the audience to collaborate in making arguments and to test claims against their knowledge. In this type of rhetorical style, the speaker adopted a personal tone, audience members were treated as peers, with an emphasis on identification, and arguments unfolded inductively. (p. xv)

Bonnie Dow and Mary Boor Tonn (1993) expand on Campbell's (1973, 1989) theory of the "feminine style" in their analysis of Ann Richards' discourse. They assert that Richards' "feminine style" is marked by reliance on concrete examples and anecdotes; use of self-disclosure and sharing of emotions; and a family model for political progress. The authors conclude that Richards' "feminine style" is different philosophically and strategically from the style associated with male political rhetors.

Jane Blankenship and Deborah C. Robson (1995) argue that the "feminine style" "is gaining legitimacy through its use by women and men in power" (p. 353). They identify a number of speakers who use the "feminine style," including President Bill Clinton and Senator Dianne Feinstein. The characteristics of the "feminine style" identified by Blankenship and Robson echo the work of Dow and Boor Tonn and Campbell. Characteristics of the "feminine style" include: political judgments grounded in "concrete, lived experience"; value placed on "inclusivity and the relational nature of being"; a view of "the power of public office as a capacity 'to get things done' and to empower others"; a "holistic" view of "policy formation"; and a commitment to foregrounding "women's issues" in public decision-making (Blankenship and Robson, p. 359).

Denise Bostdorff (1991) also focused on a female-associated style, but argued in her analysis of Geraldine Ferraro's 1984 vice-presidential candidacy that "Americans expect their vice presidents to talk in traditionally feminine/comedic ways" (p. 19). As a female vice-presidential candidate, then, Ferraro faced special difficulties in balancing female-associated and male-associated role expectations.

Other researchers have looked at women's use of metaphor and image (i.e., Blankenship and Kang, 1991; Jorgensen-Earp, 1990; Sullivan, 1989), reframing techniques (Hardy-Short, 1993), and empowerment strategies (Canas, 1995; Watters, 1994). For example, Jane Blankenship and Jong Guen Kang (1991) and Sullivan (1989) analyze the power of metaphor in framing women as "other" when they seek political office. Blankenship and Kang address the significance of press coverage of Geraldine Ferraro's 1984 Democratic vice-presidential candidacy. They argue that reporters linked the world of sports and politics metaphorically—two worlds traditionally named as male worlds—and suggested that Ferraro didn't belong in either world. Sullivan traces George Bush's use of sports metaphors during the 1984 vice-presidential debate and suggests that "Bush's word choices communicated that the present political contest should be viewed as yet another contest on the athletic field" (p. 333). When Bush linked sports and politics, he metaphorically established a framework for the debate that cast Ferraro as an outsider. Both analyses of the vice presidential debate claim that because the language defined the political world as male, Ferraro as a female was immediately cast as "other."

In all these works the emphasis rests on women's struggle to give voice to different messages in different forms than traditional male leaders. Although women have been on the margins of the political world—cast as the "other"—they have prevailed in making their voices heard in the public forum.

In this book, we are concerned both with the barriers that women have faced in public life and with the ways women have chosen to cope with these barriers. Thus, we situate our work between some of the concerns previously addressed by political scientists and communication researchers. In Chapter 2 we establish our framework for analyzing rhetorical approaches utilized by political women in their efforts to obtain a hearing in the public sphere. Further, we examine the boundaries that necessitate special strategies on the part of women, strategies that are not needed for men to secure a public voice.

NOTES

1. Bem refers to the first two waves of feminism, but does not use the term "third-wave" feminism to describe her own efforts. We agree with Bem's characterizations of the first two waves of feminism and the accomplishments associated with those movements. Bem does not use the term third-wave feminism in her book, and we also hesitate to use the term. The text of a 1993 roundtable discussion published in *Ms.* ("Let's get real about feminism") speaks to difficulties in defining the next wave of feminism. Panelists bell hooks, Gloria Steinem, Urvashi Vaid, and Naomi Wolf discussed a number of possibilities for the next wave or waves of feminism. Because there exist these possibilities and varieties, we consider the term third-wave feminism ambiguous and avoid its use.

2. Bem (1993) cautions that not all males in the United States are empowered and says "the term *male power* should thus be construed narrowly as the power historically held by rich, white, heterosexual men, for it is they who originally set up and now primarily sustain the cultural discourses and social institutions of this nation" (p. 3).

3. Bem (1993) echoes Schutz and Luckmann's (1973) observations concerning the intersubjectivity of the socially constructed life-world. Schutz and Luckmann argue: "The world of daily life is given to us in a taken-for-granted way.... The province of meaning of this world retains the accent of reality as long as our practical experiences confirm its unity and harmony. It appears to us as 'natural' reality, and we are not prepared to give up the attitude that is based upon it unless a special shock experience breaks through the meaning-structure of everyday reality and induces us to transfer the accent of reality to another province of meaning" (p. 35). Bem's remarks concerning enculturation also correspond with Schutz and Luckmann's observations concerning "biographical articulations." Schutz and Luckmann define "biographical articulations" as "categories which are formed intersubjectively and established within the relative-natural

worldview. They are basically imposed upon the individual and become interiorized by him [sic]" (p. 57).

4. Bem, in tracing the roots of androcentrism, acknowledges her debt to feminist scholars in a number of fields. Her discussion of Judeo-Christian thought credits Pagels (1976, 1977), Phillips (1984), Sanday (1981), and Lerner (1986). For feminist reconstructions of Judeo-Christian religious texts, she recommends Plaskow (1990), Reuther (1985), and Sjoo and Mor (1987). Bem's discussion of the androcentric legacy of ancient Greek philosophical thought relies upon Okin (1979) and she also recommends Saxonhouse (1985) and Bullough, Shelton, and Slavin (1988). For her analysis of the embodiment of androcentrism in U.S. law, Bem turns to Pateman (1988), Estrich (1987), Lingren and Taub (1988), Rhode (1989, 1990), Russell (1982), and Sachs and Wilson (1978). For feminist responses to Freud, see Figes (1970), Friedan (1963), Irigaray (1985, 1991), Millett (1969), Mitchell (1974), and Montrelay (1977).

5. Walker (1983) explains that Pandora's box was actually a honey-vase or a *pithos*, "from which she poured out blessings: a womb-symbol like the Cornucopia, anciently used as a vessel of birth and death" (p. 767). The vase became a box—Pandora's Box—when Erasmus "mistakenly translated *pithos* as *pyxis* in the late Middle Ages (p. 767). The box, of course, became associated with the vagina, sexual carnality, and all things evil. Just as Pandora was that pathway for all things evil, Eve in the words of Church father Tertullian, became "the Devil's gateway" (quoted in Reuther, 1983, p. 167). "Eve," the label for a douching product developed for women to cleanse the vagina or "the Devil's gateway," speaks to taken-for-granted cultural assumptions about Eve (and woman).

6. For a fuller explanation of misogynistic *interpretations* of sacred texts in the Judeo-Christian tradition, see Reuther (1983). She traces, for example, the foregrounding of particular interpretations of Genesis that scapegoated woman and cast her as "other." For example, she discusses the Watcher story of Genesis 6: 1–4 in which the Watchers or angels copulate with human females and produce giants (which become demons in later interpretations). She traces the scapegoating of women through Pauline theology as well as Augustinian theology. Additionally, she says Judaism had its own "ways of mythologizing women's inferiority and potential for subverting male definitions of good humanity" (p. 168) and she cites the story of Lilith (Adam's first wife who refused to submit to his wishes). In this story, Eve was the wife God provided for Adam to replace the evil Lilith. In sum, Reuther argues: "In the stories of Pandora, the Watchers, Lilith, and Eve the female is seen as the enemy of harmony, good order, and felicity in human affairs. These myths reveal a tremendous male fear of women's suppressed power, which, having been once unleashed, overthrew original paradisal conditions and introduced disease, mortality, hard work, and frustrating struggle for survival in place of what was ease and happiness in the midst of spontaneous plenty" (p. 168).

7. Even Jean Jacques Rousseau, as Bem notes, who is often cited as an Enlightenment advocate of equality, argued that women should be subjugated due to their powers to seduce men and influence their decisions.

8. Many scholars in communication studies and linguistics have discussed consequences of male control over language. In particular, see: Kramarae (1981), Kramarae, Schultz, and O'Barr (1984), Kramarae, Thorne, and Henley (1978),

McConnell-Ginet, Borker, and Furman (1980), Pearson, West, and Turner (1995). More specifically, a number of feminist scholars in communication studies echo Bem's call for an examination of the deep structures or frameworks that support and reproduce male power. These scholars discuss the need to reframe the study of communication by challenging androcentric and eurocentric assumptions. See, for example: Cirksena (1987); Cirksena and Cuklanz (1992); Condit (1993); Edson (1985); Fine (1988); K. Foss and S. Foss (1983, 1989, 1994); S. Foss and K. Foss (1988); S. Foss, K. Foss, and R. Trapp (1991); S. Foss and Griffin (1992, 1995); Gearhart (1979); Griffin (1993); Houston (1992); Rakow (1986); Spitzack and Carter (1987); Sullivan and Goldzwig (1995); and Wood (1992, 1994).

9. In her chapter on gender polarization, Bem addresses the role that research on "sexual deviance" played in privileging heterosexuality as well as androcentricity in U. S. culture. Although her analysis is provocative, this dimension of gender polarization is less relevant for our analysis than her analysis of "gender schematicity."

10. Gilligan (1982) tried to remediate the androcentric bias in Kohlberg's (1981) research. Kohlberg generalized about human moral development from only male research participants, assuming the male as standard. Gilligan challenged this omission and theorized from a woman's perspective. Ironically, however, Gilligan's critics (see, for example, Broughton, 1983; Larrabee, 1993, and Wood, 1994) observe a gender-polarizing bias in her work because she implied that women share an essential nature.

11. The term "old symbolic mold" is borrowed from Bennett and Edelman (1985, p. 169).

12. We are intrigued by the "out of shape" remark. The *New York Times* published a center-column front-page article on Faulkner's first day at the Citadel. She was pictured marching in the midst of male cadets. The picture is open to two interpretations. The first interpretation suggests Faulkner has the "wrong body image" for the Citadel. Her "womanly" body appears "flabby" and "out of shape." Another interpretation, however, suggests that Faulkner looks incredibly similar to other "out of shape" male cadets.

13. Interestingly, Bill Clinton, a U.S. President with no military experience, received somewhat mixed treatment from the press, who constructed his situation rather differently from Ferraro's. He was criticized during the 1992 campaign for dodging the draft, and following the election, reporters suggested he needed "to get up to speed" on military matters; however, it was not suggested (as in Ferraro's case) that lack of military service equated with inability to lead. Rather, he was seen as insufficiently credible. For example, during Campaign 1992, the *New York Times* published an article questioning Clinton's veracity concerning his explanations for avoiding the draft. The *Times* quoted a Bush spokeswoman who said, "Every time Bill Clinton says something is his last statement on this issue, something else comes up and he has to change his story" (Kelly, 1992, p. A20). Further, after Clinton's election some newspapers framed his lack of service as potentially positive. An editorial in the *New York Times* (A Vietnam Veterans Day, 1992, p. A24) observed: "In effect [by electing Clinton], Americans said: Enough—let's put the divisiveness of Vietnam behind us. Perhaps now those who fought in the war and those who fought against it can come together in mutual respect" (1992, p. A24).

14. For an analysis of Schroeder's communication style in responding to constraints she faces as a woman in politics, see Sullivan (1993).

15. Jamieson (1995) notes that "The notion [double bind] has become a catchphrase to describe the dilemmas confronting contemporary women and is a commonplace in feminist scholarship" (p. 5). She also acknowledges that "masculinity has its own constellation of double binds" (p. 4). We agree with Jamieson, however, that due to androcentric biases in Western cultures, women are more likely to face double bind situations. In the final chapter of this book, we will address the double binds that men, such as President Bill Clinton, face when they adopt communication styles traditionally associated with women.

16. For provocative analyses of the links among stereotyping, biological essentialism, and social policy see Gilman (1985).

17. Arguments based on biological essentialism emerge periodically in U.S. culture. For example, in *The Bell Curve*, Herrnstein and Murray (1994) attempt to use science to justify cultural beliefs that racial differences in performances on I.Q. tests stem from genetics. As Stephen Jay Gould points out in a review of *The Bell Curve* in the *New Yorker*, "The text evokes the dreary and scary drumbeat of claims associated with conservative think tanks: reduction or elimination of welfare, ending or sharply curtailing affirmative action in schools and workplaces, cutting back Head Start and other forms of pre-school education, trimming programs for the slowest learners and applying those funds to the gifted" (1994, pp. 147–148).

18. Although our original intent in planning this study was to analyze the rhetoric of Representative Nydia Velazquez (NY), we could not obtain samples of her rhetoric. We suspect that analysis of her rhetoric would require an ethnographic study involving interviews with her constituents. This is a project we hope to pursue in the future.

19. For a thoughtful analysis of Kassebaum's rhetorical style as a political communicator, see Campbell and Jerry (1988). Campbell and Jerry observe: "Kassebaum's success is noteworthy because she has taken stands on issues of special interest to women, including favoring a woman's right to choose abortion and passage of the ERA" (p. 130).

2

Gender, Moral Boundaries, and Political Communication

> Appeals to reason or to the nature of the universe have been used throughout history to enshrine existing hierarchies as proper and inevitable.
> —Stephen Jay Gould, the *Mismeasure of Man* (1981, p. 30)

In Chapter 1, we presented an overview of factors in Western culture, and in the United States in particular, that have consigned women to the margins of political discourse. The lenses of gender are organizing principles for social life which reproduce male power. Androcentrism, gender polarization, and biological essentialism serve as taken-for-granted assumptions that define women as outsiders in the political world. This chapter maps our framework for analyzing the political discourse of contemporary women. First, using the lenses of gender as a backdrop, we outline the moral boundaries that legitimate the voices of privileged men as political communicators and in turn dismiss the voices of women as political communicators. Second, we identify three rhetorical strategies developed by political women in response to moral boundaries.

MORAL BOUNDARIES

Although Joan C. Tronto (1993) does not refer to the lenses of gender, she identifies Western "conceptions of morality" that mark social orders framed by androcentrism, gender polarization, and biological essentialism, and urges scholars to re-vision them. According to Tronto, morality is "gendered" because in Western philosophical and political traditions questions of value have been framed in patriarchal terms. She challenges, however, the work of feminist cultural theorists who have attempted to argue for women's inclusion in political life on the basis of the common assumption that women are more moral than men. Tronto suggests that twentieth-century arguments for a "women's morality"—from the suffragist claim "if women voted there would be no more war" to the 1992 cry heralding "the year of the woman"—have been unsuccessful in attaining a place for women in the political realm. Early in the twentieth century, for example, those opposed to granting women access to the world of political decision-making proposed that women were "too moral" to participate in political life. At least some women were "too moral" for politics; "other" women were excluded as too amoral for politics. Tronto observes:

A companion to the argument that "women are more moral than men" is an image of "women" that has historically (and, I shall argue, necessarily) excluded many "women" from its purview. In the United States, for example, the morality of women was tied to motherhood, and was tied to combating the influence of immigrant, Black, and working class men. As a result, the image of "moral women" often excluded women of color, immigrant women, poor women, lesbians, and women who were not "fit" mothers. The strategy of women's morality has required for all of its limited success, that some women's realities (to say nothing of their sense of morality!) be sacrificed to achieve other women's inclusion. (p. 2)

She acknowledges, however, that although the limitations of "women's morality" seem apparent, the argument continues to influence some popular and scholarly writings.[1]

Tronto attributes the appeal of "women's morality" to the ideas that form its foundation. She suggests that in the late-twentieth-century United States, consumed by an unrestricted focus on the goals of productivity and progress, many people long for a "better world" and alternative approaches to morality. She also seeks this "better world," but wants to avoid "the strategic traps" that have "doomed" the women's morality approach. In suggesting that feminist ideals could inform a good society, Tronto proposes to place at the center of moral decision-making all the values traditionally associated with women in the private sphere, and, because of the lens of gender polarization, excluded from public discourse. These values of care include attentiveness, compassion, and nurturance. Tronto is not alone in this enterprise. She joins scholars such as Sonja K. Foss and Cindy Griffin (1995), Helen M. Sterk (1995), Helen M. Sterk and Lynn H. Turner (1994), Patricia A. Sullivan and Steven R. Goldzwig (1995), and Julia T. Wood (1992, 1994) in urging that care become central in public decision making and public discourse.

A "better vision," then, will place "a care ethic" at the center of politics. Tronto agrees with Sandra Lipsitz Bem (1993) that hidden patriarchal assumptions work in a systematic fashion to reproduce patriarchy through the generations. For Tronto, the "lenses of gender" have produced "moral boundaries" in philosophy and political theory, that, as many feminist scholars have noted, have excluded consideration of questions that concern women and people who do "caring" work. Although some exceptions exist, "for the most part, questions of natality, mortality, and the needs of humans to be cared for as they grow up, live, and die, have not informed the central questions of philosophers" (p. 3).[2]

Tronto proposes to re-vision moral decision making by bringing such questions from the periphery to the center of the philosophy that informs political theorizing. She answers Wood's (1992) call for scholars to examine the philosophical implications of research conducted by feminist cultural theorists such as Carol Gilligan (1982). Although studies by Gilligan and her followers have been criticized for drawing unwarranted generalizations about "women's morality" and overlooking differences among women based on race, class, and sexual orientation, Wood and Tronto believe that Gilligan's research encourages scholars to ask questions about "Western conceptions of morality itself [that] may be critically limited by androcentric biases" (Wood, 1992, p. 16).[3]

These views of morality informing Western approaches to political decision-making are eighteenth-century conceptions. The eighteenth century was marked by social change and a shift from moral theories that relied on context to the dominance of theories that derive their moral force from universal principles. Tronto explains the different world views suggested by contextual and universalistic moral theories. Contextual moral theories propose that more is involved in moral decision-making than the use of human reason in following the rules. She notes that such theories have a long history in Western philosophical thought. Aristotle's vision of moral life, for example, depends upon citizens as members of a community making judicious decisions based upon context. Because in Aristotle's view an individual's moral sensibilities shape the moral fabric of a community, politics and ethics are inseparable. Tronto observes, though, that in the eighteenth century it was apparent to many philosophers that the Aristotelian concept of virtue described above no longer accurately depicted social and political life.

During the eighteenth century, literate Western Europeans believed in their ability to influence the world around them. Whereas Aristotle viewed moral decision-making as involving intricate interconnections among individuals in a circumscribed local community, eighteenth-century Western Europeans viewed themselves as part of a much larger and complex global community. Due to the rise of commercialism and expanding global markets, eighteenth-century European philosophers viewed their concerns as universal rather than local; therefore, they developed moral theories, grounded in human reason, to unite people around the globe.

Social transformations in the eighteenth and nineteenth centuries also changed the definitions of family and household. Stephanie Coontz (1988) refers to the period between 1870 and 1890 as the "apex of private spheres" and observes that a trend characterizing the period was the "expulsion of wives from productive labor" (p. 261). The result of this expulsion, which occurred in all classes and ethnic groups except African Americans, was to more clearly delineate wives' domestic tasks and to sharply divide wives' responsibilities from husbands'. Tronto notes that people in this period moved from existences that were primarily family oriented or "private" to existences that were more "public." Because people in this period engaged in more travel and interacted with more people on a routine basis, they conceptualized "private" and "public" spheres.[4] Tronto notes that the separation of economic life from domestic life produced two spheres—the public and the private—and the family was classed in the private domain.

Tronto thus argues that social transformations in the eighteenth century led to a vision of morality informed by the recognition of separate spheres as well as universal standards for conduct. She suggests, then, that the ideas of Immanuel Kant were viewed as definitive in the eighteenth century. Reason, seen as the higher plane of existence, represented abstract or universal standards to guide moral conduct in the public world (including the global world). The other source for standards stemmed from the "sentiments" (analogous to the emotions) grounded in the household or private sphere.

A combination of factors in the eighteenth century thereby contributed to the bifurcation of the private and the public (sentiment and reason).[5] These factors led to dualistic thinking that resulted in circumscribed worlds for women and men which closely correspond to Bem's lens of polar opposition. Interestingly, Tronto presents a cogent argument for the arbitrariness of the assignment of sentiment to women and reason to men. She notes that feelings and emotions have not always been considered the exclusive province of women. In fact, in English-speaking countries during the eighteenth century, sentiment was viewed as the hallmark of a virtuous man. As the eighteenth century progressed, however, the capacities to "reason" and "feel" became "engendered" and in the process, women and men were expected to truncate the range of their capabilities.

Tronto traces this "engendering" of qualities associated with reasoning and feeling. Eighteenth-century philosophers raised questions about women's roles in light of changes in economic organization. For example, because the household no longer served as the "prime unit of economic production" (Tronto, p. 52), arguments were made that women should be educated to assume positions in the "public world." Furthermore, Enlightenment thinkers questioned the validity of "birth-based hierarchies" (Tronto, p. 53) and proposed that people should be able to succeed in society to the extent that their reasoning capabilities permitted. In 1792, for example, Mary Wollstonecraft, argued in her treatise *Vindication of the Rights of Woman*:

I wish to persuade women to endeavor to acquire strength, both of mind and body, and to convince them that the soft phrases, susceptibility of heart, delicacy of sentiment, and refinement of taste, are almost synonymous with epithets of weakness, and that those beings who are only the objects of pity, and that kind of love which has been termed its sister, will soon become objects of contempt. (1978 [1792], pp. 81–82)

Although writers such as Wollstonecraft advocated education for women, many other eighteenth-century thinkers considered ways to "contain" women in the private sphere.

By the middle of the eighteenth century women had become highly visible in public spaces. Because women were more visible, questions were raised about their conduct (especially their sexual conduct). Tronto cites a Scottish writer in the *Lounger*, who wrote under the pseudonym Colonel Caustic and reflected nostalgically on the "good old days" when women knew their proper place. Women became subjects for satire, and apprehension concerning their sexuality was apparent in the writings of philosophers such as Jean Jacques Rousseau. Rousseau believed women, through the use of their sexual powers, could control men and short-circuit their reasoning. Because women had such powers, Rousseau argued that they should be kept out of public life lest they interfere with the rational capacities of men. As Tronto notes, Rousseau theorized that women should be confined to the private sphere due to their "sexual difference," thereby moving from biological differences to differences in social functions. Tronto observes that in *Emile, Social Contract*, and through his reading of Plato's *Republic*, Rousseau argued that a separate private sphere—delegated to women—was necessary for the moral functioning of a public sphere.

Rousseau's line of reasoning was typical for thinkers responding to women's adoption of public roles. Although Enlightenment thought seemed to suggest that people should succeed on the basis of their capabilities, especially their capabilities to reason, women were viewed as an exception to this prevailing view. In their efforts to "contain" women in private roles, particularly in the home, thinkers such as Rousseau argued for a special role for women in fostering "moral sentiments" (Tronto, p. 55). As public roles for men in the social worlds of commerce and politics became increasingly demanding, philosophers argued that women should provide a "tempering" influence in the home. As "the pre-eminent guardians of the household" (p. 55), women were supposed to serve as antidotes to the corrupting values of the public sphere. Women became associated with the world of feeling in the household, and men became associated with the world of reason and the public world—including politics.

In discussing the bifurcation of public and private spheres, Tronto echoes Bem's beliefs concerning the lenses of gender emphasizing that the relegation of women to the private world (the world of moral sentiments or feeling) and men to the public world (the world of reason) "was the outcome of an historical process, and not the result of biologically essential facts nor a necessary result from change in social structures" (p. 56). Yet, regardless of its source, this division held sway over people's thoughts and actions. Clara E. Haase, a student at a Milwaukee Women's College in 1909, illustrates the influence of this dichotomized perspective in her senior essay. She writes, "instill it into the girl that she should not be ambitious and take away a boy's proper right and place; but that she should help him to be ambitious; that her proper sphere is the home—[sic] the world is for the boy" (p. 20). Ms. Haase clearly indicates her beliefs about the proper and separate spaces for men and women.

Tronto questions these eighteenth-century engendered "conceptions of morality itself"—conceptions that continue to guide moral reasoning in Western cultures. She argues that three boundaries, reflecting the distribution of power and privilege along gender lines, have informed political decision-making in Western cultures. The bifurcation of moral sentiment (feeling) and reason led to three moral boundaries that privileged a morality of "rights," grounded in absolutes and abstract philosophical thought, rather than a morality of "care," grounded in sensitivity to context and the maintenance of relationships. These boundaries include: (1) morality and politics, (2) the moral point of view, and (3) the public and private.

The Morality and Politics Boundary

Tronto argues that the first boundary, "between morality and politics," exists because, in general, contemporary political theorists do not see the two—morality and politics—as ideas that are intertwined and consistent with one another. She identifies two manifestations of this boundary. One manifestation, the "morality first" perspective, suggests that moral principles are absolutes and all situations in political life should be made to adhere to these fixed principles. From this standpoint, moral decision-making is devoid of contextual considerations and based on abstractions, as the task of liberal political philosophers is to clearly articulate moral principles and then convince the political world to accept them as absolutes.

Liberal political philosophers, from this perspective, function in Kathyrn Pyne Addelson's (1994) terms, as Aristotle's men of "practical wisdom" (p. 39). As Addelson explains, Aristotle's man of "practical wisdom" was vested with intellectual and political authority due to his standing "in a class and gendered society" (p. 39). Because the man of practical wisdom knew what was best for society, he served as a voice of reason and arbitrator of moral issues and "represented the established, stable public face of society" (Addelson, p. 39).[6]

Rousseau also expressed faith in the voices of reason and suggested that men should be educated for public service. As Okin (1979) notes, Rousseau believed that human beings, specifically male human beings, could be educated to be good citizens. Although Rousseau criticized Aristotle's reasoning that some people, due to their natural capacities, were destined to be slaves, he argued "that servility is natural in all women" (Okin, p. 127). Women could not be educated to be "right thinking individuals"; therefore, they could not assume public leadership roles. Rousseau's arguments concerning the education of women were driven by his assumptions concerning appropriate roles for women.

Rousseau does not, however, first assert that woman is mentally inferior to man and then draw conclusions from this about her proper function and position in society. Rather, his method is to begin by assuming that woman's role is to be a desirable and faithful sexual object for man, his wife and the mother of his children, and then to draw conclusions as to what her intellectual capacities *should* be like, in order to fit her for her proper function. (Okin, p. 130)

Thus, although Rousseau argued that reason could be cultivated through education, his social prejudice blinded him to applying this argument to the education of women. Therefore, women could not be educated to serve as public moral leaders.

One manifestation of the "morality first" boundary suggests that women lack the knowledge to serve as moral leaders in society. Another manifestation of this boundary is the "politics first" or Machiavellian perspective. This standpoint suggests that political power must be maintained regardless of the costs. When politics is perceived as a power struggle over limited resources, moral principles are viewed as irrelevant—at least in the public world. Virginia Held (1993) describes the Machiavellian tradition where morality is only relevant in private interactions between family and friends. "In public, political life, 'dirty hands' are inevitable and morally irrelevant" (p. 87).

Jean Bethke Elshtain (1981) argues that Machiavelli's theory of politics maintains a relevance in contemporary Western cultures—including U.S.

culture. Because Machiavelli emphasized "means to the ends," he suspended morality as a consideration in political decision-making. Machiavelli's vision of politics diverged from the vision of politics that marked Christian thought. In Christian thought, "justice and righteousness" governed the world of politics (Elshtain, p. 93).[7]

Machiavelli circumscribed a public political sphere governed by different rules than the private sphere of the household. Because politics is inherently a dirty business, leaders in this public world should not be evaluated by the moral standards of the private world. As Elshtain notes, "thus, within Machiavelli's world, a man could be a good ruler but a wicked person if private morality were set up as the criterion by which to judge his private actions, an alternative Machiavelli rejects as suicidal to political survival" (p. 93). From the Machiavellian perspective, the moral standards of the private sphere interfere with power in the political world.

Machiavelli, however, argued that moral standards should be applied in the proper realm—the private sphere. This line of argumentation had serious consequences for women. For Machiavelli, the private and public spheres complemented each other. Elshtain explains Machiavelli's philosophy: "Women are not of politics per se, but provide, in their capacities in the private sphere, a refuge from public life for men when they share in the private sphere" (p. 94). From this perspective, "A 'good' woman makes a 'bad' citizen by definition. . . . Women are morally superior *because* they are publicly inferior" (p. 94). Women *and* men thus function as apolitical agents in the private sphere; however, women are confined to the private sphere whereas men have the opportunity to move in both spheres.[8]

In the nineteenth-century United States, members of the female benevolence movement framed their rhetorical appeals using taken-for-granted assumptions concerning the moral superiority of women. Lori D. Ginzberg (1990) explains that "the ideology of women's higher standard of virtue was self-fulfilling, since authors defined virtue itself to conform to women's visible world" (p. 13). Because women had been shielded from the "dirty" world of politics, they seemed to be "more moral" than men. Ginzberg says: "Excluded from political process, women had little opportunity to behave as corruptly as male politicians who bought votes. Rarely achieving positions of economic power, they were not among the merchants who profited from faulty or frivolous goods" (p. 13). Thus, because public and private spheres were bifurcated and women were associated with the "more moral" private sphere, members of the benevolence movement used this assumption to argue for the special influence of women in society.[9]

The Moral Point of View Boundary

The "moral point of view," the second boundary, mandates that moral decisions be grounded in a point of view of objectivity, distance, and disinterest. According to Tronto, most political theorists since the eighteenth century have embraced Immanuel Kant's position that superior moral judgments are objective and disinterested. From this perspective, moral decision-making "should arise not out of the concrete circumstances of any given society, but out of the requirements of reason" (Tronto, p. 9). Decision-making based on the "moral point of view," in sum, suggests that sound decision-making is divorced from the arena of feelings. Additionally, Tronto points out that the "moral point of view" implies that decision-making should not be contextualized or influenced by situational diversity but should instead appear as universal. The ideal moral decision-maker remains detached and denies the significance of "emotion, daily life, and political circumstances" (Tronto, p. 9). Virginia Held (1993) explains that Kant's categorical imperative requires the decision-maker to apply "an impartial, pure, rational principle to particular cases" (p. 50). A set of universal rational principles exists that may be utilized in making moral decisions.

Held also suggests that reason, in the guise of the detached and autonomous decision-maker, takes another form in the modern era. The Utilitarian approach to moral decision-making "recognizes that persons have desires and interests, and suggests rules of rational choice for maximizing the satisfaction of these desires and interests" (p. 50). Although the Kantian and Utilitarian approaches differ in their assumptions about the role of reason in moral decision-making, Held notes that both philosophies "share a reliance on a highly abstract, universal principle as the appropriate source of moral guidance, and they share the view that moral problems are to be solved by the application of such an abstract principle to particular cases" (p. 50). Both approaches privilege the role of reason and "denigrate emotional responses to moral issues" (p. 50).

Addelson (1994) discusses a detached and autonomous approach to decision-making that she believes makes serious, responsible research difficult. For Addelson, the "individualist perspective" in social scientific research suggests "the ideal knower is a judging observer, not a participant in the world being judged" (p. 138). In this paradigm, the assumption is that judgment, guided by the individualist perspective, allows the social world to become as predictable as the scientific world. The detached and autonomous judge views the past as an entity to be studied and the future as an entity to be defined. In sum, when individuals serve as judges and ground decisions in "professional authority" (p. 139), devoid of contextual considerations, they provide solutions based upon abstract standards of reason.

A number of feminist thinkers have traced consequences for women when authority is associated with the detached and autonomous decision-maker. Jane Flax (1992) proposes that the epistemological power and rhetorical force of the moral point of view resides in the dream of "innocent knowledge" (p. 447). "Innocent knowledge" is defined by Flax as "the discovery of some sort of truth which can tell us how to act in the world in ways that benefit or are for the (at least ultimate) good of all" (p. 447). She refers to this knowledge as "innocent" because when individuals act in accordance with this knowledge, they are comforted by the fact that they have done the "right thing." "Innocent knowledge" provides moral legitimation for those who "act as the servant of something higher and outside (or more than) themselves, their own desires and the effects of their particular histories or social locations" (p. 447). Flax also suggests that many feminists have grounded their arguments for equality in "innocent knowledge" and the "Enlightenment discourses of rights, individualism, and equality" (p. 447).[10]

Martha Minow (1990) challenges the Enlightenment discourses of rights, individualism, and equality as they inform legal reasoning in the United States. She says that "much of legal reasoning demands familiarity with legal terms, practice in perceiving problems through categories, and acceptance of the consequences assigned to particular legal categories" (p. 1). The mark of the effective legal reasoner is the ability to remain detached and autonomous in sorting problems and assigning them to categories. Minow argues that legal analysis is analogous to other forms of analysis and says: "When we analyze, we simplify. We break complicated perceptions into discrete items or traits. We identify the items and call them chair, table, cat, and bed. We sort them into categories that already exist: furniture and animal. It sounds familiar. It also sounds harmless. I do not think it is" (p. 3). Legal reasoners are distant and disinterested parties who make decisions in accordance with the categories. These categories function as truths that provide a rationale for classifying individuals as inside or outside the boundaries of the legal system. Minow argues that these categories are value laden and may "express and implement prejudice, racism, sexism, anti-Semitism, intolerance for difference" (p. 3).

Recent examples of Minow's argument abound. The categories that legal reasoning provide may very well have obscured much of the complexity of the Anita Hill–Clarence Thomas hearings in 1991. In writing about this case, Kimberlé Crenshaw (1992) observes that the experience of black women in U.S. society can be construed as "intersectional." By this, Crenshaw means that black women are located at the intersection of two dominating hierarchies, one sexual and one racial. At this intersection, some experiences of black women are unexplainable in terms of race or gender alone. Crenshaw continues by noting that legal doctrine does not provide well for this intersectionality and "black females.... sometimes fall between the existing legal categories for recognizing injury" (p. 404). Black women may be required to choose between two competing identities to be legally recognized. Crenshaw's thesis is that Anita Hill suffered "intersectional disempowerment" during the hearings.

More recently, the reactions to O. J. Simpson's acquittal also illustrate Minow's perspective that legal categories are value laden. The lines of gender and race clearly informed the values people brought to this case, yet it is also clear that gender and race intersected to make reactions to the acquittal more complex than the black–white issue the media represented it to be. In her *New York Times* column, Maureen Dowd (1995) observes: "This week polls show that we are still two separate societies, that whites cannot fathom the distrust that blacks feel given their day-to-day experiences, and accumulated rage that can counter rational arguments" (p. A29). Ironically, in the same column Dowd quotes Robert Coles, who questions the efficacy of depicting the situation in polarized black–white terms. Coles said: "It [the reaction to Simpson's acquittal] is the anatomy of all the tensions, polarizations, suspicions, distrust, grudges and reasons for the grudges writ large" (quoted in Dowd, 1995, p. A29). Coles advocates a contextualized approach to decision-making that most reporters and members of the general public seem to have missed.

Mary Daly (1973) claims that the categorizer, the detached and autonomous decision-maker, worships the false god of "methodolatry" (p. 11). According to Daly, theologians, philosophers, and many academics embrace methodolatry and decontextualize their decision-making. When abstractions guide decision-making, "it commonly happens that the choice of a problem is determined by method, instead of method being determined by the problem" (Daly, p. 11). Abstract decision-makers disregard "ideas that do not fit into pre-established boxes and forms," and disregard and view them "as nondata" (Daly, p. 11). Furthermore, Daly argues that the false god of methodolatry is used to exclude women from decision-making processes.

It should be noted that the god of Method is in fact a subordinate deity, serving higher powers. These are social and cultural institutions whose survival depends upon the classification of disruptive and disturbing information as nondata. Under patriarchy, Method has wiped out women's questions so totally that even women have not been able to hear and formulate our own questions to meet our own experiences. Women have been unable even to experience their own experience. (pp. 11–12)

Daly thus argues that taken-for-granted assumptions, grounded in abstract claims and legitimated by appeals to reason, preclude consideration of women's experiences in developing approaches to decision-making. Carol P. Christ (1980) concurs with Daly and comments that women have been in the difficult position of trying to understand their experiences through a male (and thus rational) perspective. This is the case, according to Christ, because women have not been in control of shaping their own experience into story.

For Mary Field Belenky, Blythe McVicker Clinchy, Nancy Rule Goldberger, and Jill Mattuck Tarule (1986), Daly's methodolotry is an epistemology based on "separate knowing." They argue that separate or "impersonal knowers espouse a morality based on impersonal procedures for establishing justice" (p. 102). During their interviews with women, Belenky and her colleagues discovered that it was "easy to hear" (p. 102) the voices of separate knowers. Because psychologists such as Piaget (1951, 1952, 1965, 1973), Kohlberg (1969, 1981, 1984) and Perry (1970, 1981) have argued for the superiority of the voice of separate knowing in moral development, the markers of this voice are clearly defined. Separate knowers do not perceive relationships between themselves as knowers and the objects/subjects of knowing. For example, separate knowers, as detached and autonomous voices, see themselves as critical thinkers and gatekeepers at "exclusive clubs"—clubs for people "tough enough" to suspend their emotions and engage in reasoned discourse. Separate knowers are tough on themselves. They "assume that everyone—including themselves, may be wrong" (p. 104).

Belenky and her colleagues do not argue that the voice of "separate knowing" is associated exclusively with men in Western cultures; however, they agree with Tronto, Daly, and Christ that this voice has been privileged in Western cultural experience. They suggest that when women and men embrace the voice of "separate knowing," there is a recognition that detached and autonomous reasoning is associated with power and important decisions.[11]

The Public and Private Boundary

The final moral boundary separates issues associated with public and private life. Clearly, the boundary between public and private life is instrumental in maintaining the other two boundaries identified by Tronto. Tronto notes that many feminist scholars have observed that much Western thought distinguishes separate transactions for the public and private world, and confines women to the private world. This last boundary not only excluded women from public life, but created separate spheres for public and private life. Because men dominated public life, their value orientations informed public policy decisions. Elshtain (1981) describes the public world and the value orientations that excluded women from that world:

> Because women have, throughout much of Western history, been a silenced population in the arena of public speech, their views on these matters, and their role in the process of humanization, have either been taken for granted or assigned a lesser order of significance and honor compared to the public, political activities of males. Women were silenced in part because that which defines them and to which they are inescapably linked—sexuality, natality, the human body (images of uncleanness and taboo, visions of dependency, helplessness, vulnerability)—was omitted from political speech. (p. 15)

Thus, in Western philosophical thought, women's biological or "natural" characteristics were used to confine them to a private world.

The world of women—the household—is "an island beyond politics" (Held, 1993, p. 54). Feminists reject the bifurcation of private and public worlds and note that "the personal is highly affected by the political power beyond [i.e., abortion legislation]" (Held, p. 54). Patricia J. Williams (1991) points out that we confuse the personal with the private. While private issues may not be appropriate for public discourse, the personal "is where our most idealistic and our deadliest politics are lodged, and are revealed" (p. 93). All the moral boundaries, as noted earlier in this chapter, are legitimated through philosophical discourse that aligns women with the world of emotion and men with the world of reason. Women, as Held explains, have been associated with the "natural" world and defined in accordance with their biological natures (i.e., childbearing). The private realm, that of the household, "is seen as the natural realm where women merely reproduce the species" (p. 54). Men, on the other hand, are associated with the public world, the world of reason, "the distinctively human realm in which man transcends nature" (p. 54). In the Western philosophical tradition, these worlds are clearly delineated and "these associations are extraordinarily pervasive in standard concepts and theories, in art and thought, and cultural ideals, and especially politics" (p. 54).

Held argues, then, that in Western philosophical thought, men have been associated with a "specifically human activity" (p. 55)—politics—and women have been associated with an activity—childbearing—that is not specifically human. Women engage in "natural" activities and men engage in "rational discussion in the polis" (p. 55).

Linda Nicholson (1993) cites the work of Roberto Unger (1975) and explains that the identification of separate spheres for private and public activity is basic to liberal political theory shaped by the ideas of Machiavelli, Thomas Hobbes, John Locke, and John Stuart Mill. The foundation for liberal political theory is dichotomous thinking where "on the one hand stands the order of reason, thought, form, rules, and means. On the other exists the order of desire, feeling, content, substance, and ends" (Nicholson, p. 93). Citizens are united in their public concerns or those governed by reason, but divided in their private concerns or those that "constitute our particularity" (Nicholson, p. 94). Based on this perspective, reason is associated with the public world "because knowledge, to the extent it is true, does not vary among persons. When desiring, however, men are private beings because they can never offer others more than a partial justification for their goals in the public language of thought" (Unger, quoted in Nicholson, p. 94). This world view precludes the possibility of caring from an objective perspective or reasoning from a subjective vantage point.

For our purposes in studying political communication, it is especially significant that women were excluded from rational discussion in the polis. Public speaking, associated with the realm of politics, was viewed as unnatural for women. Karlyn Kohrs Campbell and E. Claire Jerry (1988) argue that "public speaking and femininity were perceived as mutually exclusive" (p. 123). In the nineteenth century, women fought for the right to express themselves in public. Furthermore, "Because gender roles persist, contemporary women who seek leadership positions face barriers that make it particularly difficult for them to succeed" (p. 123). Kathleen Hall Jamieson (1995) discusses the historical roots of the "double bind" of silence and shame that Campbell and Jerry refer to. Jamieson writes of the Biblical injunctions to silence for women, citing Paul's comment 'Let a woman learn in silence with all submissiveness' (quoted in Jamieson, p. 80). Jamieson further notes the persistence of the notion that silence is a mark of a virtuous woman by observing, for example, that Anita Hill was criticized for being a "relentless debater."

A number of factors coalesced in the middle of the nineteenth century to consign women to the nonpolitical, private sphere of the household. In the commercialized, industrialized, and urbanized nineteenth-century United States, sentiment was out of place in the public world. Two conceptual ideals, "true womanhood" and "woman-belle ideal," defined women "as suited only for gender-based roles as wives and mothers and as a repository for cherished but commercially useless spiritual values" (Campbell and Jerry, p. 123).[12] The private world of the home and woman's sphere served as a refuge from "amoral capitalism and dirty politics" (Campbell and Jerry, p. 123). In 1909, Clara E. Haase, a student at Milwaukee Downer Women's College, reflected prevailing nineteenth-century views when she wrote in her senior essay on education for girls that "we need to protect our girls from the corroding and destructive side of money-making" (p. 2).

Although taken-for-granted cultural assumptions in the nineteenth century suggested that women embodied spiritual values and occupied a higher moral plane than men, women were not permitted to speak out publicly about social problems such as slavery. When women entered the public world of politics, they "lost their claim to purity and piety" (Campbell and Jerry, pp. 123–124). Campbell and Jerry suggest that the movement for women's rights "grew out of this contradiction" (p. 124).

When women sought public platforms and spoke out about social injustices, Scripture was used to justify silencing them. Because Eve was responsible for the "fall" and bringing sin into the world, "she was placed under the dominion of her husband and prohibited from speaking" (Campbell and Jerry, p. 124). Women speakers in the nineteenth century, however, challenged the prohibition against public speaking. Early speeches by Angelina and Sarah Grimké were presented before women in the private sphere of the home; however, as they attracted larger audiences, their speeches were moved to churches. When the American Anti-Slavery Society admitted all interested parties (including women) to its ranks, women became more visible as speakers. Critics of highly visible speakers such as the Grimkés charged them with violating their "duties" as set forth in the New Testament and engaging in "unnatural activities" (quoted in Campbell and Jerry, p. 124).[13] When Lucy Stone and Antoinette Brown were students at Oberlin, they "horrified the community by debating each other in rhetoric class" (Campbell and Jerry, p. 124). Stone came close to being denied graduation at Oberlin when she insisted on presenting her own oration rather than permitting a male faculty member to read the oration for her.[14]

Campbell and Jerry explore the significance of the controversy over women as public speakers. They argue that the issue was not public speaking per se, but the challenge that females in public speaking roles presented to "male authority and rationality" (p. 124). When women sought influence beyond the private, domestic realm of the home, they sought equality and violated male authority in the public realm. When women spoke in public, they violated the culturally shared value that "rhetorical action is, as defined by gender roles, a masculine domain" (Campbell and Jerry, p. 125).

Speakers operate in the public sphere; women's concerns are domestic. Speakers call attention to themselves, aggressively take stands, affirm their expertise; "true women" are retiring, their influence is indirect, they have no expertise on matters outside the home. The public realm is driven by ambition; similarly speaking is competitive, energized by the desire to persuade others. These are traditionally masculine traits related to man's allegedly lustful, competitive nature. In other words, a woman who speaks affirms her "masculinity"; more precisely, she affirms her possession of qualities that are ascribed only to males. (p. 125)

In sum, women speakers challenged audience assumptions concerning masculinity and femininity and the spheres of conduct appropriate for women and men.

Throughout U.S. history, women who spoke publicly and violated the culturally defined spheres of conduct for women and men have been labeled heresiarchs, hysterics, and witches (Jamieson, 1995, pp. 86–91). Anne Hutchinson was banished from colonial America when she attempted to assume a leadership role in the Boston church (discussed in Jamieson, p. 87). Elizabeth Cady Stanton's *The Women's Bible* was attacked by a member of the clergy who argued the book was "the work of woman, and the devil" (quoted in Jamieson, p. 87). When Mrs. E. P. W. Packard disagreed with her husband, a clergyman, on religious matters, he committed her to the Jacksonville State Hospital for the Insane in Illinois. She kept a diary during her internment in the mental institution and wrote:

Had I lived in the sixteenth instead of the nineteenth century, my husband would have used the laws of the day to punish me as a heretic for this departure from the established creed—while under the influence of some intolerant spirit he now uses this autocratic institution as a means of torture to bring about the same result—namely a *recantation of my faith*. (quoted in Jamieson, p. 88)

Other women were labeled witches when they spoke out. "Assaultive speech" was the most common accusation against "witches" in colonial America. Because women were confined to the private sphere, the sphere aligned with emotion rather than reason, their accusers charged they were more susceptible to appeals from the devil. As Jamieson observes, "witches died in ways that symbolized the extinction of their speech. At the stake, fire (a metaphor for speech) consumed the witch and her capacity to speak. Alternatively, fiery words were drenched permanently by drowning. Hanging simultaneously choked the ability to speak and the speaker" (p. 89).

Finally, women were labeled hysterics. Many women in the nineteenth-century United States were subjected to "rest cures" designed to cure their hysteria. The disease (particular to women) was labeled hysteria by Hippocrates, who derived the term from the Greek word for uterus. Because women were assumed to be emotional and associated with the natural world (i.e., reproductive functions), any disorder of the mind was linked with a disorder in the reproductive system. "Rest cures" contained and silenced women in order to restore their bodily (i.e., reproductive functions). Of course, ironically, the "rest cure" put the woman in the position of dominating her family's life.

Even as the twentieth century closes, women face barriers when they speak out in public. Because women speakers span the boundaries for masculinity and femininity embraced by the audience, they face special challenges. A woman must be "all things" to all audience members and meet traditional expectations for *female* and *male* conduct in a public speaking situation. In order to establish her credibility, a woman speaker must project "expertise, authority, and rationality" (male-identified traits) (Campbell and Jerry, 1988, p. 125) *and* softness, warmth, and deference (female-identified traits). If a woman projects male-associated traits devoid of the tempering female-associated traits, she may be perceived as "unwomanly, too aggressive, and cold" (Campbell and Jerry, p. 125). As we discussed in Chapter 1, some empirical research on women political candidates corroborates Campbell and Jerry's assertion.

The three moral boundaries, thus, exert considerable force on women's lives, especially on those women who wish to assume leadership positions. The boundary between public and private life contains human beings in gender-associated spheres where male-associated and female-associated characteristics are clearly delineated. The boundary between public and private life legitimated the other two boundaries identified by Tronto—the boundary between morality and politics and the moral point of view. The division between public and private life philosophically framed women as unsuited to public (including political) life. Women were destined to be on the margins of public life for the following reasons: (1) They lacked capacities for reason, and therefore were considered intellectually inferior to men; (2) they represented sentiment (emotion) and therefore were morally superior to men; and (3) they (due to their limited reasoning capabilities and abundant sentiments) were incapable of autonomous and detached decision-making.

Although contradictions abound in the reasoning concerning women (and men) in the intellectually bounded and bifurcated world described by Tronto, philosophers legitimated patriarchal power by providing a rationale (supposedly grounded in nature) for containing women in the private world. Women, however, have struggled, and continue to struggle against the boundaries constraining them from the public domain. The women we profile in the succeeding chapters have taken several approaches to the constraints placed upon them by the current positioning of the boundaries.

CONTEMPORARY POLITICAL WOMEN AND MORAL BOUNDARIES

In seeking roles in the public world of politics, women have developed rhetorical strategies responding to the moral boundaries defined by Tronto. When Representative Patricia Schroeder decided against seeking the 1988 Democratic nomination for the presidency, she expressed frustration with political processes and probably spoke for many political women when she said: "I could not figure out how to run and not be separated from those I serve. There must be a way, but I presently haven't figured it out yet" (quoted in Weaver, 1987, p. 1A). As women try to "figure out" how to respond to boundaries as they enter political life, they are developing a number of approaches to making their voices heard. Three rhetorical strategies surfaced through close analysis of the research on political women communicators as well as our own case studies presented in Chapters 3 through 5. Three strategies include: (1) denying; (2) confronting and accommodating; and (3) re-visioning.

Denying

Women who deny the presence of boundaries when they attempt to enter the political world express faith in a rationalist paradigm. When women political communicators deny the barriers, they suggest that the moral boundaries are nonexistent or permeable. From the perspective of the denier, the rules for political communication are clear and success will follow if those rules are followed.

Dr. Jocelyn Elders, in her brief tenure as U.S. Surgeon General, exemplified the denying rhetorical strategy for women as political communicators. When President Clinton forced Elders to resign from her post as Surgeon General, a headline in the *New York Times* reported: "Clinton Had Warned Dr. Elders to Curb Tendency to Make Controversial Remarks" (Jehl, 1994, p. A1). Elders expressed faith in the "morality first" boundary. She seemed to assume that she spoke the "truth" and would be honored for doing so; she did not seem to understand that she spoke the wrong "truth" in her public discussion of issues associated with sexuality—issues usually discussed in private. Additionally, she did not seem to recognize that in the Machiavellian world of politics, principle ("truth telling") is not necessarily valued unless it serves particular strategic ends. During an interview for the the *New York Times Magazine*, Elders was asked about her remarks on the legalization of drugs (remarks that "ruffled some feathers" [Dreifus, 1994, p. 18] according to the interviewer). Elders responded by saying, "I served on commissions and task forces with [Clinton] for 13 years, so he couldn't say that he didn't know what I was about" (quoted in Dreifus, p. 19). Elders seemed to be saying that Clinton knew she spoke her mind and should have been prepared to hear her continue to do so.

During that same *New York Times Magazine* interview, Elders expressed faith in the support she would receive from President Clinton. The interviewer asked Elders if she was concerned that Clinton might turn on her the way he did on Lani Guinier. She replied that she had every assurance from the president that he was supporting her. She then commented that she expected that they might disagree from time to time;

she noted that she disagreed with her husband so why shouldn't she disagree with Clinton occasionally? Elders displayed a "let the chips fall where they may" attitude that may be typical of African American women (Shuter and Turner, 1992). That attitude, however, put her in a position of denying that boundaries might constrain her actions and that she could receive negative repercussions for her honesty. Whereas deniers refuse to acknowledge the existence of barriers, confronters and accommodaters recognize barriers to their participation as leaders in political processes and communicate as though they will be able to circumvent those barriers.

Confronting and Accommodating

Confronting and accommodating may be seen as separate rhetorical strategies, but we place them together here because women who are able to have a voice in mainstream politics use them in combination. Women who primarily confront (i.e., Mary Daly, Angela Davis, Andrea Dworkin, bell hooks, and Patricia J. Williams) find their voices outside of governmental politics. Complete accommodation to the boundaries results in silence. Thus, when women confront and accommodate the boundaries, they demonstrate a conscious or unconscious recognition that they are disadvantaged, but not disempowered as communicators in the political world. Campbell and Jerry (1988), for example, argue that Geraldine Ferraro and Nancy Kassebaum recognize the double binds they face as female communicators and have developed speaking strategies responding to these double binds. Ferraro and Kassebaum confront and accommodate the stereotypic perceptions of women as political communicators. In her speeches as a vice-presidential candidate, Ferraro accepted opportunities to challenge the assumption that women are "irrational" decision-makers. She spoke confidently in arguing for her leadership abilities during the vice-presidential debate with George Bush, and said: "My feeling, quite frankly, is that I have enough experience to see the problems, address them and make the tough decisions and level with people" (Transcript of Philadelphia debate, 1984, p. 4). Throughout the campaign, however, she did not hesitate to emphasize that in addition to her nontraditional role as a female politician, she also played traditional female roles as wife, mother, and caregiver for her aging mother. As a U.S. Senator, Kassebaum suggests she is "reasonable" by carefully constructing and supporting her arguments. Campbell and Jerry acknowledge that Kassebaum also accommodates by taking on traditional female roles (i.e., mediator, teacher) in the Senate (p. 131). As the Republican-controlled Senate debated overhauls of the Medicare and Medicaid programs, during Fall 1995, for example, Kassebaum emerged as a voice of moderation and a mediator.

Janis L. King (1990) suggests that Wilma Mankiller used a strategy similar to confronting and accommodating in her successful bid to become the first elected female principal chief of the Cherokee Nation of Oklahoma. King points out that Mankiller was the subject of many attacks during the campaign and she had to respond in a manner that both confronted her opponents and would not alienate her rhetorical audience. The strategy Mankiller employed was an educational one. She instructed her audience in the traditional ways of the Cherokee, showing that the attacks upon her were unfounded and that her attackers were in fact the ones out of step with Cherokee culture. King points out that the educational strategy was useful because "women are viewed often as responsible for educating children and therefore maintaining the culture" (p. 35). Thus, Mankiller employed a strategy that marries confrontation with accommodation.

Confronting and accommodating as a rhetorical strategy, however, is fraught with difficulties, as revealed in our case study of Hillary Rodham Clinton in Chapter 4. When women vacillate between confronting and accommodating, they respond as though the world is rational. In sum, this strategy suggests that the three moral boundaries, all three grounded in reason, may be finessed if the speaker simply strikes the appropriate balance between confronting and accommodating. When women rely upon this strategy, they overlook the power of double binds—the irrational "catch 22"—that they will be criticized regardless of their choices as communicators. From the standpoint of this rationalist paradigm, the woman as a political leader has ensured her own failure by making the "wrong" communicative choices.

When a political woman confronts and accommodates, she reveals awareness that the political "playing field" is not level. She also suggests in her choices that politics is a game (in the Machiavellian tradition) and that she will succeed if she discovers the appropriate "tactics" to respond to each situation she faces. Women who deny the existence of moral boundaries, on the other hand, respond to political situations as though the "playing field" is even. Yet, choosing either of the two strategies implies an endorsement of the status quo—and the values of patriarchy. The last strategy, re-visioning, represents efforts to introduce different values (i.e., care, context, culture, personal experience, and community) into public discourse.[15]

Re-Visioning

Rhetors who adopt a re-visioning strategy are in accord with Tronto's proposal that the three moral boundaries be "redrawn" (p. 11) rather than abolished. Similar to confronters and accommodaters, re-visioners recognize the existence of the boundaries, yet they are unwilling to work within them, because they disagree with the value system that undergirds them. Re-visioners engage in what Adrienne Rich refers to as "the act of looking back, of seeing with fresh eyes" (1979, p. 35). Rich suggests that "re-visioning" "is more than a search for identity: it is part of our refusal of the self-destructiveness of male-dominated society" (p. 35). Although Rich was addressing the need for feminist literary critics to identify ways in which "the very act of naming has been until now a male prerogative" and to find new ways "to see and name" (p. 35), her recommendations are equally applicable for women as political communicators.

Re-visioners recognize that naming in politics has been a male prerogative, and that the moral boundaries must be "redrawn." When the boundaries are "redrawn" and moral decision-making is re-visioned, political decision-making will take into account the value orientations of "others" (i.e., women, slaves, people of color) who have been on the margins of discourse. When she spoke at New York University School of Law before her appointment to the U.S. Supreme Court, Justice Ruth Bader Ginsburg, for example, refused to adopt the disinterested approach to decision making. She said: "The effective judge will strive to persuade and not to pontificate. She will speak in 'a moderate and restrained voice,' engaging in a dialogue with, not a diatribe against, coequal departments of government, state authorities, and even her own colleagues" (quoted in "In Her Own Words," 1993, p. A24).

Justice Ginsburg also spoke to the centrality of care as well as the importance of personal experience in decision-making when she accepted the nomination to the U.S. Supreme Court. She responded:

I have a last thank-you. It is to my mother, Celia Amster Bader, the bravest and strongest person I have known, who was taken from me much too soon. I pray that I may be all that she would have been had she lived in an age when women could aspire and achieve and daughters are cherished as much as sons. I look forward to stimulating weeks this summer and, if I am confirmed, to working at a neighboring court to the best of my ability for the advancement of the law in the service of society. (Transcript of president's announcement, 1993, p. A24)

Ginsburg enacted this contextualized approach to decision making when she created a flexible schedule for a clerk who needed to balance his responsibilities at the Court with his responsibilities for child care (Word for word: A talk with Ginsburg, 1994, p. A23).

The values expressed by Justice Ginsburg reflect Tronto's recommendations for "re-visioning" morality and replacing a "rights" approach (associated with abstractions) to moral decision-making with a commitment to "care" ("near the center of human life") (p. 101). Her definition of care, developed with Berenice Fisher, says:

On the most general level, we suggest that caring be viewed as a *species activity that includes everything that we do to maintain, continue, and repair 'our world' so that we can live in it as well as possible.* That world includes our bodies, our selves, and our environment, all of which we seek to interweave in a complex, life-sustaining web. [Fisher and Tronto, 1991, p. 40, quoted in Tronto, 1991, p. 103]

We agree with Fisher and Tronto that when care is at the center of moral decision-making in politics, it will be transformed.

The women we profile in the succeeding chapters have taken several approaches to the constraints placed upon them by the current positioning of the boundaries and have had differing ways of placing care into the political arena. We now turn our attention to case studies addressing ways political women have struggled with and repositioned the boundaries.

NOTES

1. Tronto notes that the argument concerning women's morality is viewed as important enough to be included in texts on U.S. women's history and cites Norton (1989). She also cites contemporary scholars who argue for women's morality: Browning-Cole and Coultrap-McQuin (1992); Card (1990); Gilligan (1982); Larrabee (1993); Pollitt (1992); Porter (1991).

2. Tronto claims, for example, that the work of Martin Heidegger is a "major exception" (p. 182).

3. A number of feminist theorists have been labeled "essentialist" for assuming that all women—regardless of race, class, or sexual orientation, are more similar than different. These theorists have also been criticized for arguing for polarized views of women and men. Finally, in Julia T. Wood's terms, these theorists "participate in the masculinist emphasis on differences and abstractions" (1992, p. 8). Prominent feminist theorists who have been labeled "essentialist" include: Carol Gilligan (1982); Nel Noddings (1984, 1989); Mary Field Belenky, Blythe McVicker Clinchy, Nancy Rule Goldberger, Jill Mattuck Tarule (1986); and Sara Ruddick (1989). For analyses of problems with "essentialism," see: Houston (1992); Larrabee (1993); Spelman (1988); and Wood (1992, 1994).

4. Tronto (1993) cites Polanyi (1957), Habermas (1989), Laslett (1983).

5. Tronto also suggests, however, that the Scottish Enlightenment thinkers offered an alternative moral vision to Kant's and "represent the 'losing' side in moral thinking in the eighteenth century" (p. 36). Frances Hutcheson, David Hume, and Adam Smith, Scottish philosophers of the eighteenth century, grappled with reconciling Aristotelian concepts of virtue with the changing social landscape of the eighteenth century. Although the Scottish Enlightenment thinkers argued for a morality grounded in sentiments, such a moral vision seemed unworkable in a global economy.

6. From our vantage point studying women and political communication, the legacy of Aristotle is mixed. As we noted in Chapter 1, feminist theorists have highlighted misogynistic elements of Aristotle's thought. Spelman (1983), for ex-

ample, discusses the flawed reasoning whereby Aristotle uses his definition of the soul "to justify his view that women are naturally subordinate to men" (p. 21). Okin (1979) explains Aristotle's philosophy: "Thus, in accordance with his characteristic teleology, Aristotle argues that not only the entire animal kingdom, but the vast majority of humans as well, are intended by nature to be the instruments which supply to the few the necessities and comforts that will enable them to be happy in their contemplative activity. Thus, women, slaves, and artisans and traders are all subsidiary instruments for the achievements of the highest happiness of 'man' " (pp. 78–79). Tronto (1993), however, suggests that Aristotle's concept of virtue offers possibilities for questioning the moral boundaries she identifies. In Aristotle's world, for example, virtue "is a disposition" (p. 30) and the virtuous man is virtuous in private and public roles. Elshtain (1981) also sees possibilities for feminist thinkers to turn to Aristotle and observes: "Yet the manner in which explanatory theories in politics are assessed means that one can reject particular evaluations which flow from general theory (Aristotle on slavery) without repudiating an entire logic of explanation (Aristotle on politics as a form of action)" (p. 53).

7. Elshtain (1981) provides a context for Machiavelli's theorizing. Machiavelli generated his political theory in response to "fratricidal wars" that resulted in turmoil in sixteenth-century Italy (p. 92).

8. As Elshtain (1981) observes, Machiavelli did acknowledge one type of politics associated with the private realm—sexual politics.

9. Ginzberg (1990), however, notes that the ideology of the women's benevolence movement was marked by contradictions. For example, in 1837 Catherine Beecher argued for the special moral influence of women grounded in their designated sphere. She said: "Petitions to congress, in reference to the official duties of legislators, seem, IN ALL CASES, to fall entirely without the sphere of female duty. Men are the proper persons to make appeals to the rulers whom they appoint" (quoted in Ginzberg, pp. 67–68). On the other hand, however, Ginzberg explains that Beecher made direct appeals to legislators in support of her causes. Ginzberg also argues that the women's benevolent movement revealed another inconsistency in its arguments concerning women and their special influence on morality. The movement created separate spheres for women in designating them as caretakers of morality. The benevolent reformers did not assume that working-class women were morally superior. In fact, members of the benevolence movement supported conservative political interests that sought to purge cities of the influence of the working-class poor.

10. Flax (1992) argues that feminists could benefit by following the postmodernist quest to reinvent political theorizing by freeing it from its epistemological foundations in Enlightenment thought. She suggests that many feminist thinkers engage in binary thinking (or boundaries thinking in Tronto's terms) and assume they can find, in true Enlightenment tradition, "clean knowledge" (p. 457). Because much feminist thought is grounded in the "metanarrative" of the Enlightenment (p. 457), many feminists believe that one set of absolute, but faulty truths, can be replaced with another set of absolute, but valid truths.

11. Belenky et al. (1986) note that most of the "separate knowing" women interviewed were recent graduates of "elite, liberal arts colleges" (p. 103). The researchers suggest that the "separate knowers" recognized what it would take

to succeed at such institutions (a commitment to detached decision-making grounded in reason). Belenky et al. summarize the approach of these graduates as recognizing the significance of internalizing *"the way They want you to think"* (p. 103).

12. Campbell and Jerry (1988) cite Welter (1976) and Scott (1970) on the concepts of "true womanhood" and "woman-belle ideal" (p. 11).

13. Campbell and Jerry (1988) cite Lerner (1967) on the speaking careers of the Grimkés. They cite Stanton, Anthony, and Gage (1887) and Barnes and Dumond (1934) on religiously based objections to the Grimkés as public speakers.

14. Campbell and Jerry (1988) cite Gurko (1976) on the experiences of Lucy Stone and Antoinette Brown at Oberlin.

15. Dow and Boor Tonn (1993) argue that Ann Richards' "feminine discourse reflects a philosophical standpoint" (p. 298) and "offer[s] alternatives to patriarachal modes of thought and reasoning" (p. 299). Dow and Boor Tonn's analysis suggests they see Ann Richards as a re-visioner. We believe Richards' style is much closer to accommodating and confronting.

3

Denying Politics: The Strange Case of Lani Guinier

> At the height of the furor over Lani Guinier's appointment, a colleague described her as comporting herself like "a black Jacqueline Kennedy." Although their circumstances were so very different, I think I understand the temptation to such an analogy. What has made both women not just graceful but great has been their ability to stay focused on the good and meaningful priorities in their lives even while negotiating paths filled with political land mines—and to do so without apparent anger or mean-spiritedness. But it did make me wonder when we will stop turning America's most eloquent, intelligent, and committed women into test sites for the ability to endure abuse elegantly.
> —Patricia J. Williams, *The Rooster's Egg* (1995, p. 151)

When Lani Guinier was nominated to serve the Clinton administration as Assistant Attorney General for Civil Rights, her credentials seemed unquestionable. After President Bill Clinton withdrew her nomination, a commentary in the *New Yorker* chronicled Guinier's stellar qualifications to fill the civil rights post. She had attended Radcliffe and Yale Law School, served a clerkship with the Chief Judge of the United States District Court in Michigan, and held a post as a professor of law at the Pennsylvania Law School. Furthermore, she had experience with civil rights litigation. She was a special assistant during the Carter administration to Drew Days, who occupied the top civil rights post in the Justice Department, and she served as a litigator for the N.A.A.C.P. Legal Defense and Educational Fund.

"Something" happened, however, and President Clinton removed

Lani Guinier. By permission of Jose Lopez/NYT PICTURES.

Guinier's name from nomination for the post. The "something," as observed in a *New Yorker* commentary, had nothing to do with her credentials, but with "her ideas . . . [o]r, rather, a caricature of her ideas" (Idea Woman, 1993, p. 4). Although Guinier was a highly qualified candidate, mainstream media forces coalesced around this caricature defining her candidacy as "in crisis."

Guinier was additionally misrepresented in the media because, as an African American woman, she found herself "at the crossroads of gender and race hierarchies" (Crenshaw, 1992, p. 403). At this crossroads, African American women experience "intersectionality"—being the target of both racial and gender discrimination. Intersectionality further implies that African American women are limited in their abilities to conceptualize this double burden because the dominant discourse focuses on *either* race or gender in isolation.[1] Anita Hill (1995) comments on her own experience with intersectionality. The ease with which she "lost" her own substantial credentials as a respected law professor and had her image distorted closely resembles the process Guinier endured through media (mis)representations. Hill observes:

At the beginning of the hearing, as for the previous ten years, I was viewed as a person holding a position of relative social respectability, a law professor at a state university. The rhetoric used to discuss my claim of harassment made my credentials irrelevant. Through their "cross-examination," the senators attempted to show their power in relationship to my powerlessness. In the end I was characterized as a contemptible threat, a vindictive pawn of radical feminists, a victim of erotomania, someone to be viewed at best with pity, at worst with disdain. (p. 273)

Hill asserts that this transformation of her image rested on the concept of power. She suggests that African American women only receive power at the will of the mainstream and their license to possess power is easily revoked. Demonizing the African-American woman is one sure way to simultaneously revoke her power while reminding her of the "tenuousness" of her association with it.

The media's use of ideological hegemonic rhetorical appeals grounded in and playing on stereotypic images of African American women illustrates the problem of intersectionality for Guinier. A headline in the *Wall Street Journal* referred to "Clinton's Quota Queens," which as a commentary in the *New Yorker* observed, contains nasty overtones of "welfare queens" (Idea Woman, 1993, p. 5). A *U.S. News and World Report* article opened with "strange name, strange hair, strange writing—she's history." As Guinier noted in a speech at the 1993 N.A.A.C.P. Annual Conference: "I endured the personal humiliation of being vilified as a madwoman with strange hair—you know what that means—a strange name and strange ideas, ideals like democracy, freedom and fairness that mean all people must be equally represented in our political process" (all quoted material in Labaton, 1993, July 14, p. A12). Guinier points out the double discrimination (racial and gender) that comes from being described as having "strange hair." Certainly, few male political figures receive media attention on their hair styles. Further, the comment "strange" encodes associations of "out-of-place," prompting the notion that people with kinky, African hair do not belong on the public stage assuming positions of power.

Yet, despite Guinier's eloquence and intellectual grasp of her situation as she spoke to the N.A.A.C.P. after her nomination was withdrawn, during the short period while she remained a nominee, her silence implied an acceptance of and a faith in the mainstream power structures. We argue that her silence was part of a strategy of denial; a denial of the power the boundaries had to constrain her assumption of the Assistant District Attorney post. Guinier's rhetorical choices from the time she was nominated until her nomination was withdrawn reflected a faith that she was on a level playing field and that the essential "rightness" of her ideas would allow her to prevail. She did not show a recognition that boundaries were in place that would cause her difficulties in attaining her goals.

This chapter will explore how media appeals reinforced the boundaries Joan Tronto (1993) delineates and used multiple marginalities or intersectionality to cast Guinier as a "madwoman" or "other," a person on the fringes of society whose ideas were unworthy of consideration. This despite several arguments that her ideas concerning "proportional representation" were not novel or "radical," but simply were defined as such by her opponents, many of whom had not read her work. Additionally, we explicate how Guinier's strategy throughout the nomination process was a denial of these boundaries. She cooperated with her "handlers" in the Clinton administration who silenced her; she was not permitted to respond to her media critics or to testify before the Senate Judiciary Committee. Our purpose in this chapter is not to "set the record straight" concerning Guinier's views; instead, we attempt to "set the record straight" concerning how the media's instantiation of the boundaries and Guinier's initial use of denial combined to constrain her, disallow her a hearing, and consign her to the margins of discourse.

First, we explain how moral boundaries legitimated the rhetorical appeals that cast Guinier as "other." Second, we analyze Guinier's rhetorical responses to attacks from media sources. Finally, we explore implications for future women, particularly African American women, who seek access to the political stage. Throughout, we suggest that rhetorical critics have special responsibilities to respond to, unmask, and define the contours of racist and sexist appeals that are used to exclude capable individuals, such as Guinier, from playing important public roles.

MORAL BOUNDARIES AND APPEALS TO RACISM AND SEXISM

A host of writers have traced the cultural roots of hegemonic codes that support racism and sexism in North America. Antonio Gramsci (1971), in drawing distinctions between civil and political society, suggests that societies are composed of a civil component that includes voluntary affiliations among its citizens. Schools, families, and unions, for example, constitute voluntary affiliations. Political affiliations are involuntary for citizens and include institutional structures such as the army, the police, and central government. Whereas political society provides obvious domination over its citizens, Gramsci argues that civil society (including culture) provides a more subtle and powerful domination over its citizens. Although cultural ideas may seem voluntary because they function through the general agreement of members of a society, Gramsci suggests that particular ideas become hegemonic or dominant in a culture. These ideas are taken for granted and encode the interests of those who are in power in a culture.[2] The moral boundaries defined by Tronto (1993), set within the context of the lenses of gender explicated by Bem (1993), function as taken-for-granted ideas that serve the patriarchal interests of those in power in U.S. culture. The attacks on Guinier found grounding in attempts to maintain all the moral boundaries. Guinier, according to her critics, was not qualified to lead because: (1) she was not a right-thinking individual, (2) she depended on context to situate her arguments, and (3) she did not belong on the public stage, although her race preempted her from a protected place in the private sphere as well.

The Morality and Politics Boundary

In labeling Guinier as not a "right-thinking" individual, her critics implied she violated the boundary between morality and politics. "Right-thinking" individuals recognize proper "moral principles" (grounded in reason) and apply those principles without consideration of context (Tronto, p. 7). Edward Said (1994) offers an explanation for the importance in the United States that "right-thinking" people "conform" to particular moral principles. He observes that "[a]n alarming defensiveness has crept into America's official image of itself, especially its representation of the national past" (p. 314). Said contends that societies protect their "sanctioned narratives" which are parables revealing embedded cultural values. For example, in the United States two sanctioned narratives include "America as a pioneering society and American political life as a direct reflection of democratic practices" (p. 314). "Right-thinking" people uphold these narratives.

Guinier's law review articles challenged the shortcomings of the legislative system of representation in the United States; therefore, her critics suggested that she was questioning basic democratic practices at the heart of our sanctioned narratives, and thus she could not be, by definition, a "right-thinking" person. In an article for the *New York Times Magazine* (February 27, 1994) adapted from her book, *The Tyranny of the Majority* (1994), Guinier explains her proposals and suggests that they do advance democratic principles. She summarizes her views concerning proportional representation: "My point is simple: 51 percent of the people should not always get 100 percent of the power; 51 percent of the people should certainly not get all the power if they use that power to exclude 49 percent. In that case we do not have majority rule. We have majority tyranny" (Guinier, 1994, February 27, p. 54). As Guinier explains her views in *The Tyranny of the Majority*, she speaks in accordance with Said's observations concerning sanctioned narratives: "Talking about racial bias at home has, for many, become synonymous with advocating revolution. Talking about racial divisions, in itself, has become a violation of the rules of polite society" (Guinier, 1994, p. 18). Here

Guinier voices a recognition that the boundary of morality and politics prevented her from expressing views seen as challenging sanctioned narratives. Anthony Lewis (1993, September 27) comments on this challenge within a political framework. He observes that Guinier's "insistence that race is still a corroding factor in American life clashed with the desire of Bill Clinton and the New Democrats to play down that issue" (p. A17).

A column in the *Wall Street Journal* by Clint Bolick set the tone for attacks on Guinier as a "wrong-thinking" person, unworthy to serve in the U.S. Justice Department. Bolick distilled a few statements from a 1989 law review article and quoted Guinier as arguing that "fundamental flaws exist in our democracy" (Bolick, 1993, April 30, p. A12). He also charged her with suggesting "certain social goods—health care, day care, job training, housing—must be recognized as basic entitlements" (p. A12). His most damaging charge, however, and the one that haunted Guinier before her nomination was withdrawn, was that she supported predicating judicial appointments on racial quotas.

It should be noted that Bolick cited the following statement from Guinier's 1989 article to support his conclusion that Guinier advocates quotas. "She proclaims that anti-discrimination laws mandate 'a result-oriented inquiry,' in which roughly equal outcomes, not merely an apparently fair process, are the goal" (p. A12). As Laurel Leff (1993) observed in the *Columbia Journalism Review*, the phrase "quota queen," the title of Bolick's opinion piece, never actually appeared in the article. Yet, Leff also observed that "much of the press corps seemed unable to resist this alliterative label" (p. 38). Guinier became the "quota queen" according to a number of news sources, including the *Los Angeles Times*, *USA Today*, the *Chicago Tribune*, and the *Washington Post*, among others. Ironically, as a number of Guinier's defenders noted, she was opposed to quotas. Anthony Lewis commented in the *New York Times*, for example, that Guinier has been highly critical of gerrymandering to create "so-called minority districts" (1993, June 4, p. A31).

Guinier was similarly misrepresented on the issue of "authenticity." Paul Gigot (1993), in a column for the *Wall Street Journal*, said Guinier had written that Douglas Wilder, the governor of Virginia, was not an "authentic" representative of black interests because he had to appeal to white constituents in order to win election. Leff (1993) remarked that "Guinier's views on authenticity are convoluted" (p. 39) and not easily understood by those outside the legal profession.[3] As Patricia J. Williams (1995) contended, this misrepresentation began to take on gigantic proportions. "For those familiar with Lani Guinier's work, this [misrepresentation] begins to resemble some drunken party game in which each person whispers a message to his [sic] neighbor, each embroidering 'the story' until there is no story left, only the leavings of inebriated malice" (p. 140). Williams asserted that Guinier's ideas were maliciously distorted. Lewis (1993, June 4) agreed and attributed the inaccurate representations of Guinier's work to "ideological zealotry" with little concern for the truth. We believe this "ideological zealotry" was in the service of maintaining the sanctioned narratives and keeping the morality and politics boundary in place.

Anna Quindlen not only criticized media coverage, but decision-makers who relied upon that coverage and did not question Bolick's credibility as a challenger to Guinier's candidacy. As Quindlen observed, "Mr. Bolick is a conservative who has worked with William Bradford Reynolds, the Reagan Administration official who removed the teeth from the civil rights division and didn't even bother to replace them with cosmetic dentures" (1993, June 6, p. E19). Quindlen, however, reserved her harshest criticism for "those who made chitchat on the appointment, perhaps even who were expected to vote upon it, who used newspapers and television coverage as a kind of Cliff Notes of the advise-and-consent process" (p. E19). Through this process of distortion and inadequate research, Guinier's critics placed her on the outside and solidified the morality and politics boundary.

Guinier was demonized and criticized in an effort to show her as a non–right-thinking individual prohibiting her from a position of power and thus protecting the morality and politics boundary. Bolick (1993, June 2) argued: "Ms. Guinier's opinions place her at the cutting edge of 'critical race theory' (CRT), a profoundly left-wing school of thought that has defined the outer boundaries of radicalism in legal academia" (p. A15). Ray Kerrison (1993) referred to her as "loony Lani" and indicated that no matter how right-thinking she might appear we should not be fooled into thinking that she is anything but crazy. "In a word, Lani Guinier may appear to be learned, presentable and articulate, but at heart she is a crackpot" (Kerrison, 1993, p. A18). Williams (1995) noted the odd comparisons of Guinier to Anita Hill and Tawana Brawley, "all those loony, out-of-control black women crazed by the repeated spurnings of men they just couldn't let go of" (p. 143). Guinier was cast as "other" and outside of the mainstream. The word "exotic" was used by more than one writer to characterize her views. "Ms. Guinier's writings in professional journals suggest that she would interpret the Voting Rights Act in novel, even exotic ways" (A civil rights struggle, 1993, p. E14). John Leo (1994), in a column for *U.S. News and World Report*, referred to Guinier's "exotic remedies" for legal problems. "Exotic" is an unusual word choice for someone's legal views with its connotations of primitivism, nativeness, and sexuality. It is the same word that was used to describe the performer Josephine Baker, an African American woman known for her sexually explicit dances. With this association, Guinier was seen as outside the morality and politics boundary.

The morality and politics boundary can take two forms, one that suggests that there are fixed "moral principles" that right-thinking individuals adhere to. The second manifestation of this boundary argues that women are too moral for the dirty political world. Interestingly, although Guinier was attacked along the first dimension of the boundary, she was not cast as morally superior to the rough world of politics. We believe this approach was not used to critique Guinier because of her race.

Using the notion of intersectionality, Marsha Houston (1992) argues that African American women face "multiple, interlocking identities" and "multiple, interlocking oppressions." She contrasts the sanctioned narratives associated with white women with those associated with black women. While white women historically have been valued as sexual objects, invested with all that a patriarchal culture defines as positive femininity (for example, physical beauty, passivity, and sexual purity), African American women historically have been despised as "sexual laborers," invested with all that a patriarchal culture defines as negative femininity, including physical unattractiveness, domineeringness, and sexual promiscuity (p. 49).[4] Other scholars (for example, Alexander, 1995; Collins, 1991; Painter, 1992) have concurred with Houston's observations about the symbolic depictions of African American women.

K. Sue Jewell (1993) has written that cultural depictions of African American women as Mammy, Aunt Jemima, Sapphire, and Jezebel abound. Mammy was submissive to her master, satisfied with her station in life performing domestic duties, and "the antithesis of the American conception of womanhood" (p. 39). Mammy "is portrayed as an obese African American woman, of dark complexion, with extremely large breasts and buttocks, and shining white teeth visibly displayed in a grin" (p. 39). Aunt Jemima is the cantankerous version of Mammy (i.e., Mammy in *Gone With the Wind* is an Aunt Jemima). Sapphire (i.e., Sapphire in *Amos 'n' Andy*) engages in verbal point making with African American males, emasculates them, points out their inadequacies, and suggests they are shiftless.[5] The Jezebel, "the bad black girl" or "tragic mulatto" meets Eurocentric standards for attractiveness, but manifests qualities associated with masculinity (independence, aggressiveness, decisiveness) and is derided by the dominant white culture for possessing those characteristics, although as Jewell notes, African American women themselves view these traits positively.

Jewell also observes that in the media "new images of African American women [emerged] during the 1980s" (p. 36), but she says those images invariably were undercut by two strategies. When new positive images were introduced, they were accompanied by the old negative images of African-American women (i.e., Mammy, Aunt Jemima, Sapphire, Jezebel). The other strategy was to introduce positive images of African American women, but then to systematically destroy such images, thereby legitimating the old stereotypes associated with African

American women. To illustrate these strategies, Jewell cites the case of Vanessa Williams, the first African American woman crowned Miss America. Although mainstream media coverage initially treated Williams favorably, "there were many who felt that this historic event was too good to be true" (p. 52). The media, then, relentlessly pursued the stories that Williams had posed for nude photos prior to her participation in the pageant. Jewell refers to the media "witch hunt" and asks if reporters would have been so eager to discredit a white Miss America. She says: "In effect, the mass media that had been successful in constructing a positive image of an African American woman also contributed to the destruction of this image" (p. 53).

It is worth noting that when President Clinton announced he was withdrawing Guinier's nomination, his statement, widely reported in the media, praised her, but at the same time appealed to stereotypic constructions of African American women. He said, "I just love her" followed by "if she called me and told me she needed $5,000, I'd take it from my account and send it to her no questions asked" (quoted in Branan, 1993, p. 57). His statement was puzzling in suggesting that Guinier, a highly accomplished and successful lawyer, might need funds. The statement, however, is less puzzling when viewed in terms of stereotypes that follow African American women, even professional women. He seemed to speak as the master of the Big House—the White House—overseeing a slave. "As one observer remarked, 'He was treating her like a welfare queen—looking for a handout. It had the instant effect of putting her in a subservient position and him in a position of great generosity'" (quoted in Branan, 1993, p. 57).

Given President Clinton's response to Guinier and Jewell's observations concerning mainstream media coverage of African American women, it is not surprising that Guinier became "loony Lani," the purveyor of "exotic remedies." In consideration of the portrayals of African-American women as "on the take" and possessing "negative femininity," it is no wonder that no critics tried to portray Guinier as too pure for the dirty world of politics, but rather focused on her as an outsider—not a right-thinking individual.

The Moral Point of View Boundary

Guinier demanded attention to context in all of her writing, for example, in articulating remedies for voting rights problems she spoke to highly particular issues. In writing about a permanent majority, Guinier was concerned with situations such as the one in Etowah County, Alabama, where white county commissioners voted to give control of road work in the black commissioner's district to a white commissioner. Thus, as Guinier pointed out, in such situations the representation of blacks was effectively undercut. William Coleman (1993) noted that Guinier wrote "attempt[ing] to solve these difficult, deeply embedded problems in local jurisdictions; [her writings] are not blueprints for revamping political systems nationwide" (p. 31). Guinier's goals were situated in a particular context but her critics insisted they be interpreted as absolutes. Ted Koppel questioned her on *Nightline* by saying, "We were talking about majority rule before. It's one of those sacred phrases that anyone who believes in Jeffersonian democracy holds dearly, and I'm still not altogether clear I understand what your quarrel with it is" (In her own defense, 1993, p. 9). Koppel obviously suggested that Guinier had challenged an absolute of democracy.

On this same episode of *Nightline*, Cokie Roberts said in a voice-over that Guinier was challenging basic democratic principles. "It's exactly Guinier's interpretation of the Voting Rights Act that makes her so controversial. She questions such fundamental aspects of American government as majority rule. She looks for ways to change the way elections work and legislatures work to give more votes to racial minorities. Even liberal senators call some of her writings crazy" (p. 4). Again, Guinier's ideas were attacked as absolutes with no consideration for the context Guinier herself so carefully constructed.

Guinier's critics also refused to acknowledge the context in which she was writing—academic law reviews. The *New York Times* alleged that Guinier herself was at fault for the criticism that was leveled at her because her "articles about voting rights [were] poorly written, provocative and easy to caricature" (The Lani Guinier Mess, 1993, p. A20). Guinier, however, was not writing for a lay audience who would have difficulty with her legal prose and find her "writing . . . not the stuff of bedtime reading" (Sachs, 1993, p. 24). The *New York Times* critique did not take Guinier's intended audience into consideration.

Guinier did have her defenders. For example, Coleman (1993) argued that when Guinier's proposals were contextualized, they were not "radical and exotic" (p. A31). Furthermore, he compared the responses to Guinier with those to Thurgood Marshall when he fought against segregation and biased laws. Two attorneys writing in defense of Guinier in the *Wall Street Journal* argued that "as specialists who struggle with these difficult issues, we are familiar with Prof. Guinier's detailed academic work. The complexity of the problems and the seriousness of her scholarship have been lost in the caricatures of her views we have read" (Aleinikoff & Pildes, 1993, p. A15). Yet, these defenses mainly came too late to undo the negative impressions that her critics had made in instantaneous soundbites.[6]

Guinier herself recognized that her problems stemmed from decontextualization. On *Nightline* on June 2, 1993, when she had her one and only chance to speak before Clinton withdrew her nomination she said, "my own mother does not recognize me, in terms of the press and the media that I've been receiving. So if there is a senator who only knows me through the media, I wouldn't blame them if they expressed reservations about confirming somebody who may have said some of the things that I have not said, but which have been attributed to me in the press" (p. 8). Furthermore, when Guinier delivered the 1994 Commencement Address at Hunter College she said that having her ideas represented in the media devoid of their context was her "worst nightmare" (Newman, 1994, p. B5).

George Will's (1993) comment that "[m]any of Guinier's ideas are extreme, undemocratic, and anticonstitutional" (p. 78) was representative of critiques that treated Guinier's statements as attacks on absolute principles; absolute principles embodied in sanctioned narratives. Yet, when it served his argumentative purposes, Will was capable of employing contextualizations such as Guinier's. In *The Tyranny of the Majority* (1994), Guinier points to this irony. She notes that Will, himself, has argued that minority interests must be protected in the face of tyrannical majorities. Guinier observes that her argument and Will's are very similar except that she wrote about a disempowered black minority while Will was concerned with the minority of well-to-do landlords in New York City.

The moral of this story is that context can be ignored or employed differentially to serve the interests of the powerful, white, male majority in the United States. As Mary Daly (1973) argues, the false God of Methodolatry serves the interests of the powerful by "the classification of disruptive and disturbing information as nondata" (pp. 11–12). Thus, Guinier's contextualized application of voting rights remedies was classified as nondata by critics such as George Will because its message of inclusion for the disempowered threatened hegemonic interests. At the same time, Will's argument in favor of the affluent posed no threat to hegemony. Guinier was caught in the confluence of race and class. Her message did not serve the powerful, and therefore the moral point of view boundary was firmly erected to keep her from gaining a position of power.

The Public and Private Boundary

Inherent in this boundary is the bifurcation of many issues and the assignment of one of the two parts to males and its opposite to females. One primary duality is that of reason and emotion. In the case of Guinier, critics often referred to her as "a madwoman" or a "separatist crackpot" indicating, despite her academic credentials, that she was not rational nor were her ideas grounded in reason. Thus, Guinier was shown to belong to the private domain where emotion dominates and was prevented from fully entering the public sphere where reason prevails.

Additionally, the boundary between public and private entails silence on the part of women. Silence is imposed on women as a punishment for bringing sin into the world. Williams (1995) asserts that Guinier was silenced to prevent her presumed sins. "The public was warned not to look too closely, as if investing her with the power of truthful speech might release some mythic contagion; as if she were a siren guiding the ship of state onto the shoals of destruction; as if she were Pandora or Eve or Lilith or Jezebel" (p. 141). Further, as we noted in Chapter 2, silence is also perceived as the mark of a virtuous woman. Guinier was both punished for deigning to speak out in her published works and muzzled by the Clinton administration into adhering to the model of silence. She was instructed that she could not speak to the public about the nomination until the Senate Confirmation Hearings, which, of course, in her case, never arrived. The White House reluctantly lifted this gag order and allowed her to speak on *Nightline* the night before her nomination was withdrawn. Williams (1995) observes, "her voice was [completely] obliterated at that moment in history when she came close to assuming a position invested with the power of law" (p. 139). Further, in the absence of her own speech, others appropriated her story and misrepresented her ideas, as we have discussed previously in this chapter. Thus, Guinier found herself in the position that Toni Morrison ascribes to all blacks in the United States, "[o]ur silence has been long and deep.... In canonical literature, we have always been spoken for. Or we have been spoken to. Or we have appeared as jokes or as flat figures suggesting sensuality" (quoted in Gates, 1993, p. 89). Guinier was unable to tell her own story during the period she was a nominee and so she did become a joke and a dehumanized figure, and she was kept off the public stage, at least as an assistant attorney general.

Finally, the public and private boundary is maintained by characterizing women as pure and pious. As Adele Logan Alexander (1995) notes, however, African American women are not perceived in this manner but rather are seen "primarily as sexual beings who have not modesty, virtue, or intelligence, and little claim to respect or power" (p. 5). She also observes that the chivalrous treatment extended to white "ladies" was not offered to black women. Black women did not have the protection of the private sphere as a retreat. Patricia Hill Collins (1991) states, "[o]ne key feature about the treatment of Black women in the nineteenth century was how their bodies were objects of display. In the antebellum American South white men did not have to look at pornographic pictures of women because they could become voyeurs of Black women on the auction block" (p. 168). African American women do not have the history of being mistresses in the domestic sphere, they were part of the possessions of white families. Consequently, Guinier was not constrained by this application of the public and private boundary.

GUINIER AND DENIAL

In responding to her critics, Guinier seemed to act out of what Jane Flax (1992) refers to as "innocent knowledge." Individuals who act out of "innocent knowledge" believe they are doing "the right thing." Ironically, Guinier embraced the democratic principles that were used to classify her as "other" and unfit to serve. She expressed a belief in the democratic ideals of rights, individualism, equality, and fairness. When she spoke out on *Nightline* on June 2, 1993 (In her own defense: Lani Guinier), in her only opportunity to explain her views before her nomination was withdrawn, she expressed faith in the system. She seemed to assume that when she would have her "day in court" (i.e., her day before the Senate Judiciary Committee), her views would be clear and she would be vindicated. During the *Nightline* interview with Ted Koppel, she said:

I believe that—well, I guess I would say that I believe in fairness, I believe in democracy, and I think that fairness requires that I be given an opportunity to present my views to the Senate. I believe in the legislative process and I think that the Senate, if given an opportunity to hear me speak, would be persuaded that I should be confirmed. (1993, p. 8)

Guinier's faith could have been shaken, however, by Koppel's handling of the final question. He asked her, "you still think you have a chance?" (p. 10). She responded with "I have every expectation that, if given a chance, I will succeed" (p. 10). Koppel closed the interview by offering the following judgment on Guinier's response: "Okay. We close where we began, on that elegant evasion" (p. 10). Where Guinier chose to speak in nuanced fashion, making a statement that was context-dependent, Koppel chose to hear evasion.

As Guinier discovered the morning following the *Nightline* interview, her critics had prevailed. President Clinton withdrew her nomination. A *Newsweek* article reported that Guinier should have known her nomination was in trouble, but she did not understand the signals she was receiving from members of the Clinton administration (Cohn, 1993). Faith in innocent knowledge had shielded her from the reality that her nomination was in trouble and prompted a rhetorical strategy of denial on her part.[7] In *The Tyranny of the Majority* (1994), Guinier said: "I have always wanted to be a civil rights lawyer. This lifelong ambition is based on a deep-seated commitment to democratic fair play—to playing by the rules as long as the rules seem fair. When the rules seem unfair, I have worked to change them, not subvert them" (p. 1). Thus, even after she had reclaimed her voice, she still expressed a belief in "playing by the rules." However, at this point she is talking about transforming the system when it is unfair. Her strategy during the period of her nomination did not focus on this transformation.

Because Guinier trusted the Clinton administration and had faith in the rules, she denied that the boundaries could be operating to put her nomination in jeopardy. She accepted the administration's ban on her speech (and her ability to defend herself), and remained silent as her accusers labeled her "the quota queen." Since her nomination was withdrawn, however, Guinier has moved beyond the denial strategy. She seems to have lost her faith in innocent knowledge and is speaking out, acknowledging that "[w]hat I was always interested in was to have a debate on the issue. And so maybe the debate is coming a year later. That's fine" (quoted in Applebome, 1994, p. E5).

IMPLICATIONS

We believe Lani Guinier is no longer completely following the strategy of denial. She now speaks out and is being heard but she is not Assistant Attorney General for Civil Rights. So she has a voice on the public stage but not a legitimate power role in governance. As Williams (1995) observes, Guinier is taking back her story and actually achieving "star status." Williams also comments, though, that one has to be optimistic to see the forum that Guinier now occupies as being anything like the national stage she might have had.

Following her initial strategy of denial and silence allowed others to define her and tell her story inaccurately. Many in the media tried to set the record straight but they came into the discussion too late and the inaccuracies were already fixed in many people's minds. Thus, her initial denial and belief in the power structure, which had, after all, served her well up until the loss of her nomination, combined to keep the boundaries in place. Keeping the boundaries secure ensured that Lani Guinier would remain on the margins.

In *The Tyranny of the Majority* (1994), Guinier voices the hope that "we can learn some positive lessons from this experience, lessons about the importance of public dialogue on race in which all perspectives are represented and in which no one viewpoint monopolizes, distorts, caricatures or shapes the outcome" (p. 190). She, herself, seems to have regained her voice—she is a popular speaker on campuses and her book is selling well—yet she also expresses the hope that people will continue to work within the system to resolve issues of unfairness. We assert that she may be remiss in not suggesting that what remains to be done is the transformation of the system in order to make a place for her and others like her to speak.

NOTES

1. For an analysis of a popular television text that reflected the tendency of the dominant discourse to focus on *either* race or gender in isolation, see Sullivan and Goldzwig (forthcoming, 1996). An episode of *Designing Women*, "The Strange Case of Clarence and Anita" (first broadcast November 4, 1991), illustrated how Anita Hill's charges of sexual harassment were essentialized as mirroring the experiences of *all* women regardless of race, class, or sexual orientation. The episode did not address Hill's standpoint as an African American woman bringing sexual harassment charges against an African American man. Further, as Sterk and Turner (forthcoming, 1996) note, this same episode of *Designing Women* failed to allow even the African American character (Anthony) to speak about the Hill/Thomas hearings as a nexus of several vectors of discrimination. Instead, Anthony presents a point of view devoid of nuances of intersectionality.

2. We are indebted to Said's (1978) application of Gramsci to Western cultural constructions of the Orient.

3. A number of commentators, writing in Guinier's defense, pointed out that her critics often turned to footnotes to decipher Guinier's views (hardly the place to look to make judgments about a scholar's views). Leff (1993), for example, explained that Bolick highlighted the term "authentic," introduced in Guinier's *Michigan Law Review* article, and misrepresented her views. Leff said Guinier, in the text of her article, questioned the term "authentic" defined as black representatives "elected by blacks" (p. 39). Bolick turned to a footnote in the same article referring to Governor Douglas Wilder of Virginia, that raised questions about whether electing blacks to office would ensure that black interests would be honored. Bolick combined statements Guinier made about authenticity and applied them to Wilder, suggesting that the article proposed that Wilder is an "inauthentic" representative of black interests (see Leff, 1993, pp. 39–40). Leff also noted that "most press accounts, however, didn't even provide the basic definition of 'authenticity' as used in voting rights terminology" (p. 40).

4. Houston (1992) cites a number of writers to support her arguments for "interlocking oppressions and interlocking identities." See, for example: Brittan and Maynard (1984); Bulkin, Pratt, and Smith (1988); Collins (1991); Dill (1979); hooks (1981, 1984); Lont and Friedley (1989).

5. hooks (1992) describes her response to the Sapphire of *Amos 'n' Andy*—"the first screen representation of black femaleness I saw in childhood" (p. 120). She wrote: "We did not long for her. We did not want our construction to be this hated black female thing—foil, backdrop" (p. 120). She notes, however, that adult black women had an entirely "different response to Sapphire; they identified with her frustrations and woes" (p. 120). Adult black women thus claimed Sapphire as one of their own—a strong figure responding with anger to the injustice of her situation.

6. Additionally, when it became clear that Guinier's nomination was in trouble, a number of commentators rushed to her defense—too late to save the nomination. Coleman (1993) pointed out that a number of Guinier's "remedies" for "voting rights problems" were adopted by the Department of Justice in the Reagan and Bush administrations. Some "remedies" that Coleman suggested that were not "radical or exotic" included: cumulative voting, majority rule, appli-

cation of the Voting Rights Act to legislative rules, and enforcement of current law. Applebome (1994) wrote in the *New York Times*, as Guinier was assuming a high profile on the speaker circuit, that "some of her writings, which were widely depicted by critics as radical" are receiving serious attention (p. E5). The title of Applebome's article, "Guinier's ideas, once seen as odd, now get serious study," referred to cumulative voting and proportional representation. A *Time* article did not rush to Guinier's defense, but did suggest that "Her proposed solutions are complicated, at least when compared with conventional electoral rules" (Sachs, 1993, p. 25). These comments, however, came too late to save her nomination.

7. hooks (1992) suggests that Anita Hill operated out of a similar strategy in denying the reality of her situation in testifying before the Senate Judiciary Committee. hooks observes: "While I have talked with many women of various ethnicities who admired Hill's calmness, her steadfast monotone as she gave rational testimony, such admiration need not obscure the reality that Hill's performance suggests that she brought to the hearings misguided faith in a system that has rarely worked for women seeking justice in cases of sexual harassment" (p. 80).

4

Power and Politics: A Case Study of Hillary Rodham Clinton

> Like horse-racing, Hillary-hating has become one of those national pastimes which unite the elite and the lumpen.
> You might say it takes a village to demonize a First Lady.
> —Henry Louis Gates, "Hating Hillary" (1996, pp. 116, 131)

Much of Hillary Rodham Clinton's public persona seems to consist of shifts and feints as she morphs herself into many images that the media reflect back to her and to the public. A brief inquiry into the state of her hair styles shows the myriad of images she has tried on since becoming the First Lady in 1992. Her shifts have not been confined to appearances, however. Her rhetoric also is by turns appeasing and combative. Kathleen Hall Jamieson (1995) reads Rodham Clinton's maneuvering as a way of successfully transcending the double binds that often constrain women. Jamieson argues that "[Rodham Clinton] established her competence without sacrificing her femininity" (p. 47). We, however, are not as sanguine about Rodham Clinton's success as Jamieson is, and argue that her strategy of choice, confrontation and accommodation, carries dangers that she has not been able to evade completely.

Because the First Lady seems to believe in a rationalist paradigm, we see her rhetorical choices as respecting the boundaries that Joan Tronto (1993) explicates. Rodham Clinton's rhetoric does not challenge the righteousness of having boundaries in place. Instead, her rhetorical style suggests a belief in women's abilities to study situations, figure out where the boundaries are, and then educate themselves to surmount them. Her actions reveal a liberal feminist belief in the strivings of the individual to overcome obstacles.[1] Therefore, we observe in Rodham Clinton a

Hillary Rodham Clinton and Senator Bob Dole discussing health care reform, February 1993. By permission of Paul Hosefros/NYT PICTURES.

movement back and forth between (and sometimes the simultaneous encoding of) the strategies of accommodation and confrontation. Accommodation strategies acquiesce to the boundaries in general while confrontation strategies challenge the practice of keeping women out of the public sphere. Yet, the use of these strategies reflects an underlying belief that public speakers should be right-thinking, rational, and grounded in absolute values. Interestingly, this combination of accommodation and confrontation manages to push back some of the restrictions inherent in boundaries while maintaining the lenses of androcentrism, polarization, and biological essentialism (Bem, 1993). We assert that Rodham Clinton, through her use of this strategy, provides a model of illusory change. Some boundaries are moved, but the lenses that perpetuate sexual inequality remain in place.

Rodham Clinton's strategy of confrontation and accommodation is reflected both in her own actions and in media coverage of those actions. For example, an article in the the *New York Times* (1995) carried the headline: "For Mrs. Clinton: Cookies, Tea and a Dash of Policy" (Burros, 1995, December 5, p. B10). Burros points out that Rodham Clinton assumed a more traditional First Lady role after the defeat of the health care bill. Rodham Clinton's acquiescence to tradition in displaying the White House Christmas decorations, however, was tempered by her attention to policy issues. "But tradition only goes so far: while only one question was asked about politics, Mrs. Clinton made plain her intention to take an active part in the President's re-election campaign and said that uppermost in her mind was Bosnia and the United States' peace-keeping mission there" (p. B10). Here Rodham Clinton makes plain that although she is playing a more circumspect role (i.e., accommodating) she still maintains a nontraditional interest in U.S. policy (i.e., confronting).

Yet, as we have just suggested, by being both confrontative and appeasing, Rodham Clinton has simply received a combination of positive and negative responses from the media and from the people in the United States. Because we do not believe Rodham Clinton has successfully found a transformational strategy, but instead is simply using confrontation and accommodation together to find her place on the playing field, she has been unable to fix on a consistent image or to receive consistent feedback. For example, in 1995, when Rodham Clinton traveled to Mongolia, she visited a center for homeless children, stopped to drink mare's milk ("a drink that has the foretaste of cow's milk and the aftertaste of rank sweat" [Faison, p. A10]), and announced that the United States would contribute one million dollars to UNICEF. From stop to stop she accommodated by demonstrating interests traditional to first ladies. The eighteen U.S. reporters assigned to Rodham Clinton's trip had many photo opportunities but not much in terms of "what journalists call hard news" (Faison, p. A10). The *New York Times* coverage of her trip was positive, unlike other coverage she received for her perceived intrusions into U.S. policy.

Dale McFetters, for instance, opines in the *Chicago Tribune* (1995), one month after Faison's approving article in the *Times*, "First Lady Hillary Clinton is wrong. Americans do not have a problem with, or find threatening, the fact that she is a woman, that she is bright, that she is independent, that she is her husband's closest confidante. They do have a problem with the idea of an unelected, unaccountable co-president of the United States, the role Clinton seems to have envisioned for herself" (p. 17). McFetters is responding to Rodham Clinton's statements blaming the defeat of the White House's health care plan on the public's resentment of her partnership style marriage with the president. Thus, as Rodham Clinton moved to the offensive, the commentators responded negatively.

Both Blanche McCrary Boyd (1995) and Anna Quindlen (1994) have commented on Rodham Clinton's difficulties in finding a suitable style, and her need to do so. They have taken a more sympathetic view of Rodham Clinton's strategic shifts, however. McCrary Boyd claims Rodham Clinton has been able to accomplish more by "focusing on women in other countries" and concentrating on "politically peripheral subjects: women, children, the arts" (p. 17). McCrary Boyd attributes some of Rodham Clinton's shifts to political acumen. She does mention one concern in her conclusion. "My only concern is about Socks the Cat. Witches have cats. What Hillary needs is a dog, a Lassie look-alike. Lassie was brave, nurturing, and a good citizen, and she conveyed these qualities despite her very small vocabulary. Lassie was heroic without being threatening, and that is the image Hillary Clinton is trying to find" (p.

Hillary Rodham Clinton speaking on health care reform. By permission of Stephen Crowley/NYT PICTURES.

17). It is worth noting that despite the general tone of optimism that McCrary Boyd conveys, she does evoke the image of Hillary as witch, suggesting that finding her appropriate image may be difficult. Quindlen argues that Rodham Clinton may be changing not out of weakness, but from a position of strength to take advantage of her "bully pulpit" as First Lady.[2]

McCrary Boyd, Quindlen, and Rodham Clinton seem to share a belief in a rationalist paradigm that overlooks the power of double binds (i.e., that women will be criticized regardless of the choices they make). We assert that the quest for the right style, the right strategy without concern for transforming the male-centered system makes women participants in their own vilification. They are easily co-opted by the media and labeled saint or sinner. A cover of *Newsweek* (January 15, 1996), for example, featured a story on Rodham Clinton carrying the headline "Saint or Sinner?"

Regardless of the reviews of her accommodating and confronting strategy, the strategy itself is worth examining in a specific context. We have chosen to observe this strategy in Rodham Clinton's discourse on health care reform, especially her testimony before Congress, which provides an excellent case study for our purposes. It is not our intention to evaluate the White House health care plan, but rather to illustrate Rodham Clinton's use of rhetorical strategy in presenting it. We contend that Hillary Rodham Clinton's rhetorical choices indicate that she is well aware of the issues suggested by Joan Tronto (1993) and Sandra Lipsitz Bem (1993). Her awareness, however, does not prevent her from making the shifts we document in her public discourse. In fact, it is possible that her awareness motivates her rhetorical choices. Her rhetorical stance implies a belief that by alternatively abiding by the constraints posed by the boundaries and directly railing against them, she will be able to operate without all of the restraints the boundaries entail.

Yet, we wish to show that although the initial response Rodham Clinton received after her appearance on the Hill was overwhelmingly positive, later public opinion and media representations hardened against her. We argue that this is the inevitable result of the strategic choices Rodham Clinton adopted.

From the moment President Clinton announced that the task force on America's health care system would be chaired by the First Lady, public opinion has shifted frequently concerning Rodham Clinton's role and competence. Clinton spoke glowingly in an exchange with reporters on January 25, 1993, about the First Lady's credentials for heading this task force. He said:

I am grateful that Hillary has agreed to chair this task force and not only because it means she'll be sharing some of the heat I expect to generate. As many of you know, while I was Governor of my State, Hillary chaired the Arkansas Education Standards Committee, which created public school accreditation standards that have since become a model for national reform. She served as my designee on the Southern Regional Task Force on Infant Mortality, was also chair of our State's rural health committee in 1979 and 1980, a time in which we initiated a number of health care reforms that benefit the people of my State to the present day. And on the board of the Arkansas Children's Hospital, she helped to establish our State's first neonatal unit.

I think that in the coming months the American people will learn, as the people of our State did, that we have a First Lady of many talents, that who most of all can bring people together around complex and difficult issues to hammer out consensus and get things done. (W. J. Clinton, 1993, pp. 96–97)

Although Clinton spoke in glowing terms about his spouse's credentials and expressed confidence in her unique capabilities to chair the health care task force, her appointment was somewhat controversial.

An article in *The Economist* (1993) entitled "Nepotism for the Nineties" that appeared immediately after Rodham Clinton's appointment expressed the perspective that the president erred in appointing his own wife to such a position. The article criticized Rodham Clinton as "on the soft left of the Democratic Party, more worried about extending entitlements than cutting costs. Nothing wrong with wives, so long as they do not have expensive tastes" (p. 26). A *Wall Street Journal*/NBC News Poll indicated that public opinion was divided almost equally on the topic of Rodham Clinton's appointment (47% approved, 45% disapproved) (reported in First Lady's First Job, 1993, p. 16).

Much of the news coverage following Rodham Clinton's appointment was positive. For example, *U.S. News and World Report* commented: "Mrs. Clinton not only receives praise for her role as commander in chief of the White House's battle for national health care, she gets respect" (Cooper, Walsh, Dentzer, & Toch, 1993, p. 30). This article concurred with the generally congratulatory tone adopted by *The Lancet* (January 30) in reporting on Rodham Clinton's appointment. Despite this positive tenor, it is worth noting that even the most laudatory articles contained a double-edged sword in their coverage of the appointment. For example, the *U.S. News and World Report* (1993) article that claimed respect for Rodham Clinton carried the headline, "Co-President Clinton?" indicating that there is at least a question about the legitimacy of Rodham Clinton's authority. Additionally, *The Lancet* (Greenberg, 1993) reported that "Washington is becoming accustomed to Hillary Clinton as de facto co-president, with her own well staffed suite in the political wing of the White House" (Greenberg, p. 295). Again, although the article generally praised Rodham Clinton, the phrase "de facto co-president" undercut the positive message suggesting she was undeserving of the appointment and the power base she occupies.

HILLARY CLINTON'S DISCOURSE OF CONFRONTATION AND ACCOMMODATION

When Hillary Rodham Clinton appeared before the Congress in the fall of 1993, to provide the White House's position on health care reform, she spoke from a position of power but with the clear recognition that many of her listeners believed that this was power she had neither earned nor was entitled to. Yet, after her appearance she received rave reviews for her performance. Her abilities to reason (and thus confront the "morality and politics" boundary) were lauded. Shortly after her testimony, Alissa J. Rubin (1993) praised Rodham Clinton in the *Congressional Quarterly Weekly Report*, saying, "when Hillary Rodham Clinton testified before Congress on health care, she came across as a negotiatorand a promoter, a policy analyst and a teacher. She was a mother who cared about her daughter, a daughter who cared about her parents. She was also a proxy for presidential power unlike any first lady in history" (p. 2640).

Some commentators, in contrast, noted that she had been praised too highly, observing that it was patronizing to fawn over the First Lady's intelligence as though it was completely unexpected and anomalous.

Ruth Mandel offered the following explanation for responses to Rodham Clinton's testimony on health care reform.

> If you find that . . . they are bending over backwards to be more courteous, more flattering, then you have to say it's partly their way of dealing with the fact that she's not an ordinary witness or expert; she is the first lady; she is married to the president of the United States. But some of it may be a sign that they haven't had much experience dealing with a woman who is this strong, this articulate, this competent. (quoted in Rubin, 1993, p. 2643)

Mandel's observation speaks to Rodham Clinton's anomalous status; however, she does not address the insidious quality of the remarks.

A member of the House Ways and Means Committee staff, Tim Crippen, seemed more aware of subtexts masked by the fawning over Rodham Clinton's appearances and testimonies. He held two mugs that the First Lady had used during her testimony before the committee and said: " 'This one has a better lipstick print on it,' he said, holding one and grinning. Maybe I'll auction it off" (quoted in Dowd, 1993, p. A18). Maureen Dowd (1993) also seemed to recognize questionable subtexts when she referred to "a sense of wonder" (p. A18) over the appearances and noted: "Everything about Hillary Rodham Clinton—what she said, how she said it, how she sat and even what sort of feminine imprint she left drinking tea out of the blue Ways and Means Committee china—caused a great stir on Capitol Hill today" (p. A18). Patrice Buzzanell and Bren Ortega Murphy (1993) concur and note, "[t]he current over-emphasis on Hillary's intelligence and competence affirm the degree to which intelligence is viewed as deviant from women's nature. While we celebrate the accolades bestowed upon Hillary for her work, we are reminded that public praise is short-lived" (p. 31).

Crippen and Dowd and Buzzanell and Murphy imply that the overly positive reception received by Rodham Clinton on the Hill carried risks. We believe that Rodham Clinton's accommodating and confronting rhetoric invited the reception she received on the Hill. Our discussion of the First Lady's rhetorical choices during the hearings will highlight the risks of rhetoric that at one turn accommodates and at another turn confronts the moral boundaries defined by Tronto.

Dual Rhetorical Approaches

Our analysis of Rodham Clinton's testimony will reveal a dual strategy of accommodation to moral boundaries. Her responses to questions during the hearings honored the morality and politics boundary. In speaking with authority as a "right-thinking" individual, she respected male-associated norms for public discourse, thereby demonstrating that she could serve as a moral leader. By "playing the game" and honoring the "rough and tumble" world of politics, she acknowledged the practical (i.e., Machiavellian) requirements of politics, thus undercutting the assumption that women are "too good" for politics. As a right-thinking, savvy politician, she also paid tribute to "the moral point of view" by appealing to reason and speaking from an objective, distanced, and disinterested standpoint.

Our analysis will also suggest that although she demonstrated she could "act like a man," she also accommodated by proving she could "act like a woman." She was testifying in the public sphere of politics, but she behaved in stereotypic female ways associated with women's place in the private sphere. Thus, her accommodating communication was quite intricate. Because Rodham Clinton adopted a dual strategy of accommodation, she had access to the public political stage. For example, if she had not tempered her reason-based policy presentations with stereotypic, female-associated communication patterns (i.e., references to family and her roles as mother, wife, and sister) she might have been silenced due to her threatening presence.[3]

Rodham Clinton's confronting communication, in contrast, is apparent only in the most fundamental sense. Her very presence on the Hill constituted confrontation; however, because she is a liberal feminist she agreed to honor male-associated norms in testifying (i.e., rhetorical appeals grounded in reason and abstractions). When she appeared on the Hill, she was "heroic without being threatening." It must be noted that Rodham Clinton was not an antagonistic confronter. Whereas confronters such as Mary Daly, Angela Davis, and Patricia Williams challenge moral boundaries by urging their audiences to examine the core values that undergird U.S. institutions, Rodham Clinton seems willing to accept the frameworks of the status quo as long as she (and other right-thinking women) can gain access to them.

Accommodating and Confronting

As a witness before the House and Senate committees, Rodham Clinton presented herself as a person vested with the wisdom to make recommendations concerning health care reform. She adopted what Kathryn Pyne Addelson (1994) refers to as the standpoint of the liberal political philosopher. Of course, traditionally the liberal political philosopher was male and was the embodiment of reason "represented[ing] the established, stable public face of society" (Addelson, p. 39). Rodham Clinton represented an anomalous female embodiment of the voice of reason. After Rodham Clinton completed her opening statement (brimming with statistics) before the Senate Committee on Finance, the chair, Robert Packwood (Republican-Oregon), complimented her on her performance. His statement that "we observe you no longer have a text and you do not even use notes at this point" (1993, p. 8), highlighted her anomalous position.[4] Clifford B. Stearns, a member of the Subcommittee on Commerce, Consumer Protection, and Competitiveness, adopted a similar tone in praising Rodham Clinton and said: "I want to congratulate you. I have watched Federal Reserve Chairman Greenspan show up at tables like that with a whole list of people helping him, so you are making a winning statement by showing up all by yourself. I want to compliment you on that" (House Committee on Energy and Commerce, 1993, p. 13). As we analyzed this exchange, we were reminded of Samuel Johnson's famous statement that the terms woman and preacher were so incongruent that a woman preacher was akin to a dog standing on its hind legs.[5]

From committee to committee, Rodham Clinton cited statistics such as those from the Consumer Guide to Coronary Artery Bypass Graft Surgery (Senate Committee on Finance, 1993, p. 34). In addressing the Senate Committee on Finance and the House Committee on Energy and Commerce, for example, she emphasized the Clinton health plan would emulate that of Germany's by becoming more cost-effective.

They [Germany] spend less than 9 percent of their gross product on health care and they insure all of their citizens and guarantee better benefits to all their citizens. We spend $1 trillion every year, leaving millions of Americans lacking insurance and millions on the verge of losing it because of the changes in the economy. And too many Americans get the most expensive health care in the most expensive place—the emergency room. (Senate Committee on Finance, 1993, p. 4)

She also emphasized that the Clinton plan would emulate the German model by providing coverage for all citizens.

Additionally, Rodham Clinton derived credibility by citing statistics offered by Dr. C. Everett Koop, a highly respected former U.S. Surgeon General. She mentioned that Dr. Koop "has estimated maybe $200 billion worth" could be saved on U.S. health care costs by reducing waste (House Committee on Energy and Commerce, 1993, p. 10). In highlighting the risks the uninsured face when they need hospital care, she said: "I heard Dr. Koop say the other day that an uninsured person who enters a hospital with the same problem as an insured person is three times more likely to die than the insured person. That is a shocking statistic" (House Committee on Energy and Commerce, 1993, p. 27).

Thus, Rodham Clinton honored the first dimension of the morality and politics boundary by presenting herself as a "right-thinking" person by appealing to reason in citing evidence (particularly statistics) and a highly revered "right-thinking" person, Dr. Koop. She also proved that, even though she is a woman, she could play the political (i.e., Machiavellian) game. When she appeared before the House Committee on Energy and Commerce, Joe Barton seemed to question her rationality by saying, "I am a registered professional engineer. I believe that one must identify the problem before trying to develop a solution" (1993, p. 19). He then challenged the Clinton administration's statistics on the number of uninsured in the U.S. "at some point in time" (p. 19). She continued to cite evidence, and although Barton refused to relent in challenging her data, she continued to defend herself. In one of the most widely reported exchanges during the health care hearings, Rodham Clinton demonstrated that she could "play tough." Dick Armey (Republican-Texas) had referred to the Clinton health plan as "the Kevorkian prescription for the jobs of American men and women" (reported in Lewin, 1993, p. E1). As a preface to his questions for Rodham Clinton, Armey said he planned to make the debate "as exciting as possible" (House Committee on Education and Labor, 1993, p. 24). She responded with, "You and Dr. Kevorkian" (p. 24). Armey came back with "I have been told about your charm and wit, let me say, the reports on your charm are overstated. The reports on your wit are understated" (p. 24). Another member of the committee, Harris W. Fawell, praised Rodham Clinton's performance in the "rough and tumble" world of politics by saying, "After seeing how you impaled my comrade-in-arms . . . " (p. 28).

Rodham Clinton thus demonstrated, through her appeals to reason, that she could speak as a man of "practical wisdom" even though she is a woman. By adopting a style that has served men well in the board and legislative rooms, she suggested that she belonged on Capitol Hill. She also made it clear that she could "dirty" her hands with politics.

In honoring the boundary between morality and politics, Rodham Clinton also paid homage to the moral point of view boundary. For the most part, she spoke as an objective, distant, and disinterested observer of the health care scene. She seemed detached and autonomous as she relied on appeals grounded in the realm of reason rather than emotion. She wanted what was "best" for the country in an abstract sense. For example, she emphasized the need for people to do what is right by saying, "every individual will have to take responsibility and pay something" (Senate Finance Committee, 1993, p. 5) and "no one is able to escape some responsibility. Everyone participates" (House Committee on Education and Labor, 1993, p. 5). When she stressed the need for all U.S. citizens to have reliable health care, she appealed to another abstraction in the form of a maxim, "and I always am of the philosophy that there but for the grace of God go I" (House Committee on Education and

Labor, p. 16). In addressing a question concerning the affordability of the Clinton health care plan, she referred to cost containment as "the key" (House Committee on Energy and Commerce, 1993, p. 10) to "better quality to be given the citizens of this country" (p. 10).

Rodham Clinton's appeals to abstractions may have revealed a faith in the "innocent knowledge" described by Jane Flax (1992). As the First Lady spoke in terms of a "good" that transcended particular circumstances or contexts, she seemed to "act as the servant of something higher and outside (or more than) themselves [herself]" (p. 19). Although some news accounts credited Rodham Clinton's ability to personalize policy issues, we remain skeptical of the extent to which she communicated in this way. Maureen Dowd described the First Lady's testimony before the House Ways and Means Committee and speculated on her rhetorical choices:

During the campaign, Mrs. Clinton was surprised to learn from polls that many Americans did not picture her in a maternal way and did not even know that she had a daughter. Today, she was careful to lace her testimony with personal references, beginning in the morning by telling the Ways and Means Committee that she was "here as a mother, a wife, a daughter, a sister, a woman." (1993, p. A19)

We attach less rhetorical significance to Rodham Clinton's personal references than Dowd does. In response to a question from Bill Bradley (Democrat-New Jersey) about the possibility of taxing firearms to fund health care, she revealed that she privileges evidence grounded in reason and the "moral point of view" over evidence grounded in personal experience. She said, in what seemed to be an apologetic tone: "Speaking personally—and that is all that I can do with respect to your second proposal—I am all for that.... Friend.... We will look at your proposal and be happy to talk with you about it. I am speaking personally, but I feel strongly about it" (Senate Committee on Finance, 1993, p. 35). The First Lady seemed to be saying that "speaking personally" did not "count" to the extent that speaking abstractly "counts." Her remarks reflected an epistemology based on "separate knowing" as described by Belenky, Clinchy, Goldberger, & Tarule (1986).[6] By apologizing for her "personal" beliefs, Rodham Clinton foregrounded her presumption that reason-based, empirical evidence is superior to other types of evidence (i.e., evidence grounded in the personal or particular). Her rhetoric thus reflected her faith in the Enlightenment values of rights, individualism, and equality.[7]

Rodham Clinton's rhetoric, in sum, accommodated two of the moral boundaries, and although she entered the public world of politics, we argue her rhetoric accommodated the public and private boundary.

Clearly, she moved outside the traditional world of women—the household (i.e., the "island beyond politics" according to Held, 1993, p. 54). We ask, however, to what extent her public political performance was tempered by deference to a stereotypic rhetorical style associated with the private "island beyond politics." Stan Greenberg, President Clinton's pollster, said of Rodham Clinton's style during the hearings: "It's just the right combination of—I hate to say this—a woman's touch with a real mastery of the policy" (quoted in Ifill, 1993, September 22, p. A24).

Greenberg's discomfort in identifying "just the right combination" speaks to our reservations about Rodham Clinton's accommodating and confronting style. Although she confronted the public and private moral boundary by defining a new type of public role for a First Lady, she deferred, sometimes demurred, and played the role of a female witness from the "island beyond politics." For example, she engaged in banter with committee members that made her "serious" testimony seem less threatening. When Donald W. Riegle, Jr., complimented Rodham Clinton by using intensifiers ("You are just giving terrific leadership to this country"), she responded by mirroring his intensifying language.

Oh, Senator, that is *such* a good question. And it is made *so* complicated by the way the federal budget is structured and operates because it is *very* hard to achieve savings based on investments in prevention or savings based on competition in the private sector as part of the budget analysis and projections.... It has been one of the issues that I have *really* struggled over as I have tried to understand it.... (Senate Committee on Finance, 1993, p. 37, emphasis added)

As a number of studies of communication and gender have noted, women are more likely to use words that intensify a noun or verb.[8] Rodham Clinton, of course, responded to Riegle's intensifiers. Riegle's use of intensifiers in questioning Rodham Clinton may have indicated deference to the First Lady's status.

During the hearings, Rodham Clinton also manifested another feature stereotypically associated with females. Although Dowd (1993) wrote that Rodham Clinton "did not show any exultation at the reception she was given on her big day" (p. A19), she did remind her listeners that she plays traditional female roles. For example, during her opening statement before the House Ways and Means Committee, Rodham Clinton highlighted her roles (most of them caretaking roles).

As a mother, I can understand the feelings of helplessness that must come when a parent cannot afford a vaccination or a well-child exam or cannot pay for that x ray or prescription for a sick child.

As a wife, I can imagine the fear that grips a couple whose health insurance vanishes because of a lost job, a layoff or an unexpected illness.

As a sister the inequities and inconsistencies of a health care system that offers widely varying coverage depending on where a family member lives or works, and as a daughter I can appreciate the suffering that comes when a parent's treatment is determined as much by bureaucratic rules and regulations as by a doctor's expertise. As a woman who has spent many years in the work force I can empathize with those who labor for a lifetime and still cannot be assured they will always have health coverage. (1993, p. 12)

Rodham Clinton thus reminded her audience that she brought "a woman's touch" to her policy statements. Although her appearance before congressional committees was anomalous—not what we expect of First Ladies—her references to her life as a woman reminded listeners that she is not anomalous in every way.

In other communication settings, Rodham Clinton's "woman's touch" has assumed another rhetorical form. When interviewers pose challenging questions about serious matters (i.e., Whitewater and her financial dealings when she worked at the Rose Law Firm in Little Rock, Arkansas), Rodham Clinton often responds by smiling and laughing at seemingly inappropriate moments thereby undercutting the seriousness of her message.[9] Barbara Walters (1996) asked Rodham Clinton a number of difficult questions during a *20/20* segment. Throughout the interview, when Walters posed challenging questions, Rodham Clinton smiled (at what seemed inappropriate moments) and tilted her head, thus playing the role of innocent. When Walters warned that a difficult question was coming, the First Lady said, "Oh dear [poor me], all your questions are tough." Rodham Clinton used a similar strategy during a 1996 interview with Terry Gross on National Public Radio's *Fresh Air*. The First Lady fielded questions about Whitewater and her new book, *It Takes a Village and Other Lessons Children Teach Us* (1996). Gross posed the following question: "You know a lot of men growing up—a lot of boys growing up are supposed to aspire to be President. Mothers are supposed to look at their boys and say, someday he'll be President, I know it. Did you ever aspire to be First Lady? Did you ever." Rodham Clinton's response (overlapping with Gross's question):

[laughter, 4 seconds alone and in her voice throughout most of this response] It never crossed my mind. I cannot imagine—you know, once jokingly in high school, I thought of the least likely thing that I would ever end up doing and I said, "Oh, I'm going to grow up and be a Senator's wife and live in Washington." And I did it totally tongue in cheek, because I thought it was such a ridiculous thing to even think about. Well, here I am and I'm living in the White House. (1996)

Her critics have depicted her as a woman hungry for power; her laughter suggested, "Oh, little me?" Maybe Rodham Clinton is aware that a number of communication and gender studies report that women face the cultural expectation that they should be more nurturing and sensitive than men and that they should smile and laugh more than men.[10] This expectation corresponds with Phyllis Chesler's (1989) finding that women and men feel threatened by women who smile infrequently.

Gross and Rodham Clinton both looked through Bem's lenses of gender. After all, Gross did not ask the First Lady if she ever aspired to be president. The First Lady played along with the question and seemed flattered. If Rodham Clinton had looked at the lenses of gender she would have asked Gross why she asked a question that linked her fortunes with her husband's career choice.

Our analysis, then, suggests that although a number of media commentators identified Rodham Clinton's testimony before Congress on health care as a rite of passage for First Ladies, her communication choices may be questionable. Tamar Lewin (1993) seemed to summarize a popular perception of Rodham Clinton's style: "Few women in American political life have so publicly and so seamlessly incorporated the disarming charm once called 'feminine' with the steely confidence associated with powerful and persuasive men" (p. E1). Although Lewin does not identify an accommodating and confronting style, that is the style she seems to be describing. Rodham Clinton's testimony before Congress on health care served as our case study for the purposes of this chapter; however, we contextualized our analysis by suggesting that the accommodating and confronting style characterizes her communication as First Lady.

Rodham Clinton, our analysis proposes, is a confronter only in the most obvious sense. She did, in Dowd's (1993) words, signal "the official end of the era in which Presidential wives pretended to know less than they did and to be advising less than they did" (p. A19). She played a highly visible role in shaping policy. Furthermore, she confronted conservative Republican efforts to cast her as a "radical" feminist—a woman who did not even bake cookies. We believe, however, that Rodham Clinton's belief in "innocent knowledge" has led her to accommodate to the moral boundaries rather than redraw them. Our analysis suggests that her accommodating and confronting rhetoric is fraught with hazards for her position as a woman on the public political stage.

LIMITATIONS OF ACCOMMODATING AND CONFRONTING RHETORIC

We admire Rodham Clinton's efforts to redefine the role of First Lady. As she struggles to redefine the role, however, she faces the historical, philosophical, psychological, and political forces (discussed in the first two chapters of this book) that have coalesced to keep women on the

Hillary Rodham Clinton overseeing preparations for the Clintons' first state dinner, February 1993. By permission of Suzanne Dechillo/NYT PICTURES.

margins of the political world. In her attempts to reframe the role of First Lady as first person, she is grappling with the taken-for-granted assumption "that the president's wife should exemplify the most conservative notions of a woman's place" (Wills, 1992, p. 6). Additionally, as Frank Rich (1995) argues, Rodham Clinton is "the nation's No. 1 scapegoat" (p. E17). Writing in the wake of the release of Hollywood's latest adaptation [interpretation] of *Little Women*, Rich said misogynistic responses to Rodham Clinton tell us more about ourselves than about the First Lady. He acknowledges that Rodham Clinton erred in holding "secret" meetings of the health care reform task force she chaired.

Yes. But the depth of rage directed against her far exceeds the crimes. You don't have to love Mrs. Clinton, or share her politics, to feel that her demonization tells us much less about who she is than it does about a country that still feels threatened when its little women grow tall. (1995, p. E17)

A report in *Time* indicated that a Republican consultant is aware that the country still feels threatened by strong women and that his charge is to undermine Rodham Clinton's credibility before the 1996 campaign (Carlson, 1992, p. 30).

News accounts speak to Rodham Clinton's efforts to communicate in ways that will make her listeners feel less threatened. From 1992 to the time we are writing this chapter early in 1996, Rodham Clinton confronted, then accommodated when her behavior was questioned by critics (for the most part, conservative critics). After her cookie comment became an issue during the 1992 primary season, she came to understand the power of the sound bite. Her remark, "I suppose I could have stayed home, baked cookies, and had teas" (Carlson, 1992, p. 30), provided an ideal sound bite. Few news sources, of course, contextualized her remark by reporting the rest of her statement: "The work that I have done as a professional, a public advocate, has been aimed . . . to assure that women can make choices . . . whether it's full-time career motherhood or some combination" (Carlson, 1992, p. 30). We can imagine Rodham Clinton saying to herself, "There must be some way to avoid the sound bite trap and the attendant misrepresentation of my views."

We suspect that accommodating and confronting has been her response to avoiding the "traps" of discourse. Headlines speak to what media commentators widely interpret as strategic shifts in her presentation of self. A few examples to illustrate the perceptions of her shifts: "First Lady Stars in Spotlight on Health" (Clymer, 1993, September 26, p. A32), "Hillary Clinton Seeking to Soften a Harsh Image" (Burros, 1995, January 10, p. A1), "Contrition as Weapon" (Dowd, 1994, p. A10).

Although she presented herself as a witness guided by reason and cognizant of the facts during her health care testimony before Congress, we noted her efforts to soften her image. She has attempted to soften her image in other situations. For example, Dowd (1994) described Rodham Clinton's stereotypic female appearance and demeanor when she met the press to discuss Whitewater in Spring 1994. In her article, Dowd suggested that the meeting with the press was carefully orchestrated to avoid any hint of a co-presidency. She wore a soft pink suit and sat in a chair providing no barrier between herself and the press. The set-up suggested a chat between the press and the First Lady. As she denied any wrongdoing in Whitewater, she spoke softly and assumed the role of a First Lady unjustly accused. The setting seemed designed to diffuse serious questions.

Everything was soft and warm, the sweater with the long, black knit skirt and the black high heels; the beige-and-gold decor of the State Dining Room, which is often used for private dinners; the profusion of ferns in the fireplace behind the First Lady, and the brass vases full of pink and white flowers. (Dowd, 1994, p. A10)

In this stereotypically feminine environment, the woman who demonstrated her command of specialized documents on health care simply denied that she was an expert in the investment questions surrounding Whitewater.

Furthermore, she explained that she saw nothing wrong with trying to make money; she personalized her explanation by saying her father encouraged her to read stock tables when she was a child and she invites her daughter to do the same thing. All these responses were uttered in a tone that suggested "poor me, I just did not understand what was going on with Whitewater. We trusted our friends." Dowd described Rodham Clinton's demeanor:

She appeared as comfortable as if she were sitting at her kitchen table chatting over tea and cookies, an impression heightened as she called the reporters by their first names, an effective technique except when she called Newsday's Susan Page, "Ann." (Dowd, 1994, p. A10)[11]

Dowd thus implies that Rodham Clinton softens or accommodates to female stereotypes when it is to her advantage to do so.

When Rodham Clinton in turn accommodates and confronts, however, she frames herself in polarized terms (i.e., as saint or sinner). Her shifts supply media commentators with easy sound and photo bites. When she invited reporters, such as Marian Burros and Ann Landers (not the reporters who cover "hard news") to a luncheon at the White House, the event was featured on the front page of the *New York Times*. She met with the "soft news" reporters during the same week *Newsweek* published her article criticizing Republican proposals for welfare reform. Burros (1995) implied that the First Lady was seeking advice on reinventing herself so her critics would "like" her more (pp. A1, 15).

The White House luncheon with the "soft news" reporters provides additional evidence that Rodham Clinton seems to believe that she can finesse every boundary and lens of gender if she discovers the appropriate rhetorical formula. When she presents herself as the "tough" policy wonk (i.e., testifying on Capitol Hill) or the perfect mother (i.e., making Chelsea's favorite scrambled eggs when she's sick), she suggests she can be all things to all people. Where is the real (the human being) Hillary Rodham Clinton? In a commentary for the *New York Times Magazine*, Frank Rich highlighted Linda Ellerbee's observation that Rodham Clinton should beware that "the Superwoman myth [framing her] is dangerous" (1993, p. 70). Rich summarized the dangers of the myth: "Hillary the icon, the ideal working mother and wife, is as fake (and punishing) an image as the caricature of Hillary as a killer-lawyer too busy grabbing power to answer a phone call from Chelsea's school nurse. The Hillary hagiography, like the Hillary demonology, is designed to serve a political agenda" (p. 70).

Rich wonders where the human Rodham Clinton may be found—the one who knows it is impossible to balance all her responsibilities. Where is the person in the midst of hagiography and demonology? When she accommodates and confronts, she serves the interests of those who seek to cast her as an anomaly. As Henry Louis Gates (1996) observes, "At times, it seems that Hillary has been labeled Saint in order that she may be found guilty" (p. 132). In upholding the moral boundaries in all but the most superficial of ways (i.e., moving in the public sphere usually associated with men), Rodham Clinton plays a game she can never win. As saint or sinner, she is a freak, and, as Susan Stewart (1984) observes, "through the freak we derive an image of the normal; to know an age's typical freaks is, in fact, to know its points of standardization" (p. 133). The freak "is a freak of culture" (p. 109) rather than a "freak of nature" (p. 109). When viewers feel distanced from the "freak" as other, they feel normal.

The saint or sinner *Newsweek* cover, for example, in highlighting all Rodham Clinton's contradictions, implies she is a freak. Her pose, on the one hand, suggests glamour—the tilted head and the hairstyle reminiscent of Marilyn Monroe. When we look at Rodham Clinton, however, we see glamour without the airbrush—her witch's warts are showing. She is a stereotypical grotesque representing a "female iconography" (Russo, 1994, p. 14) of deviance. In particular, Rodham Clinton, although she seems "radical" (i.e., testifying before Congress presenting the administration's health care plan), is an "average" woman because she has "seemingly ordinary female trouble with processes and body parts: illness, aging, reproduction, nonreproduction, secretions, lumps, bloating, wigs, scars, make-up, and prostheses" (Russo, p. 14).[12] The First Lady, then, has ordinary female troubles; the stereotypic female iconography comforts audiences by suggesting that the world really has not changed to any great extent. In some respects, Rodham Clinton is an anomaly (i.e., she testifies before Congress), but she is still a woman with all those female-associated problems.

The moral boundaries and lenses of gender constitute the points of standardization (measures of normalcy) against which Rodham Clinton gets measured. In accommodating and confronting, the First Lady is "stunting"—a rhetorical approach that carries the dangers we have described in this chapter. Russo (1994) suggests that strategies are not possible in "certain risky situation[s]" (p. 22). Risky situations call for "stunts" or "grotesque performances" (pp. 20–21). For example, Russo discusses Amelia Earhart's "stunt flying" and her awareness of the symbolic significance in labeling women as stunt flyers rather than flyers in the early years of aviation (i.e., the norm for flying would be defined by making reference to stunt flying as other or aberrant). Earhart, however, defended her stunt flying by arguing that at least she could carve out her own space in the male-dominated field of aviation (as could other women aviationists) by stunting.

Rodham Clinton might argue that her stunting—her accommodating and confronting—permits her to carve out a rhetorical space in the male-dominated political world. We believe it would be wiser for the First Lady to avoid the stunting that has marked her discourse. If she spoke forthrightly and addressed the female iconography that follows her, she might be able to move through the political world as a human being rather than as a saint or sinner. Stunting honors the boundaries and lenses by denying problems with our socially constructed life world. A First Lady speaking as a human being could highlight the double binds women face when they enter the political world or any male-associated world (i.e., business).

Interestingly, a reporter who covered the Arkansas political scene suggests that Rodham Clinton was not always the accommodater and confronter we have described in this chapter. In his defense of the First Lady, Anthony J. Moser (1996), emphasizes that he is a conservative who has never voted for Clinton. Moser's editor at the *Arkansas Democrat* assigned him to investigate the fringe benefits Clinton received as the governor of Arkansas. The Governor's office denied Freedom of Information requests and refused to supply Moser with the records; however, Rodham Clinton contacted the reporter and told him to come to her office at the Rose Law Firm to examine the records. Moser concludes:

The Hillary Rodham Clinton I covered during her husband's 12 years in office championed openness and freedom of information. She was not an arrogant ice queen, as now depicted. She was the most accessible member of the administration and the friendliest to the press.

If that has changed, if she has become secretive, Washington must have done it. (p. A13)

Moser thus suggests that he does not recognize the Rodham Clinton depicted in the media as "a secretive, dissembling dragon lady" (p. A13).

IMPLICATIONS

We understand that Rodham Clinton probably assumed she needed a different strategy when she moved to the White House. In efforts to carve out her rhetorical space in the White House, we do believe she faced extraordinary double binds. It is difficult for us to envision a more challenging communication situation.[13]

Our analysis, however, proposes that her rhetorical stunting has been misguided. Rodham Clinton herself made the comment in 1993 that she has "often thought of [her]self and [her] friends as transitional, maybe more sure of where [they] were coming from than where [they] are going" (quoted in Martin, 1993, p. 43). We would like to hear Rodham Clinton asking questions that speak to complex human realities and that reveal a clearer sense of where we are going. If she asked these questions, she could use her platform as First Lady to urge us to think about a "better vision" of politics as proposed by Tronto (1993). Although Rodham Clinton might claim she is advocating a transformed politics, her efforts ring hollow for us. Too often the First Lady's efforts parallel her advice in *It Takes a Village and Other Lessons Children Teach Us* (1996). Richard Bernstein (1996) offers the following observations concerning the book: "Her book is often abstract, bromidic, tepid, precious. Mrs. Clinton seems so eager not to stir controversy that she avoids most of the tough stuff, taking harbor instead in a mix of smallish recommendations, heartwarming personal anecdotes and, above all, civics-lesson platitudes" (p. C9).

Rodham Clinton could embrace controversy and use it to her advantage in asking us to consider the following questions. What does it mean to be a person of practical wisdom (rather than a man of practical wisdom)? What would it mean to give more attention to context in political decision-making? What does it mean to serve as a moral leader in the United States? Is politics inherently a dirty business? How do we move beyond the vision of the detached, autonomous political decision-maker? How can reason and emotion come together in political decision-making? How do we bring together bifurcated private and public spheres in political decision-making? How do we move beyond androcentric models of political decision-making? We urge Rodham Clinton, then, to look "at" rather than "through" the lenses of gender to ask how her discourse and her images in the media have been framed by the moral boundaries identified by Tronto. She could turn to Representative Barney Frank (Democrat-Massachusetts) for inspiration. He is not a rhetorical stunter; instead, through his discourse he challenges the boundaries and lenses that constitute our cultural frameworks. We realize Frank has a narrower constituency than Rodham Clinton; however, she might study his communication choices. In 1987, Frank "came out," although advisers warned him that the announcement could mean the end of his career. He acknowledged that he was in a relationship with a man. During 1989, he faced a scandal when a male prostitute claimed he had been in a relationship with Frank. He spoke forthrightly and today says he was "dumb and indiscreet" (quoted in Dreifus, 1996, p. 23). Frank cleared his name before the House Ethics Committee and "now relishes his outspokenness, political and personal" (p. 23). After the Republicans assumed control of Congress, Frank remained one of the few representatives willing to stand by his liberal positions.

It was unimaginable that I could live as a gay man with someone like Herb and have an emotionally satisfying private life that was not an interference with public life. In my own life, things have moved forward. (quoted in Dreifus, p. 23)

Through his discourse Frank continues to question the "common sense" logic of the private and public boundary—the logic that said a human being could have one face in private life and another face in public life. When he was interviewed for the *New York Times Magazine*, he asked that a photo run of him with his partner. He explained the request to the interviewer: "[b]ecause I think the fact of gay couples is important. There are so few stories in print of gay people that aren't tragedies, scandals or disasters" (p. 24).

Frank not only pushes the private and public boundary, but the other boundaries. He asks his audiences to go beyond an abstract label—gay man—and to look at him as a human being (i.e., contextualize his life). By speaking forthrightly, he forces us to question whether politics is inherently a "dirty business." When he speaks and foregrounds his standpoint as a gay man, he invites us to question the heterosexist power relations that undergird the lenses of gender. Because Bem (1993) argues that Western cultural belief has privileged heterosexuality as the "normal" or "natural" sexual orientation, Frank is a "gender nonconformist"—an individual who looks "at" the lenses of gender and refuses to live according to society's scripts.

We exhort Rodham Clinton to question society's scripts and speak as a person rather than as an abstract embodiment of what she believes U.S. audiences want from the First Lady. She has come to represent tensions over gender roles in the United States. Regardless of the twists and turns she makes in accommodating and confronting—regardless of the stunts she performs—she will fall short.

In closing, we ask Rodham Clinton to consider what her rhetorical stunting communicates to young people. Following the health care testimony before Congress, Tamar Lewin (1993) said that Rodham Clinton was "feminism's first mainstream icon: a powerful, smart woman with mass-market appeal" (p. E1). Lewin, though, questioned the First Lady's rhetorical choices and said: "Sometimes the effort not to offend leaves her sounding a bit like a Miss America contestant, looking for an answer bland enough to please everyone" (p. E3). Eleanor Smeal, president of the Fund for a Feminist Majority, in contrast, viewed Rodham Clinton as a positive role model and suggested a number of girls might be inspired to become lawyers when they grow up. Lewin was more skeptical and said some girls might "get a message that they should try to marry the president" (p. E3). An Ellen Goodman column speaks to this problem. She reports that U.S. Supreme Court Justice Sandra Day O'Connor received a letter from a schoolboy praising her accomplishments. Goodman, along with a lot of other people, wonders what is being taught in the nation's schools. The letter said:

Dear Justice O'Connor. We read a book about you. You're the first woman on the Supreme Court. You learned to ride a horse. You must be the fairest judge in the U.S.A. I hope that someday you can become a President's wife. Love, Chris. (quoted in Goodman, 1996, p. 36)

It appears some girls and boys might assume that First Lady, the ultimate appendage to a powerful male, is an admirable goal for women, young and old. Goodman says Justice O'Connor sent a copy of the letter to Rodham Clinton and she was not "amused" (p. 36). We hope the letter encouraged the First Lady to reflect on the consequences of her accommodating and confronting rhetoric.

NOTES

1. Josephine Donovan (1992) traces the development of liberal feminist thought and summarizes the problems with it. Liberal feminism is grounded in the Enlightenment belief that human beings, women and men, have "natural" rights based upon their abilities to reason. Liberal feminists assume that if these reasoning capabilities are recognized in women as well as men, equal opportunities will follow in the workplace and all other areas where inequities have existed. Donovan identifies Mary Wollstonecraft's *Vindication of the Rights of Woman* (1792) as the earliest articulation of liberal feminist thought. Donovan cites the 1966 Statement of Purpose issued by the National Organization for Women (NOW) to illustrate liberal feminist views. "NOW is dedicated to the proposition that women, first and foremost, are human beings, who like all other people in our society, must have the chance to develop their fullest human potential. We believe that women can achieve such equality only by accepting to the full the challenges and responsibilities they share with all other people in our society, as part of the decision-making mainstream of American political, economic, and social life" (quoted in Donovan, p. 25). As Donovan observes, however, liberal feminist thought does not address problems in the private sphere. For example, if women are expected to "uphold the domestic world" (i.e., take primary responsibility for child care), they may have difficulty moving in the "public" world of the workplace. Additionally, liberal feminists do not address the possibility of ontological differences between women and men. Because men have been in power, they have created the institutional structures and women may not fit into those structures (i.e., institutional structures may need to change). Finally, Donovan notes that liberal feminist thought does not address ethical problems with private and public spheres (i.e., Machiavellian "split between fact and value" [p. 28]) that suggest the public realm is amoral (the morality and politics boundary identified by Tronto, 1993).

2. Anna Quindlen (1994) refers to Rodham Clinton's "bully pulpit." We have

reservations about the use of this term. "Bully pulpit" connotes images of male politicians engaging in verbal fisticuffs.

3. Sullivan and Levin (1995) discuss the use of familial tropes by powerful political women. Rodham Clinton is in company with a long line of powerful political women (i.e, Queen Elizabeth I) who have used familial tropes to reassure the public that, although they operate in the public, male-associated realm of policy, they also dwell in the private, female-associated world.

4. Over a three-day period in September 1993, Rodham Clinton testified before two Senate committees. The Labor and Human Resources Committee met on September 29 and the Finance Committee on September 30. She testified before three House committees. Ways and Means met on September 28, Energy and Commerce on September 28, and Education and Labor on September 29.

5. In *The Madwoman in the Attic* (1979), Gilbert and Gubar provide one of the earliest and most insightful discussions of the biases against women as speakers and writers. They note, for example, that authors from Tertullian and St. Augustine to Richard Brinsley Sheridan, Samuel Johnson, Horace Walpole, and Jonathan Swift "implied that language itself was almost literally alien to the female tongue. In the mouths of women, vocabulary loses its meaning, sentences dissolve, literary messages are distorted or destroyed" (p. 31). For an analysis of parallels between misogynistic attacks on political women in the Renaissance and Hillary Rodham Clinton, see Sullivan and Levin (1995).

6. In reading Rodham Clinton's remarks concerning "speaking personally," we were reminded that Belenky, Clinchy, Goldberger, and Tarule (1986) said: "Most of the women who leaned heavily toward separate knowing were attending or had recently graduated from a traditional, elite, liberal arts college" (p. 103).

7. Lewin (1993), in her coverage of the hearings for the *New York Times*, explained that Rodham Clinton belongs to "the leading edge of a generation of women who faced far less of the overt sex discrimination that older women had to overcome" (p. E3). She also observed that Rodham Clinton "never, ever sounds the note of woman-as-victim" (p. E3). In 1987, Rodham Clinton was skeptical that women actually faced discrimination in the legal profession, but changed her mind when she chaired the American Bar Association Commission on Women in the Profession. After hearings were held in 1988, Rodham Clinton was convinced that women faced discrimination, according to Lynn Hecht Schafran, a lawyer at the NOW Legal Defense and Education Fund. Schafran claims: "Since then, she has worked very hard to help make things better for women lawyers" (quoted in Lewin, p. E3). A report issued recently by an American Bar Association Commission on Women in the Profession indicated that although many younger male lawyers believe women have received preferential treatment, a chilly climate exists for women in the field of law. A *Times* article summarized the findings: "Though women now sit on the Supreme Court, head the Justice Department and preside over the bar association itself, the stubborn barriers faced by rank and file female lawyers are reflected in pay disparities at every level of experience and in all types of legal practice, the report found. And in the profession's highest echelons, in law firm partnerships, law school faculties and on the bench, the percentage of women, while increasing, remains inexcusably low, the report says, when measured against huge increases in the numbers

of qualified women" (N. Bernstein, 1996, p. A9). Rodham Clinton's response to the Commission's findings was reported in the *Times* as "hopefully, the Administration is leading by example" (p. A9).

Rodham Clinton's response in 1987 indicated a liberal feminist belief in "innocent knowledge." A capable person would succeed regardless of barriers in the legal workplace. Although Schafran observed that Rodham Clinton "came around" and acknowledged discrimination in the law profession, we believe her communication suggests faith in Enlightenment ideals. We also wonder if her response to the recent report downplays problems with discrimination in the legal profession. Her book, *It Takes a Village and Other Lessons Children Teach Us* (1996), also suggests a naive belief in Enlightenment ideals. The tone of the book implies that Rodham Clinton speaks from a high moral ground—the moral point of view. All the world's children could be cared for and nurtured if we would assume responsibility for them. She also offers maxims for child rearing based on her reading of the "experts" and her own experiences. Although she is writing at the end of the twentieth century, her tone is similar to Benjamin Franklin's.

8. A number of studies support language intensity as a female-associated communication style. See, for example: Key, 1975; Lakoff, 1975; McMillan, Clifton, McGrath, and Gale, 1977; Mulac, Wiemann and Gibson, 1988; Mulac and Lundell, 1980; and Schultz, Briere and Sandler, 1984. The latest studies of language intensity consider context. Mulac and Lundell caution that language intensity alone was not an accurate predictor of a speaker's sex in their study.

9. We have observed, by the way, that Rodham Clinton tends to use this strategy when faced with difficult questions. As we finished this chapter, she was facing a new round of questions concerning Whitewater and had testified before a Grand Jury. She had also appeared on a number of television and radio shows to respond to questions about Whitewater and to discuss her new book, *It Takes a Village and Other Lessons Children Teach Us* (1996). Goodman (1996) pointed out that Rodham Clinton adopts a "blame-somebody-else refrain that she resorts to when the going gets hot" (p. C19). we have noticed that the "blame somebody else" statement is accompanied by smiles and laughter. When we listened to an interview on NPR's *Fresh Air*, we were struck by her serious utterances followed by laughter.

10. For an overview of research in this area, see Pearson, West, and Turner (1995); and Wood (1994). Wood traces the history of cultural expectations that women are designated caregivers. She also argues that "we urgently need to revise longstanding, but outmoded views of caring as strictly a private matter and of women as the ones who should care for others" (p. 15).

11. It is interesting to note that Dowd's front page article on Rodham Clinton's press conference carried the headline, "Contrition as Weapon" on p. A1 and "Contrition as Weapon against Public Doubts" on p. A10.

12. Russo (1994) mentions one tabloid representation of Rodham Clinton in an endnote. The tabloid photo shows the First Lady with a gigantic baby alien that she was supposed to be adopting. Russo, however, does not focus on the depiction of Rodham Clinton, but rather on the status of the baby alien as "freak." Using Russo's frame of reference concerning female iconography, it is interesting to note the number of times that photos of Rodham Clinton drew attention to her "bloated" legs. For example, a photo in the *New York Times* published just

before she started testifying before Congress on health care reform featured Rodham Clinton's "bloated" legs and the caption "Hillary Rodham Clinton is solidifying her position as the power beside, rather than behind, the throne" (Ifill, 1993, September 22, p. A24). Another front page *Times* photo (captioned "A Club of Her Own) featured the First Lady's "bloated" legs and "wide" hips (1993, August 28, p. A1).

13. Elizabeth Hanford Dole indicates she has learned from the problems faced by Rodham Clinton. She announced that, although she is on a one-year leave from her position as president of the American Red Cross, she will return to her job even if her husband is elected president. She says that the United States no longer needs a First Lady (Lehigh, 1996, p. 6). We suspect that Hanford Dole operates out of the same rationalist liberal feminist paradigm that has informed Rodham Clinton's rhetorical choices. More than one critic of Hanford Dole's statements, however, has suggested that she will not be able to circumvent the issues that have followed Rodham Clinton. As one reporter observed, "And while some may see Mrs. Dole's proposal as courageous and refreshing, it could also create her own set of problems and potential conflicts of interest" (Seelye, 1996, January 16, pp. A1, B7). She declines to answer the "tough" questions about how she sees the role of First Lady. Additionally, just as Rodham Clinton has been dogged by questions concerning her finances, Hanford Dole will face similar questions. When Dole sought the Republican nomination in 1988, albeit briefly, questions were raised about his wife's financial dealings. Indeed, the *New Yorker* published an article in January 1996, raising questions about Elizabeth Hanford Dole's finances (Mayer). Ruth Mandel, director of the Eagleton Institute of Politics at Rutgers University, suggested that Hanford Dole's finances would become an issue as campaign 1996 progresses (reported in Seelye, 1996, p. B7). Money is associated with power in U.S. culture, and as our study of women and political communication points out, many people seem uncomfortable with women in power. Hanford Dole's critics have argued that she exercised her political power in managing the Red Cross (Frantz, 1996).

Janet Reno. By permission of U.S. Department of Justice.

5

Re-Visioning Moral Boundaries: A Case Study of Janet Reno

> Transforming what care means and who does it requires dislodging it from its historical embeddedness in only the private sphere and the realm of personal concern. Simultaneously, the association among women, caring, and the personal realm must be qualified by men's increased involvements in caregiving roles and family life. The exigence now is to situate the issue of caring squarely within public consciousness.
>
> —Julia T. Wood, *Who Cares? Women, Care, and Culture* (1994, p. 145)

When President Bill Clinton nominated Janet Reno to serve as United States Attorney General, in the wake of the Zoë Baird and Kimba Wood debacles, an article in the *New York Times* noted that the third choice seemed "safe." Baird and Wood withdrew their nominations after it was revealed that they had hired undocumented workers to provide child care.[1] The *Times* article observed: "Ms. Reno is single and has no children, and White House officials said they were absolutely certain she had no problem with hiring illegal immigrants or not paying taxes on household help" (Berke, 1993, p. A22). Reno, in the words of one essayist, did not have "'the Zoë Baird problem,' meaning child-care infractions" (Wallis, 1993, p. 76). The lack of a "Zoë Baird problem," in sum, "helped pluck the childless and unmarried Janet Reno from relative obscurity to become the president's nominee for the job. No kids, no nanny, no Zoë Baird problem. Reno, 54, who appears to be well qualified for the post, doesn't even have an immigrant gardener; she mows her own lawn" (Wallis, 1993, p. 76).[2]

As one reporter suggested, President Clinton fulfilled his promise to his wife, Hillary Rodham Clinton, and some women's groups, by selecting a woman to fill the post of Attorney General (Berke, 1993, p. A22). He selected a woman, however, who did not have a "woman's problems" (i.e., Zoë Baird problems)—the entanglements of family responsibilities. Indeed, the top female appointees in the Clinton administration fit the Reno profile: "Of Clinton's top female appointees, Health and Human Services Secretary Donna Shalala and now Reno are unmarried and have no children; Energy Secretary Hazel O'Leary and U.N. Representative Madeleine Albright have grown kids; only EPA chief Carol Browner has to worry about child care. So much for the President's vaunted vow to create a government 'that looks like America' " (Wallis, 1993, p. 76).[3]

Although Reno was Clinton's third choice for the attorney general post, she became one of the "stars" of the administration due to her "straight talk" after the fire at the Branch Davidian complex in Waco, Texas. As Clinton distanced himself from the tragedy and the plan to spray tear gas into the complex, Reno went on a media marathon and answered questions about her decision-making processes. When Larry King asked her whether the decision had been a mistake, she admitted: "Obviously, as you look at all the information that we had, as you consider everything we knew at the time, we made the best decision I think that we could, based on everything that we knew. Based on what we know now, it was wrong" (An interview with Janet Reno, 1993, April 19, p. 3). A *New York Times* article described Reno as "shaken and somber" as she responded to questions from reporters (Labaton, 1993, April 20, p. A1).

Reno emerged as a powerful and forthright speaker, a public figure who was willing to take responsibility for her actions. In the weeks and months following Waco, media narratives cast her as a folk hero—the last of the courageous and ethical political figures. One cartoon depicted Reno (singing "Stand by Your Man") shielding the cowardly Clinton from media arrows (Bok, 1993, p. E6). A *Time* cover story referred to "Reno: The Real Thing" and "Truth, Justice and the Reno Way" (Gibbs, 1993, July 12, pp. A20–27). Another *Time* article featured Reno as "Standing Tall: The Capital is All Agog at the New Attorney General's Outspoken Honesty." Reno's "true grit" was linked with her unusual upbringing by a mother who was an alligator wrestler (Cloud, 1993, pp. 46–47). A *Lear's* cover promised a story on Reno and "how she got her grit" and provided an explanation of what it meant "Growing Up Reno." Growing up Reno meant having an eccentric mother who "drank like a fish, cursed like a sailor, and refused to wear a bra" (Laughlin, 1993, p. 51).

Reno had been in office barely six weeks when she, in her own words, made one of "the hardest decisions in the world to make" (Press Conference on the Branch Davidians Crisis, 1993, p. 3). Her discourse, if not her decision itself, earned her a reputation for courage and honesty. A *New York Times* article summarized her position after Waco: "President Clinton stopped by the Justice Department to praise her grit. A friend from her undergraduate days at Cornell sent yellow flowers with a card saying, 'Hang in there, Janet.' And during a speech, an employee held up a sign echoing a remark by the Attorney General's sister, who had called from Florida on the night of the Waco fire to say, 'That-a-girl' " (Johnston, 1993, May 1, p. A9).

Approximately six weeks after Waco, Reno's reputation for courage was enhanced when she chastised Clinton staff members for bypassing her when seeking help from the F.B.I. in investigating the White House travel office. She said: "There are ways these things should be handled" (quoted in Friedman, 1993, p. D20). During the intervening months, however, stories circulated in the press questioning Reno's competence as Attorney General. Articles about her true grit gave way to articles with titles such as "Drift and Turmoil in Justice Department" (Johnston, 1994, January 29, p. A6). One article noted: "Interviews with dozens of other former and current lawyers at the department indicate that in contrast to the public image of competence and compassion, Ms. Reno's stewardship has resembled a shakedown cruise under a novice captain and pick-up crew of political appointees still uncertain of their roles" (Johnston and Labaton, 1993, p. A18). Other criticisms centered on Reno's reliance on "long, unprioritized lists as her chief tool of management" and that her "immersion in detail meant that some major decisions didn't get made" (Caplan, 1994, p. 51).

In the months following Waco, Reno's competence in running her office was questioned. She continued, though, to keep a high public profile in the midst of mixed press reviews. When Lani Guinier, Clinton's nominee for Assistant Attorney General for Civil Rights, was attacked for her writings, Reno came to her defense and proclaimed the writings "thought-provoking efforts . . . to invigorate debate" (quoted in Gibbs, 1993, July 12, p. 23). On August 28, 1993, she was the only member of the Clinton cabinet to walk with the Rev. Jesse Jackson to commemorate the thirtieth anniversary of the March on Washington. She testified before a Senate Commerce Committee hearing on violence on television and criticized television executives for promoting shows that have "ground [violence] into us, day in and day out" (quoted in Wines, 1993, A1). A *New York Times* editorial, "Janet Reno's Shameful Delay," criticized the Attorney General for failing to expedite the appointment of a special prosecutor to investigate the Whitewater charges against the Clintons. An article in the *Times* indicated that Reno had responded to "strong political pressure" in calling for an investigation of the slaying of a rabbinical student in Crown Heights (Labaton, 1994, pp. A1, B2).

Columnist Anthony Lewis questioned Reno's "silence on the crime bill" (Lewis, 1993, November 22, p. A11). In August 1994, an article in the *Times* emphasized that the Clinton administration valued Reno's counsel concerning refugees from Cuba. Because of her direct experience with Cuban refugees as a Miami prosecutor, Reno's advice was sought and a writer covering the Justice Department said: "Not since Ms. Reno's commanding performance after the Federal Bureau of Investigation's disastrous assault on the Branch Davidian Complex in April 1993 has she found herself so visibly in the limelight" (Johnston, 1994, p. A6). Despite mixed reviews since Waco, her stance following the fire at the Branch Davidian complex remains as a positive example of Reno's grit and integrity.

As Peter Boyer (1995) points out, "Reno's decision on Waco was made, it seems in retrospect, under impossibly difficult circumstances" (p. 39). The stalemate at the Branch Davidian complex started before Reno was confirmed as U.S. Attorney General. When Reno was asked, in April 1993, to make a decision about pumping nonlethal gas into the complex, she "was in a new job, in a new town, and was taking advice from a roomful of virtual strangers" (Boyer, p. 40). Public debates will continue concerning Reno's decision and the F.B.I.'s conduct in Waco. During summer 1995, Congressional hearings explored "what happened at Waco." Our analysis does not focus upon evaluating the appropriateness of Reno's decision-making concerning Waco, however, nor do we attempt to assess explicitly her success in the role of Attorney General.

In our analysis of Reno's discourse immediately following the fire at Waco, we do not concentrate on the efficacy of her decision. Rather, we highlight the values she brings to moral decision-making and define her as a pathbreaker in re-visioning the patriarchal moral boundaries that we argue have framed political interaction. Her discourse reveals that, in challenging patriarchal moral boundaries, she is articulating a "different" vision of what it means to be a public political servant.

Attorney General Janet Reno's discourse suggests she is engaged in challenging the moral boundaries identified by Joan Tronto (1993). The Attorney General is weaving "a complex, life-sustaining web" through her discourse, encouraging listeners to look *at* rather than *through* Sandra Lipsitz Bem's (1993) lenses of gender in order to expand the moral boundaries. After the fire at the Branch Davidian complex, Reno spoke from a morality grounded in "care" rather than a morality grounded in "rights."

JANET RENO'S LIFE-SUSTAINING WEB OF DISCOURSE

When Janet Reno "stood tall" and accepted responsibility for decision-making concerning the Branch Davidian complex in Waco, reporters expressed surprise at her candor. A reporter for *Time* said: "Washington, a city that pulses with conformity loves exotic visitors with colorful pasts, which helps explain the reception Reno has received in her two months on the job. But it is her performance under pressure that has sealed her stature in the capital" (Cloud, 1993, p. 46). Another *Time* article referred to Reno's "personal geometry" and "ethical hygiene" that set her apart from other members of the Clinton administration (Gibbs, 1993, July 12, p. 24). The same article noted that "the peculiar laws of politics ensured that she would get all the credit for taking all the blame" (p. 24). In "Reno's Popularity Rises from the Ashes of Disaster," a *New York Times* reporter remarked: "Her plain-vanilla style and unstudied demeanor seemed to connect with ordinary Americans, and she was cast in a sympathetic light as someone who tried to deal peaceably with a zealot, David Koresh" (Johnston, 1993, May 1, p. A9). A *New York Times Magazine* profile of Reno described her presence:

Outside Washington, she has assumed larger-than-life stature because of the way she has projected herself as the nation's top law-enforcement officer. There, she seems compassionate, honest, and real. In March, Reno inspected crime-fighting programs in Atlanta. Eldrein Bell, then the Police Chief, said to me [the reporter] "She represents a break from tradition. She's the most refreshing law-enforcement leader I've met in my whole career and I've been in this field for 33 years." (Caplan, 1994, p. 42)

The credit Reno received for her honesty and her willingness to accept responsibility suggests that "ethical hygiene" is not a quality usually associated with public figures—especially political figures. Indeed, her conduct was contrasted with, in the words of a *Time* reporter, that of President Clinton "who vanished hours before surfacing [after the fire in Waco] to claim responsibility" (Gibbs, 1993, July 13, p. 23). "Lies, Lies, Lies," claimed a cover story in *Time* that commented upon ethics and politics: "The public may now assume lying on the part of its Representatives because it expects them to lie. Clinton himself reflected this cynical view recently, when he whimsically entertained reporters with his laws of politics, including this one: " 'Nearly everyone will lie to you, given the right circumstances' " (quoted in Gray, 1992, p. 34).

Perhaps many United States citizens, including reporters, share Clinton's ideas concerning the "laws of politics." Cynical views associated with public life, particularly politics, may have led to Reno's "full-fledged folk-hero status" (Cloud, 1993, p. 46) following her responses to Waco. Whereas Clinton's statement seemed to support moral boundaries as defined by Tronto in suggesting that politics is a dirty business devoid of ethics, Reno's statements following Waco seemed to challenge those moral boundaries. An analysis of Reno's discourse in response to Waco reveals that by contextualizing decision-making, taking personal responsibility for her actions, and honoring the maintenance of relationships in communities, she challenged the boundaries between morality and politics, the moral point of view, and public and private life (the political and the personal).

Morality and Politics

Reno's discourse after Waco challenged both versions of the morality and politics boundary. She rejected the "morality first" approach when she acknowledged that mistakes had been made in analyzing the situation at the Branch Davidian complex. Instead of asserting a "morality first" position and arguing that the decision was correct in light of particular principles, she addressed the shortcomings of the decision-making process. Rather than suggesting that it was necessary to carry out the F.B.I. plan on a particular day, Reno said:

We made a decision today—there is no perfect timing, there is no perfect day, and there is no trigger—that we would increase the pressure today, but today was not meant to be the day, or the days. We were prepared to carry it out tomorrow, and the next day, and do everything we could to effect a peaceful resolution of this matter.

It was not today; this was just a step forward in trying to bring about a peaceful resolution by constantly exerting further pressure to shrink the perimeter. (Press Conference on the Branch Davidians, 1993, p. 5)

In sum, during a press conference following the fire at the complex, Reno did not defend her decision in absolute terms. She said consultation took place. She had "approved the plan which had been developed by the FBI, after very careful study, and discussion with people in the field, a unanimous representation from the field, that this was the best way to achieve a resolution of this matter without further loss of life" (Press Conference on the Branch Davidians Crisis, 1993, p. 2). She did not try to deny that mistakes were made and claimed that the decision was "made based on the best information that I had" (Press Conference on the Branch Davidians Crisis, 1993, p. 17). During the House Judiciary Committee Hearing on the Waco Incident, Representative Hamilton Fish, Jr. (Republican-New York) asked Reno to comment on suggestions by Richard Restak, a neurologist and neuropsychiatrist, that David Koresh was psychotic and his behavior was "unpredictable." In responding to Fish, Reno expressed an openness to examining her decision concerning Waco in light of Restak's work. She said: "[I want to] talk with any other expert I can, brief them on everything we tried to do, and try to understand whether a man like David Koresh, whom he calls unpredictable and whom everybody agrees was unpredictable, if there is any other way to have done it" (House Committee on the Judiciary, 1993, p. 22).

Reno thus spoke with humility in reflecting on her decision to take action at the Branch Davidian complex. Her approach stood in direct contrast to a "morality first" approach to politics that suggests "right-thinking" individuals occupy privileged positions and know what is best for the country. In a speech before the Association of American Law Schools, Reno articulated the rationale that informed her approach to explaining the actions at Waco. She said:

I don't do spin. I want to try to use small, old words that everyone understands. I want to say no when I can't do something. I want to be as honest and direct as I can. And people say well, what is going to happen? I got elected five times trying to be as honest and direct as I can, and what the American people, I think, want more than anything else in the world are not shaded and false promises, but honest, candid, direct answers as to what you can do and can't do. They appreciate I don't know when you don't know. They appreciate yes to a long question, when yes will suffice more than three sentences. (1994, p. 6)

During an interview with Ted Koppel on *Nightline*, Reno actualized the approach she described during the speech when she spoke in simple terms, refused to obfuscate, and said that "nothing, nothing, can justify what happened today" (Waco: What Went Wrong, 1993, p. 8).

In refusing to frame her rhetoric in abstract "morality first" terms, Reno also questioned a "politics first" or Machiavellian approach to decision-making. She noted: "I don't do spin stuff, and I'm not distancing anybody from anything—I'm telling you exactly what happened" (Press Conference on the Branch Davidians Crisis, 1993, pp. 17–18). Rather than arguing that the situation at the complex called for expedience in justifying her decision, Reno promised: "I will analyze everything, I will look back on it, I will ask that we further review what can be done in other situations. I will look at whatever information is available in terms of other groups that might do something like this. I will carefully consider everything for the future, and review it based on what was done here" (Press Conference on the Branch Davidians Crisis, 1993, p. 18).

When answering questions about Waco, Reno went beyond justifying her decision-making. Rather than attempting to protect her reputation or the reputation of the Justice Department, Reno moved beyond "morality first" or "politics first" approaches. Her emphasis on seeking the truth challenged the boundary between morality and politics. For Reno, politics and morality are congruent and intertwined. She made it clear that public figures are accountable when she said: "I go out to seek the truth, and that's what I tried to do here, and I'm going to do everything I possibly can to seek the truth" (U.S. Department of Justice Media Conference on the Waco Report, 1993, p. 48). In seeking the truth, Reno challenged the "moral point of view" boundary.

The Moral Point of View

When Reno explained her decision-making processes following Waco, she emphasized that they were not "distant and disinterested" or divorced from the realm of "emotions and feelings." In addressing questions about the decision, she made it clear that she did not see herself as a "detached and autonomous moral decision-maker." She acknowledged her own pain and said:

These are the hardest decisions in the world to make. My heart goes out to the families of the agents killed, the agents injured, as well as to those children and the families of those who perished in the compound today. We must all reflect on how we as a society can in the future prevent such a senseless, horrible tragic loss of human life. (Press Conference on the Branch Davidians Crisis, 1993, p. 3)

During testimony before a House Judiciary Committee Hearing on the Waco Incident, Reno responded emotionally when Representative John Conyers, Jr., referred to Waco as "a profound disgrace to law enforcement in the United States of America, and you did the right thing by offering to resign" (House Committee on the Judiciary, 1993, p. 25). An account in *Time* described Reno's response to Conyers: "Listening to Conyers' attack, the 54 year-old, 6 ft.-2 in. Reno thrust out her jaw and glared" (Cloud, 1993, p. 46). The *Time* account said Reno's voice was "quavering" (p. 46). She replied to Conyers:

I have not tried to rationalize the death of children, Congressman. I feel more strongly about it than you will ever know. But I have neither tried to rationalize the death of four ATF agents, and I will not walk away from a compound where ATF agents have been killed by people who knew they were agents and leave them unsurrounded. (House Committee on the Judiciary, 1993, p. 26)

Conyers was dissatisfied with Reno's comment and charged her with offering a "non-responsive answer" (House Committee on the Judiciary, 1993, p. 26). Reno's exchange with Conyers was emotional and she said: "I will come to your office and be prepared to answer any question at any time that you may ever have about anything that I have ever done" (House Committee on the Judiciary, 1993, p. 26).

In addition to acknowledging her emotional responses following the fire at the Branch Davidian complex, Reno also *contextualized* her decision-making. During the media conference on the Waco Report, Reno was pressed to explain "the most compelling reason in your view for going in at that time, at that moment in the process" (1993, p. 51). She refused to reduce her decision to "one reason" or one rationale and identified a constellation of circumstances that informed her decision. She said:

There was no one fact that ultimately compelled me. It was reviewing all the circumstances, the negotiation, the ability of the hostage team to be prepared, the necessity to secure the perimeter, the fact that there were dangerous people in there, and that we could not walk away from it. (U.S. Department of Justice Media Conference on the Waco Report, 1993, p. 51)

Whenever Reno was questioned about her decision-making in the period following Waco, she reiterated that a host of circumstances compelled her to agree to the plan to inject the Branch Davidian complex with nonlethal gas. She claimed that she made her "best judgment" (An interview with Janet Reno, 1993, p. 3) based on the information available to her; she also acknowledged that "in some instances there are no right answers and no clear signs as to the way you work out of something, but just trying to do it" (p. 6). When Larry King asked Reno about her "frame of reference," she again contextualized her decision:

You try to talk to everybody, consider every possibility, look at the circumstances, consider that there had been, as each pressure—As the pressure began to be stepped up, we heard nothing that would indicate that he would go through with something like this. So we step up the pressure, we try to figure out how to make it uncomfortable for them, without permanently impairing anybody, without causing any deaths. And you step up that pressure because you're concerned about the children. You're concerned about the people, you're concerned about the lives of agents around the perimeter. And again, you make the best judgment you can. (p. 3)

In sum, when Reno responded to questions about Waco, she did not speak from a "distant and disinterested" moral point of view. Although she claimed that she tried to make "the best judgment" possible, it was a judgment grounded in "concrete circumstances" rather than the abstract requirements of reason. As she defined her approach to reaching "the best judgment," Reno also emphasized that her own value orientation informed her public decisions concerning Waco.

Public and Private Life

Because Reno does occupy a public office, she has managed to challenge this boundary on a fundamental level. Tronto claims that the boundary between public and private life "makes the citadel of moral boundaries even safer from incursion by women" (1993, p. 10). Reno's discourse on Waco revealed that she did not accept this boundary. As she explained her actions, she emphasized that she considers herself a private citizen, a member of a community, who has been called to assume a public leadership role. As she played the role of Attorney General in accounting for the actions at Waco, however, she made it clear that who she is as a private person informed her public actions, both in making the decision to take action at the Branch Davidian complex and in her approach to explaining those actions.

During the press conference on the day of the crisis in Waco, Reno defined her approach to answering questions in personal terms. She seemed to be saying "I am this kind of person" and this informs my decision-making as a public figure. She explained her approach:

In any situation in which something like this occurs, everyone has questions, and I think the best way to address this is to be as open, candid and as forthright as possible, I look forward to responding to anyone and everyone who has questions, because the bottom line is, there are no easy answers to a question like this, that was posed in this situation, and it's something that we should carefully consider with the point of view of being accountable, and I'm the one to be accountable, in seeing how—what we do in the future to prevent such a senseless loss of human life. (U.S. Department of Justice Media Conference on the Branch Davidians, 1993, p. 3)

In reiterating that she would be "the person who answers the questions," she said, "I always welcome reviews" (U.S. Department of Justice Media Conference on the Branch Davidians, 1993, p. 3).

Additionally, she attributed her survival as a public figure to her personal qualities and said during a speech the summer after Waco: "[I]f there is any reason why I stand here before you as Attorney General today, it is because I had to account to people. I had to be open. I had to let them know why I did things and why I didn't do things" (Speech before the National Press Club, 1993, p. 5). She emphasized that her personal integrity informs her approach to making decisions in her public role as Attorney General and said she tries to be "honest and direct" (Speech before the National Press Club, 1993, p. 3).

In the days and months following Waco, Reno gave speeches articulating how her private and public lives are intertwined. She said that people—members of the U.S. community rather than the experts in Washington—helped her cope with the tragedy. During a speech before the Association of American Law Schools, she said that too many lawyers become "indifferent to people" (1994, p. 26) and she credited people "outside the beltway" with helping her cope as a private person with her public decisions (1994, p. 28). She said:

On April the 19th, the Waco disaster took place. In the days that followed, Americans across this country would walk up to me and just put their hands on my elbow or reach out and touch me and just say, you did okay, or it was a tragedy but go on, move ahead. People reached out and made a difference; they cared; they understood; they understood the dilemma far better than a lot of people within the Beltway. And they gave me the strength to go forward. (1994, p. 28)

Reno thus challenged the moral boundary that suggests separate realms for public and private life; for her the spheres are intertwined. She vowed during the speech before members of the Association of American Law Schools that she would not forget that the spheres are interconnected and said, "I will never, ever too long be gone from the American people and what they have to say" (1994, p. 29).

During the summer following Waco, Reno also defined her relationship with the community of the press. In a speech before the National Press Club, she observed that as a public figure she feels a special personal relationship with the press "considering the family from whence I came, especially [a family of reporters]" (1993, p. 2). She explained her feelings when she faced reporters following the tragedy in Waco. Although serving in an official capacity as Attorney General, Reno said she responded emotionally and felt personally threatened when she opened her press conference at the Justice Department.

It was on the afternoon, the late afternoon, of April the 19th of this year. I walked into a press conference in which television cameramen, commentators, reporters, looked at me as if they were a bunch of hungry wolves. Their questions came fast, furious, angry. Their faces were angry as they pounded the questions at me. What spin do you think people are going to put on this? How will this be perceived? Is your job on the line? They almost roared at me. (1993, p. 2)

She commented, however, that "about halfway through the press conference" she felt that her relationship with the reporters was transformed (1993, p. 2). She was a public figure answering difficult questions, but she sensed that as persons they had entered into a dialogue about the tragedy. Even though all participants were playing their public roles, they were interconnected on some private level "because it was almost as if we had become together immersed in one horrible tragedy, to which in many cases there were no answers" (1993, p. 2). She went on to describe the dialogue with the reporters:

There was no longer competition between the press corps out there and me, but we were trying to understand together. We were trying to understand what each one of us would have done had they been standing in my shoes. We were trying to understand life in all of its complexities. For as long as I live, as I deal with the press, I will never forget that afternoon. And it carried me through into the evening, to other commentators. They weren't pulling any punches, but there was a spirit of let's talk together, let's question together. You be accountable but let's probe, let's try to understand, let's get to the ultimate truth. (1993, p. 3)

In discussing the transformed relationship with the press, Reno suggested a relationship between private and public roles. She described a point during the press conference when the give-and-take of a question-and-answer session, designed to be adversarial, evolved into dialogue. She implied that the transformation occurred because all participants realized they shared common ground as human beings trying to understand a difficult situation.

IMPLICATIONS

Tronto's (1993) criticisms of the moral boundaries that define Western political philosophy center on the value orientation that has privileged abstract thought over feelings, circumstances, and personal experiences. Each moral boundary suggests a standpoint that legitimates "proper moral accounts" grounded in reason. A philosophy grounded in "rights" or absolutes takes precedence over a philosophy grounded in "care" or a commitment to all that may be done to "maintain, continue, and repair 'our world' " (Tronto, p. 103).

In Tronto's view, the first two moral boundaries (morality and politics and the moral point of view) reflect a patriarchal value orientation that suggests that "moral views are fixed" and made from a perspective that is "distant and disinterested." These two moral boundaries imply that such moral views are objective and agreed upon by "right-thinking" human beings. From this perspective, the "detached and autonomous" political decision-maker is designated to uphold these moral views—regardless of circumstances. These moral views, of course, do not take into account the value orientations of marginalized voices in Western cultures. The final moral boundary legitimates the first two boundaries by assigning the "important" work (the public work) to one institutional realm and the "trivial" work (the private work) to another realm.

We believe that an approach such as Reno's that directly challenges and re-visions the moral boundaries defined by Tronto reflects a view of political decision-making that will lead to a "better world." In proposing that the boundaries should be redrawn, Tronto suggests that the perspectives of those who traditionally have been excluded from the public (particularly the political) realm should be taken into account. Reno's re-visioning of the boundaries, as revealed through her discourse on Waco, is marked by a number of characteristics. She refused to accept that politics is an inherently dirty business—as manifest in the morality and politics boundary. Our analysis proposes that Reno accepts responsibility and refuses to, in her words, "do spin stuff." Additionally, her discourse speaks to problems with "the moral point of view" boundary. After the Waco tragedy, she did not deny that mistakes had been made.

Furthermore, Reno did not speak in abstract terms about the tragedy; she contextualized her decision and acknowledged her own personal pain. In Kathryn Pyne Addelson's (1994) words, Reno did not respond as a distant judge or observer, nor did she hide behind the Enlightenment cloak of "clean knowledge" described by Jane Flax (1992). Reno instead acknowledged her struggles as a moral decision-maker.

Finally, as a public figure Reno did not use the trappings of her office as a shield in explaining the Waco decision. Rather, she explained her decision in private and public terms. She emphasized that her private views, her personal integrity, informed her approach in making the decision to inject nonlethal gas into the Branch Davidian complex as well as her explanations of that decision. She also made a point of speaking as a *person* who had made a difficult decision that she was trying to explain to other people.

Future research on Reno might focus on her efforts, through her discourse, to re-vision patriarchal constructions of "family." Media coverage has characterized Reno as "without family." Reno may be "without family" according to patriarchal definitions of family (spouse and children), but that definition should be challenged. Reno did care for her mother, and she has offered her own definition of family that suggests her links with particular communities and individuals. In her efforts to re-vision the definition of family, Reno echoes Stephanie Coontz (1992), who argues for expanding definitions of family and says: "For, despite making generalizations about past families, the historical evidence does suggest that families have been most successful wherever they have built meaningful, solid networks and commitments *beyond* their own boundaries. We may discover that the best thing we will ever do for our own families, however we define them, is to get involved in community or political action to help others" (p. 288).

Other gendered media coverage of Reno deserves scrutiny by popular and scholarly critics. Although many media accounts following the fire at the Branch Davidian Complex seemed to valorize Reno as a public figure possessing special integrity, we are troubled by these accounts. A cover story for the *New York Times Magazine* referred to "Reverend Reno" one year following the fire in Waco. The reporter lauded her efforts "in one public pulpit after another . . . to restore confidence in the Justice Department"; however, the same article also raised questions about her competence in running the Justice Department (Caplan, 1993, cover). The cover story was reminiscent of a cover story one year earlier that featured "Hillary Rodham Clinton and The Politics of Virtue" (Kelly, 1993). We wonder if both women have been labeled saints only in order to be found lacking in virtue, and thus sinners.

A number of parallels emerged when we examined the press coverage of three powerful women—Janet Reno, Hillary Rodham Clinton, and Lani Guinier. All three women were treated as anomalous figures. In Chapter 4, we emphasized that Rodham Clinton has been treated as a "freak." Reno is also a freak—neither man nor woman. She defies the lens of gender polarization by refusing to act and dress "like a woman." Whereas photos of Rodham Clinton feature her "female troubles"— "bloated" legs and "wide" hips—photos of Reno feature her "graceless" walk and long strides. In one photo accompanying the *New York Times Magazine* article, Reno looks uncomfortable in her high heels and is peering back into the photographer's lens seemingly puzzled by the scrutiny she is receiving. Press accounts have suggested that she is an oddity, an original, a primitive from the Everglades. The subtext seems to be, "We won't see her kind again." Media depictions of Reno as "other" (i.e., not a "real" woman) fulfill hegemonic expectations that "real" women are unsuited for politics (i.e., the moral boundaries remain in place).

Whereas Rodham Clinton's response to hegemonic expectations is rhetorical stunting, and Guinier's was denying, Reno remains constant in how she presents herself to the world. Granted, Reno is not as highly visible as Rodham Clinton, but media images of the Attorney General suggest her power has unsettled some observers. A caricature of Reno in the *New Yorker*, for example, trivialized her accomplishments as Attorney General by focusing on her inattention to clothing and style— stereotypic female pursuits. The full-page cartoon featured Reno's wardrobe choices (i.e., Reno in "Rayon acetate one-piece dress with knit bodice and back-zippered pleated skirt with attached slip" and "Elasticized nylon-lycra scoop-front bra and bike short. High-cut Danskin thong brief" [Crawford, 1993, p. 81]). The caricature reminded us of "loony Lani"—the media misfit with crazy hair and a crazy name.

As we approach the end of the twentieth century, those who create mass-mediated messages have joined philosophers, politicians, psychologists, and theologians as the guardians of moral boundaries and the lenses of gender. A *Time* story said that Washington, DC "loves a character" and that the eccentric Reno, "trailing swamp stories and reptiles" ... "invite[s] instant mythology" (Gibbs, 1993, July 12, p. 22). All the women included in our study have been covered as "characters" by the media. We believe, however, that the mythology was invited, for the most part (Rodham Clinton certainly cooperated with the mythologizing), by political frameworks reflecting moral boundaries and the lenses of gender.

With Reno, as with Rodham Clinton and Guinier, media images alert us to our "age's typical freaks" and thereby define for us a standard

"Selections from the Janet Reno Collection," October 1993. By permission of Michael Crawford/*The New Yorker*.

against which to measure what is "normal." Reno, as a character, is someone who simultaneously defies and supports androcentric norms. In her role as the first woman to serve as U.S. Attorney General, she clearly challenges androcentric norms. Media accounts, though, uphold androcentric norms concerning the political world (i.e., politics is a man's game) by suggesting that Reno "slipped in" because she is "other" as a woman—"a self described awkward old maid with a sensible name and big, sensible shoes" (Gibbs, 1993, July 12, p. 22). She has no interest in female-associated activities (i.e., attention to appearance, shopping). When a *Time* reporter described "the 54-year-old, 6-ft. 2-in. Reno thrust[ing] out her jaw and glar[ing]" in response to John Conyers during the House Judiciary Committee Hearing, the suggestion was that the Attorney General acts and looks like a man. The characterization implied that Reno is a biological aberration—an accident. Highlighting her age also drew attention to the fact that she is beyond childbearing age. In other words, she is more male than female; therefore, she is unsuited for the private world of women and suited for the public world of men.[4]

Although Reno avoided rhetorical stunting and denying, she did not escape vilification by the media. For the most part, she was lauded by the media in her role as Attorney General, but criticized as a "woman." We do believe that these patterns of coverage by media commentators reflected their taken-for-granted assumptions concerning moral boundaries and the lenses of gender. Reno's discourse offers possibilities for re-visioning moral boundaries and looking *at* rather than *through* the lenses of gender. Change will come about, however, only when media sources acknowledge their complicity in legitimating sexist ideologies.

NOTES

1. Although the Baird and Wood situations were quite different, press coverage tended to overlook the differences. Baird hired undocumented workers, a Peruvian couple, to work as live-in nanny and driver. Wood, on the other hand, did not break the law when she hired an undocumented worker from Trinidad to provide child care. When Wood hired the child care worker, it was legal to do so. Furthermore, she paid all taxes that were due and submitted required forms. Much mainstream media coverage referred to the challenges of hiring household help and the "illegal alien" problems of Baird and Wood (see e.g. Apple, 1993; Ifill, 1993, January 24; Johnston, 1993, January 14; Williams, 1993). A *Time* reporter focused on Baird's violation of the law and observed: "But as hot an issue as working motherhood may be, this was not about child care, not about motherhood, not really about much of a gender battle at all, as the furious phone calls from men and women across the country attested" (Gibbs, 1993, February 1, p. 28).

2. A number of commentators did address the "female-associated sins" or Zoë Baird problems. For example, see: Berry, 1993, p. A23; Blumenthal, 1993, pp. 53–

61; Jong, 1993, p. A23; Lewis, 1993, January 25 and February 8, p. A17; Letters to the Editor, 1993, p. A22; Resnik, 1993, p. A23; Robinson, 1993, p. 7; Quindlen, 1993, January 20 and January 27, February 10, p. A23; Wallis, 1993, p. 76.

3. Indeed, Reno has assumed care-taking responsibilities traditionally associated with women. She lived with her mother, Jane, and cared for her when she was dying of cancer. Reno has acknowledged the importance of caring for her mother and commented: "And the fact that I cared for her and made sure she was okay is as important to me as anything I've ever done professionally.... A commitment to family should be, and personally to me has been, as rewarding as anything that I've ever done" (quoted in Anderson, 1994, 126).

4. Lisle (1996) speaks to perceptions of "old maids" and "spinsters." She says: "It was not so long ago that physicians frightened spinsters with talk about how nature would punish them for not reproducing: Their unused uteruses would decay (leading to disease and mental derangement), the climacteric would be difficult (because organs had not been nourished by semen), and their overall health would deteriorate (resulting in early death)" (pp. 227–228). Mary Daly (1978) discusses connotations with the term "spinster" and argues: "The functioning of the word *spinster* to contort women's minds into double-think is clear. It has been a powerful weapon of intimidation and deception, driving women into the 'respectable' alternative of marriage, forcing them to believe, against all evidence to the contrary, that wedlock will be salvation from a fate worse than death, that it will inevitably mean fulfillment" (p. 393). Daly proposes that the term "spinster" should be reclaimed by women and used to describe "creative boundary-living energy" (p. 394).

6

Re-Visioning Political Communication

There's been this attempt to make living in Washington seem like you're volunteering to live in a cesspool. People say, "Oh, politically you don't dare do it." But I've always said to people, that's very hard on family life.

This institution tends to elect people who don't have a life to be its leaders, and they really don't know what family friendly means. I remember saying once to Tip O'Neill, "You can keep us late, but I get your dining room, and you can tell the Capitol police that when a clown comes in, and 10 5-year-olds, to get ready."
—Representative Patricia Schroeder
(quoted in Toner, 1996, p. A24)

We undertook our study of contemporary women and political communication in the wake of Campaign 1992, highly touted as "the year of the woman." Through the case studies presented in this book, we questioned optimistic media accounts, such as the one in *Time* that stated: "If the women's movement of the '70s was the lightning flash of female empowerment, then the long-awaited roll of thunder began to resound in this year's election results" (From Anita Hill to Capitol Hill, 1992, p. 21). Although Barbara Ehrenreich wrote in 1992 that "women are a more powerful political force than ever before," (p. 61), we cannot overlook the misogynistic backlash that marked Campaign 1994.

"The year of the woman" was followed by "the year of the smear." A report in *Newsweek* observed: "It [1994] is the election after the Year of the Woman, and the historic gains by women have collided with the radical right's nostalgia for the way things were. Conservative radio-talk-show hosts feed the resentment of many men over what they perceive as 'fem-centric' policies that promote women's concerns at their expense" (McCormick, 1994, p. 18). Representative Patricia Schroeder (Democrat-Colorado), a veteran of eleven campaigns for reelection, said she was unprepared for the "meanness" of Campaign 1994, and noted: "I've had people come spit on me in the airport for the first time" (quoted in McCormick, p. 18). Of course, during summer 1993, Schroeder was the target of a smear campaign that foreshadowed the tactics that would dominate Campaign 1994. As the senior Democrat on the House Armed Services Committee, Schroeder was a prominent critic of sexual harassment in the military, targeting in particular a Navy leadership that created a climate that resulted in the assault of 83 women at the 1991 Tailhook Association convention. Some Navy squadrons in the San Diego area responded to Schroeder's criticisms by dispensing T-shirts carrying vulgar statements referring to her sexuality (reported in Schmitt, 1993, p. A10).

Although we are skeptical of the gains made by women in the male-defined political world framed by the boundaries defined by Joan Tronto (1993) and seen through the lenses articulated by Sandra Lipsitz Bem (1993), we have tried to identify approaches to communication that have the potential to open up rhetorical space for women seeking roles in governance. Additionally, our case studies highlight the need to redraw political boundaries. Much was made of voter disdain for "politics as usual" in 1992 and 1994. The remedies sought by voters in 1992 and 1994, however, were radically different. Whereas many voters in 1992 seemed to rely on stereotypes of women as "more moral" than men and assumed, if elected, "women will foster cooperation instead of confrontation in domestic and foreign affairs; as nature's housekeepers, women will clean up the environment" (Kaminer, 1992, p. 65), many voters in 1994 rejected what they viewed as a radical "fem-centric" political agenda (McCormick, p. 18).

Throughout this study, we highlighted movements in Western philosophical, political, psychological, and theological thought that framed stereotypes of women as saints (more moral than their male counterparts) or sinners (more guided by base emotion than reason). As either saints or sinners, women are "other" in relation to the political order. Saints by their very nature must be cloistered, apart from the "dirty" world of political decision-making. Sinners, on the other hand, because they lack the proper moral fiber to lead, must be confined to a private sphere that will curtail their influence in the public political world.

Although Lani Guinier, Hillary Rodham Clinton, and Janet Reno made different rhetorical choices when confronted with the moral boundaries that frame women as saints or sinners and therefore unfit for the public world of politics, they all responded to their anomalous positions as women on the political stage. In our technological age, the three women took their rhetorical cues from mass-mediated messages. Whereas colonial American women were labeled witches, accused of assaultive speech and executed, and nineteenth-century women were labeled hysterics and "shut away" to contemplate their fates while peering at the "yellow wallpaper," contemporary political women face different public humiliations. When the women included in this study were caricatured in the media, as freaks or cartoon figures, they were dehumanized. Guinier, as an African American woman, was Jezebel, Sapphire, or Mammy. Rodham Clinton was an impossible mix of saint and sinner—witch, Lady Macbeth, hermaphrodite, bad mother, crusader, superwoman. Reno was the Reverend Reno, a woman "standing" by her man (President Bill Clinton, the only man she could "land" and certainly not based on her feminine charms), the daughter of a mother who wrestled alligators, and an old maid with sensible shoes.

The case studies of Guinier, Rodham Clinton, and Reno, however, emphasized their different rhetorical approaches in making their voices heard on the public political stage above the mass-mediated clamor. During the period when her nomination to serve as Assistant Attorney General for Civil Rights was contested, Guinier seemed to accept what Jane Flax (1992) has identified as the "metanarrative" of the Enlightenment (p. 457). The "metanarrative" of the Enlightenment, a "sense making" story that Flax claims guides much feminist thought, suggests that a reasonable person will triumph in the face of groundless and erratic charges. As an African American woman, Guinier faced intersectional boundaries that worked against her public redemption. She was bound to be perceived as a sinner, a transgressor against basic U.S. values (i.e., one "man," one vote). Guinier accepted the Clinton administration's efforts to silence her and seemed to assume "right" or "reason" would triumph in the end and she would be understood. Although our analysis of Guinier is confined to the period surrounding her nomination, we see evidence that she is no longer a denier. Unfortunately, the Justice Department lost a valuable voice due to the unfair media treatment Guinier received, the failure of the Clinton administration to support her, and Guinier's faith in the "system" as reflected in her rhetorical choices.

Hillary Rodham Clinton's rhetorical choices also implied basic faith in the "system." She seemed to accept the moral boundaries and the efforts of critics and supporters alike to view her activities "through" the lenses of gender. The rhetoric of accommodating and confronting suggested that the First Lady embraced what Flax (1992) refers to as "binary thinking" and assumed, in true Enlightenment tradition, that she could find "clean knowledge" (p. 457), a formula that would permit her to finesse all the barriers that have confronted women when they seek a public voice. Rodham Clinton thus performed as a rhetorical stunter, a contortionist who could "be" whatever her audience desired at the moment.

Janet Reno's rhetoric of re-visioning indicated a different approach to the "system" than that expressed by Guinier and Rodham Clinton. Whereas Guinier's rhetoric suggested that she believed she would be vindicated when her critics understood what she "really meant" in her writings, and Rodham Clinton's rhetoric implied faith that she could "win" by beating the "system" at its own game, Reno forthrightly articulated her own position in relation to the system. Reno's responses following the Waco fire indicated that she understood the "system" and the boundaries framing it. As she went from media appearance to media appearance and responded to questions from the House Judiciary Committee, her responses intimated that she recognized how people expected her to carve out her position in explaining Waco. Her interrogators made it apparent that they were waiting for her to obfuscate as she explained the circumstances surrounding her decision-making on Waco.

The questions Reno responded to following the fire in Waco were designed to put her on the defensive. As she was asked to justify her decision, the questions were framed to invite her to "stand her ground"—to defend her decision-making as "right." Although the questions invited her to honor the "morality first" boundary, to speak as a person who knew she was "right," and to defend her choices in absolute terms, Reno refused to follow this path. Instead, she admitted that mistakes had been made and accepted responsibility for those mistakes. She also spoke as a human being who said she felt humbled by the tragic consequences of her decision-making.

In responding to questions, Reno thus made it clear that she did not speak from a Machiavellian or "politics first" perspective. She explained that the circumstances at the Branch Davidian complex were unique and defied easy categorization, an unusual admission for a lawyer trained to see the world in categorical imperatives. When she explained that she did not do "spin stuff," she refused to fall back on convenient "the ends justify the means" moral reasoning to defend the actions she authorized at Waco. Not only did Reno acknowledge that what happened at Waco could not be justified, but she presented herself as a "connected" rather than a "disinterested" decision-maker. She spoke emotionally of her own pain as a decision-maker in coping with having made such a tragic decision that resulted in loss of life, particularly the lives of children.

Finally, she contextualized her decision by speaking to the constellation of circumstances that moved her to authorize intervention at the Branch Davidian complex. Her contextualized approach to decision-making also contested dualistic assumptions concerning the boundary between public and private life. As she explained her choices, she indicated that her public decision making was informed by her personal experiences. Her rhetoric suggested that she viewed herself as a private person, a member of the U.S. community, who was called to make value-laden public decisions and made those decisions based on her character that was formed through personal experiences.

Reno's rhetoric thus suggested possibilities for re-visioning moral boundaries. In contextualizing her decision-making, taking responsibility for her actions, and speaking as a person of character representing her community, Reno enacted Tronto's (1993) proposal to make "care a central concern of human life" (p. 180). Tronto (1993) and Bem (1993) suggest that our world will change only when our social institutions change. Bem argues for "a radical restructuring of social institutions" (p. 176) in order to bring about sexual equality. The lenses of gender, defined by Bem as androcentrism, gender polarization, and biological essentialism, are kept in place, as we have argued in this book, by the moral boundaries described by Tronto.

We share Tronto's broader concern with redrawing moral boundaries to bring about fundamental institutional changes that will foster sexual equality as well as equality regardless of race, class, or sexual orientation. Gloria Anzaldúa (1987, 1990) refers to the "borderlands," the places where people on the margins—the margins of discourse and the margins of mainstream society—dwell. She uses the Aztec word *la mestiza* ("torn between ways") to explain "a consciousness of the borderlands" (1990, p. 377).

Cradled in one culture, sandwiched between two cultures, straddling all three cultures and their value systems, *la mestiza* undergoes a struggle of flesh, a struggle of borders, an inner war. Like all people, we perceive the version of reality that our culture communicates. Like others having or living in more than one culture, we get multiple, often opposing messages. The coming together of two self-consistent but habitually incompatible frames of reference causes *en choque*, a cultural collision. (1990, p. 378)

For Teresa de Lauretis (1984), "borders stand for the potentially conflictual copresence of different cultures, desires, contradictions, which they articulate or delineate" (p. 98). Because the United States is composed of a myriad of co-cultures, a central question must be how people who dwell in the borderlands or on the borders will be able to move to the centers of political discourse where privileged white women, such as Reno, have managed to find space for their voices. An even more important question may be how people on the borders will maintain their integrity once they find space for their voices on the mainstream, dominant political stage.

We also believe, that, to a certain extent, all members of U.S. society experience *la mestiza*. Because U.S. culture is diverse, composed of many co-cultures, we all experience *en choque* as we struggle with ways to come together in community. Tronto's (1993) definition of care, introduced in Chapter 2 of this book, offers hope that when we re-vision the values that buttress our political institutions we will be able to honor the cultures of the borderlands, but also able to identify common ground that will make the boundaries more permeable. When care is defined as "a species activity that includes everything that we do to maintain, continue, and repair our 'world' so that we can live in it as well as possible," we will be able to cross the boundaries and honor the common elements that bring all our lives together in a "life-sustaining web" (Tronto, p. 103). Once we recognize that all our lives are interconnected, caring activities will no longer be associated "with privacy, with emotion, and with the needy" (Tronto, p. 117). When we value the private world as much as the public world (and recognize that the two worlds are interconnected), and acknowledge decision-making based on emotion *and* reason, we will contextualize our dealings with the people around us.

Re-visioning our political structures to incorporate values associated with care obviously does not mean controversies will dissolve. Our approach to those controversies might change, however. Discussion and decision-making framed by care will enable us to bring together in political decision-making the following values, all grounded in respect for the people with whom we are communicating: (1) openness; (2) reverence for diversity of opinion; (3) a commitment to understanding the language and culture of the people with whom we communicate; and (4) a pledge to monitor our language for polarizing terms and images.

Mark Lawrence McPhail (1994, 1995), in his calls for a rhetoric of coherence, has challenged "the assumption that diverse conceptions of reality are *essentially* different and *by their very nature* distinct from one another" (1994, p. 16). He argues that we must "find similarity in difference," although the Classical rhetorical tradition encourages us instead to frame the world in dualities, or in Tronto's words, boundaries. We agree with McPhail that a "postmodern conceptualization of rhetoric" must address "nonargumentative approaches to language" and ways to bring people, in all their diversity, together in community (1994, p. 129).[1]

We have argued in this book that Lani Guinier, Hillary Rodham Clinton, and Janet Reno represent important, albeit privileged voices, because they encourage us, through their rhetoric, to reconsider the values that have framed our political institutions. Although the "year of the woman" was followed by "the year of the smear," we are hearing in Congress voices from the borders that urge us to reconsider taken-for-granted institutional values. Senator Carol Moseley-Braun (Democrat-Illinois) spoke to issues of intersectionality and emphasized that she came from the borderlands as the first African American woman elected to serve in the Senate. In 1993, Moseley-Braun took to the floor of the Senate to decry efforts of Senator Jesse Helms (Republican-North Carolina) to find a "back door" route to renew a design patent, emblazoned with the Confederate flag insignia, for the United Daughters of the Confederacy. Helms had tacked on an amendment to the national service bill that would have permitted renewal of the patent. Because most Senators did not realize they were voting for renewal of the patent as part of the national service bill, Helms won the initial test vote.

After Moseley-Braun spoke, Helms's strategy was exposed and she emphasized that she spoke as an African American in expressing her outrage. The patents connote honor and prestige and, as the *New York Times* reported, Congress has authorized a limited number of patents in this century. The patent for the United Daughters of the Confederacy, however, was renewed four times by Congress in the twentieth century. Moseley-Braun responded to Helms's efforts to depict the members of the Daughters of the Confederacy as "gentle souls" (Clymer, 1993, July 23, p. B6) by saying that the flag, symbolizing the Civil War, stood for those who "fought to try to preserve our nation, to keep the states from separating themselves over the issue of whether or not my ancestors could be held as property, as chattel, as objects of trade and commerce in this country" (quoted in Clymer, p. B6). Following the debate, Senator Ben Nighthorse Campbell (Democrat-Colorado), the only other nonwhite in the Senate, spoke as a person from the borderlands, who recognized the significance of Moseley-Braun's protest.[2] Senator Howell Heflin (Democrat-Alabama) supported Moseley-Braun and said, "we live today in a different world" (quoted in Clymer, p. B6).

A *New York Times* editorial observed that Helms derided Moseley-Braun for making race an issue during the floor debate. Due to Moseley-Braun's presence and her forceful argument, many members of the Senate became aware of symbolism that had eluded them. "Once the full Senate realized that race was already implicated in the symbolism of the Civil War emblem, the affront to black Americans was clear" (Ms. Moseley Braun's Majestic Moment, 1993, p. A18).

The voices of Moseley-Braun and Nighthorse Campbell thus encouraged Senators to examine the values that informed the debate over the patent and the Confederate flag insignia. As a speaker, Moseley-Braun embodied the characteristics we recommend for re-visioning political decision-making. Her rhetoric fostered a respect for openness and invited her colleagues to honor diversity of opinion. More importantly, she urged her listeners to understand the language and culture of the people with whom they communicate. As she pleaded, though, for her listeners to understand her standpoint as an African American woman, she avoided polarizing language. She did not demonize the Daughters, and said it was their right to wave the flag of the Confederacy, but she noted that the Senate should not legitimize their insignia by granting the patent.

Our book has featured women in highlighting the role that rhetoric can play in redrawing the moral boundaries that frame political discourse. We want to emphasize, however, that males in political life are also communicating in ways that re-vision the values that frame our political institutions. As we observed in our analysis of Hillary Rodham Clinton's rhetoric in Chapter 4, her husband is often depicted as a "wimp" in relation to his powerful wife, who is evil incarnate and exercises the supernatural powers of a witch. A cartoon in the *Chicago Tribune* following the failure of the Clintons to bring about health care reform, for example, depicted Rodham Clinton as the Wicked Witch of the West in meltdown, while her husband stood to her side, functioning as one of those palace guards we all recognize from the film version of *The Wizard of Oz* (My health care plan . . . it's just been watered down!, 1994, p. A18). The President was portrayed as an oaf—overweight, flabby, with a puzzled expression on his face. The cartoonist's message was clear. Rodham Clinton tried to use her wimpish, not-too-bright spouse to bring about an "evil" political agenda.

The *Tribune* cartoon represents only one instance of Clinton's critics casting him as the henpecked husband. Although his critics charge that he vacillates on issues, we believe he often manifests "caring" values in communication, engages in dialogue, and at times offers flashes of insight concerning a re-visioned politics. President Clinton, then candidate Clinton, communicated "care" during the town meeting debate on October 15, 1992. As a *New York Times* editorial observed, Carole Simpson, the moderator from ABC News, "tried to serve the desires of the audience rather than the tactical needs of the candidates" (The Candidates, Unvarnished, 1992, p. A24). The editorial also noted: "Governor Clinton thrived in this setting" (p. A24).

During the most telling moment of the town hall debate, Clinton made it clear that he came to the debate as a member of the U.S. community, empathizing with the concerns of voters in the audience. An African-American woman in the audience posed the following question: "How has the national debt personally affected each of your lives. And if it hasn't, how can you honestly find a cure for the economic problems of the common people if you have no experience in what's ailing them?" (Transcript of 2nd TV debate, 1992, p. A12). Ross Perot responded first and said he wanted all children to have the opportunities to succeed economically in the same ways he had succeeded—coming from disadvantaged circumstances and "making it." When President Bush responded, it was apparent he did not "get" the question. The questioner kept pressing him to answer how "on a personal basis" the poor economy had affected his life. He kept saying he wanted his grandchildren to have opportunities, but could not understand what the questioner wanted to know, and finally said, "I'm not sure I get it. Help me with the question and I'll try to answer it" (p. A12).

The member of the audience pressed Bush and said she knew people who had been laid off from jobs, could not pay their mortgages, and had missed their car payments. She wanted to know how Bush could respond to these problems if he did not understand them. He never did indicate that he understood the question. Perot and Bush responded to the question by resorting to abstractions and refusing to contextualize their answers. Perot appealed to a U.S. cultural myth by indicating he had "picked himself up by his bootstraps," while Bush resorted to discussing the futures of his grandchildren, a clichéd line he used throughout the campaign that rang hollow (after all, all his grandchildren will benefit from inherited wealth).

Clinton, in contrast, walked toward the questioner and asked her to say more about how the poor economy had affected her. Then he personalized his answer and spoke as the "governor of a small state" who knows people personally who have suffered (p. A12).

I have seen what's happened in this last four years when in my state, when people lose their jobs, there's a good chance I'll know them by their names. When a factory closes I know the people who ran it. When the businesses go bankrupt, I know them. And I've been out here for 13 months meeting in meetings just like this ever since October with people like you all over America, people that have lost their jobs, lost their livelihood, lost their health insurance. (p. A12)

When he responded to the woman's question, Clinton engaged in a dialogue with her. By avoiding polarizing language and images, Clinton demonstrated respect for openness, diversity of opinion, and the language and culture of the person with whom he was communicating.[3]

As Maureen Dowd (1992) remarked in a commentary on the debate, some critics of the town meeting debate forum had worried that it would emulate the "Oprah Winfrey" format and "lower the quality of Presidential discourse" (p. A12). Quite the opposite happened, however, as audience members pressed the candidates to concentrate on issues rather than making personal attacks on each other. When critics of the format declared that they thought the debate would be too personal and "lower" presidential rhetoric thereby denigrating the office, they revealed their belief in the values that frame Tronto's moral boundaries. Critics overlooked the importance of a debate format that asked the candidates to contextualize their answers.

Clinton's rhetoric during the town hall debate embodied "caring" characteristics, as did our previous example of Moseley-Braun's. Much of our public discourse, nonetheless, encourages divisiveness. As we wrote this final chapter, Patrick Buchanan was spreading his message of hate for those from the borderlands—all of us who seek to honor our diversity by coming together in community. In Waterloo, Iowa, Buchanan, addressing an audience composed mostly of white people, talked about building a security fence to protect the United States from illegal immigration and said, "Listen, Jose, you're not coming in this time!" (quoted in Bennet, 1996, p. A22). During a debate in South Carolina, he argued that the Confederate flag should fly over southern statehouses, because it represents "defiance, courage, bravery in the face of overwhelming odds, and I believe everyone should stand up for their heritage. It didn't fly over slave quarters. It flew over battlefields" (quoted in Bennett, 1996, p. A22). Buchanan's critics suggested that he spoke in "code, using xenophobic images like those of anti-Semitic references to incite bigots without alienating mainstream voters" (Bennet, p. A22). For example, when he spoke of U.S. Supreme Court Justice Ruth Bader Ginsburg, he referred to her as the "ultraliberal Ruth Ba-der Gins-burg," emulating a Hebraic chant as he derided her (quoted in Bennet, p. A22).

Reporters performed a valuable service in drawing attention to Buchanan's divisive rhetoric. Unfortunately, our case studies of women as political communicators suggest that media coverage also plays an important role in legitimating moral boundaries and lenses of gender. In the United States, as elsewhere in the world, people are bombarded with mediated messages to the extent that we have coined the term "information overload" to describe our inability to keep up with everything we are exposed to through the media. Most journalists would agree that this barrage of information presented to us in the media offers points of view; no news is truly "objective." Simply by choosing which stories to tell, where to place them, and how to illustrate them, editors and journalists are exerting influence and (perhaps inadvertent) bias. In the realm of local televised news, Robert Entman (1990) illustrates how "modern racism" can be reinforced in viewers by the preponderance of stories about African Americans who commit crimes, the token presence of African Americans in anchor positions, and the persistence of images linking African Americans with violence and unlawful activities. Mainstream news magazine coverage of black–Latino interaction, according to Shah and Thornton (1994), is "structured by and reinforce[s] a racial ideology" (p. 141). They suggest that a racial hierarchy is "ideologically constructed" to "continually reinforce the dominant positions of the white majority" (p. 143).

John Fiske (1994) refers to "discursive guerillas" in the media who have the power to legitimate or unsettle "dominant social interests." In our case studies of women as political communicators, "discursive guerillas" representing a range of political viewpoints supported dominant interests by legitimating moral boundaries and the lenses of gender.

When the women featured in our case studies were symbolically cast as other, the hegemonic political order (male, privileged, and white) was fortified. The coverage of Guinier, Rodham Clinton, and Reno thus suggests that many media sources serve as guardians of a hegemonic view of women in relation to public discourse. Following Smart (1986), we argue that hegemony should be considered in the Foucauldian sense, which concerns a "form of social cohesion ... by way of practices, techniques and methods which infiltrate minds and bodies, cultural practices which cultivate behaviors and beliefs, tastes, desires, and needs as seemingly natural occurring qualities and properties embodied in the psychic and physical reality (or 'truth') of the human subject" (p. 160).

Thus, those who favor a political order framed to keep those from the borderlands on the margins were reassured by the media coverage that the way of the political world was as it had always been, and that Guinier, Rodham Clinton, and Reno were aberrations. Guinier was "loony Lani," a deranged interloper. Rodham Clinton, whether cast in the role of bitch, Wicked Witch of the West, or saint, was covered in the media as an anomaly—an errant figure who had transgressed on the sacred ground of tradition. Even Reno, in some respects valorized by the press for her conduct during the Waco crisis, was subjected to cruel caricatures that suggested she was more "masculine" than "feminine." In Reno's case, the suggestion seemed to be that, although she was successful on the public political stage, her presence did not "count." She was not actually "female." Thus, our analyses revealed that all the women we studied were targets of techniques that ridiculed, trivialized, and sexualized their accomplishments, and in turn dismissed them as credible political communicators.

If women and "others" from the borderlands are to gain public voices, and in the process re-vision political institutions, then media sources must play a role in opening rhetorical space for these voices. Fiske (1994) identifies the sites for what he refers to as "discursive struggles" "between the media and the public" (p. xxi). Although he argues for the power of media and urges vigilant criticism of media practices, he also emphasizes that media events become media events because audiences participate to define them as such. When we turn a critical eye on media sources, we must also turn a critical eye "upon ourselves" (p. xxi). For example, in examining the new web site "Hillary's Hair," we must ask ourselves about the "coalition of interests" (p. xxi) supporting a web site where Internet surfers vote on Rodham Clinton's "best" hairstyle.

Fiske identifies the following five arenas for "discursive struggles" and suggests that when we turn a critical eye on ourselves and the media, we should turn to these for guidance. The five include: (1) "The struggle to 'accent' a word or sign, that is, to turn the way it is spoken or used to particular social interests" (p. 5). For example, references to Rodham

Clinton as "co-president" have been "spoken" in both liberal and conservative accents suggesting images reflecting different social interests. (2) "The struggle over the choice of word, image, and therefore discursive repertoire" (p. 5). When conservative forces triumphed in labeling Guinier a "quota queen" and the term became common currency in media coverage, they won the battle over discourse by casting the candidate as a radical. (3) "The struggle to recover the repressed or center the marginalized" (pp. 5–6). In this arena, "a discourse produces its own meanings and represses others" (p. 6). The *New Yorker* cartoonist who created "The Janet Reno Collection" trivialized her accomplishments as U.S. Attorney General and in turn highlighted her "inadequacies" as a "feminine" woman. (4) "The struggle to disarticulate and rearticulate" (p. 6). As Fiske observes, "discourse not only puts events into words or images, it also links, or articulates, them with other events" (p. 6). When Rodham Clinton (wearing a soft pink suit) held a news conference at the White House during spring 1994, to address questions on her involvement in Whitewater, she rearticulated her role as First Lady. The Washington press corps cooperated as she "chatted" and presented herself as a traditional First Lady, rather than a co-president. (5) "The struggle to gain access to public discourse in general or the media in particular to make one's case heard" (p. 6). Guinier's struggle to be heard when her nomination was "in trouble" exemplifies this site of struggle.

We embrace Fiske's suggestions for recognizing the sites where we can contest media discourse. As we close this book, however, we are also aware of the need to contest our own rhetorical critical practices. In Chapter 1, we addressed our rationale for focusing on the public realm of leadership in studying women as political communicators. We acknowledge that our critical framework for analyzing discourse produced its own meanings and repressed others. For this study, we heard from privileged women who have gained empowerment through the same political channels (i.e., elite educational institutions, connections with the powerful, and public speeches) traditionally used by men. Our critical approach did not permit us to hear from less privileged women who are making their voices heard and re-visioning politics in different ways than a Reno is re-visioning politics.

By virtue of their gender, Guinier, Rodham Clinton, and Reno come *from* the margins or the borderlands, but we need to develop rhetorical critical approaches that will permit us to study communication *in* the borderlands. In order to understand community-based, nonhierarchical power, we challenge our own assumptions concerning political power and how it is generated. Representative Nydia Velazquez (Democrat-New York), for example, defeated Democratic incumbent Stephen Solarz in the 1992 primary by exercising power through kinship networks and local neighborhood organizations. The 12th Congressional District had been redrawn to include many Latin communities and, "[a]s a native Puerto Rican, she [Velazquez] was in touch with communities she wanted to represent" (Lacayo, 1992, p. 45). Because she had served as a city council member, Velazquez "knew her way through the tangles of local politics" (Lacayo, p. 45). She made it clear, however, that she did not intend to follow the rules for "politics as usual." After she won the primary, she visited then House Speaker Thomas Foley in Washington to communicate to him that she would request assignment to the House Appropriations Committee—an assignment virtually unheard of for a new representative. She emphasized: "I'll come back tomorrow and tomorrow and tomorrow until they get tired of seeing me" (quoted in Lacayo, p. 45).

Our next step as rhetorical critics of political communication is to develop the frameworks that will permit us to study Velazquez and other political figures who enact community-based, nonhierarchical political power. In studying this politics of empowerment, we must move beyond the texts (i.e., public speeches) usually studied by critics of political discourse. As we expand the range of texts used to study community-based political power, we will turn to ethnographic research involving interviews with the constituencies of political figures, such as Velazquez.

We end this book with the hope that women are making a difference and are making their voices heard. Yet, we realize that these voices may sound faint because of the boundaries that constrain women and the lenses of gender that distort our hearing as well as our vision. Guinier, Rodham Clinton, and especially Reno offer examples of strategies that allow women to speak a little louder and let us all hear a little more clearly. It cannot fail to enrich all of humanity to hear the sounds of caring and community ring out in the public arena.

NOTES

1. We are sympathetic to McPhail's (1994) critique of the rhetorical tradition, his call for a rhetoric of coherence, and his suggestion "that racism, like other languages of oppression, arises out of an agreement to disagree that is grounded in judgments distinguishing positions and persons in terms of negative difference" (p. 18). In a later study, McPhail (1995) further develops his vision of a rhetoric of coherence and presents a reconceptualization of rhetoric grounded in Eastern thought, particularly Zen Buddhism. Although we agree with McPhail's critique of the Western rhetorical tradition, we are uncomfortable with the conceptualization of rhetoric using Eastern martial arts as a reference point. In the preface of *Zen in the Art of Rhetoric*, McPhail notes that one reviewer of the book in manuscript objected to his use of the term "warrior" "as peculiarly masculine and aggressive" (p. vii). McPhail suggests that he is contesting "accepted definitions and divisions" (p. vii.) and is going beyond patriarchal associations with the term warrior. We are open to his efforts to reconceptualize the term "war-

rior," but as feminist writers we are less than comfortable with the martial arts model he proposes for a rhetoric of coherence.

2. Ben Nighthorse Campbell joined the Republican Party in March 1995.

3. Kathleen Hall Jamieson (1988) describes a rhetorical style that is particularly suited to "the intimate medium of television that requires those who speak comfortably through it to project a sense of private self, unself-consciously self-disclose, and engage the audience in completing messages that exist as dots and lines on television's screen" (p. 81). Furthermore, Jamieson refers to Karlyn Kohrs Campbell's (1973, 1980) definition of the "feminine style" that is nonlinear, organized around examples, and evokes personal experience. Jamieson claims this "feminine" style is more suited to television than the impersonal, linear "manly" style that appeals to reason. Clinton used the "feminine" style during the debate.

References

Addelson, K. P. (1994). *Moral passages: Toward a collectivist moral theory.* New York: Routledge.
Aleinkoff, T. A. & Pildes, R. H. (1993, May 13). In defense of Lani Guinier. *Wall Street Journal*, p. A15.
Alexander, A. L. (1995). "She's no lady, she's a nigger": Abuses, stereotypes, and realities from the middle passage to capitol (and Anita) Hill. In A. F. Hill & E. C. Jorgan (Eds.), *The legacy of the Hill-Thomas hearings: Race, gender, and power in America* (pp. 3–25). New York: Oxford University Press.
Allen, M. (1995, August 23). In Virginia, 42 female cadets report for duty, but march to their own drum. *New York Times*, p. B6.
Anderson, P. (1994). *Janet Reno: Doing the right thing.* New York: John Wiley & Sons.
Anzaldúa, G. (1987). *Borderlands/La frontera: The new mestiza.* San Francisco: Aunt Lute Books.
———. (1990). La conciencia de la mestiza: Towards a new consciousness. In G. Anzaldúa (Ed.), *Making face, making soul (haciendo caras): Creative and critical perspective of women of color* (pp. 377–389). San Francisco: Aunt Lute Books.
Apple, R. W., Jr. (1993, January 23). Early damage control. *New York Times*, pp. A1, A9.
Applebome, P. (1994, April 3). Guinier ideas seen as odd, get serious study. *New York Times*, p. E5.
Aristotle. (1961). *The politics of Aristotle.* E. Barker (Ed.). London: Oxford University Press.
Barnes, G. H., & Dumond, D. L. (Eds.). (1934). *Letters of Theodore Dwight Weld, Angelina Grimké Weld, and Sarah Grimké, 1822–1844 (vol. 1).* Gloucester, MA: Peter Smith.
Beecher, C. C. (1937). *An essay on abolition with reference to the duty of American females.* Philadelphia: Henry Perkins.

Belenky, M. F., Clinchy, B. M., Goldberger, N. R., & Tarule, J. M. (1986). *Women's ways of knowing: The development of self, voice, and mind.* New York: Basic Books.

Bem, S. L. (1993). *The lenses of gender: Transforming the debate on sexual inequality.* New Haven: Yale University Press.

Bennet, J. (1996, February 25). Candidate's speech is called code for controversy. *New York Times,* p. A22.

Bennett, W. L., & Edelman, M. (1985). Toward a new political narrative. *Journal of Communication, 35,* 157–171.

Berke, R. L. (1993, February 12). Clinton picks Miami woman, veteran state prosecutor, to be his attorney general. *New York Times,* pp. A1, 22.

Bernstein, N. (1996, January 8). Equal opportunity recedes for most female lawyers. *New York Times,* p. A9.

Bernstein, R. (1996, February 4). A few hints on nurture from the First Lady. *New York Times,* p. C9.

Berry, M. F. (1993, February 10). The mother of all debates: The father's hour. *New York Times,* p. A23.

Blankenship, J., & Kang, J. G. (1991). The 1984 presidential and vice presidential debates: The printed press and "construction by metaphor." *Presidential Studies Quarterly, 21,* 307–318.

Blankenship, J., & Robson, D. C. (1995). A "feminine style" in women's political discourse: An exploratory essay. *Communication Quarterly, 43,* 353–366.

Bleier, R. (1984). *Science and gender: A critique of biology.* New York: Pergamon Press.

———. (1986). Sex differences research: Science or belief? In R. Bleir (Ed.), *Feminist approaches to science* (pp. 147–164). New York: Pergamon Press.

Blumenthal, S. (1993). Letters from Washington: Adventures in babysitting. *New Yorker,* pp. 53–61.

Bok, C. (1993, April 25). *Akron Beacon Journal* cartoon reprinted in *New York Times,* p. E6.

Bolick, C. (1993, April 30). Clinton's quota queens. *Wall Street Journal,* p. A12.

———. 1993, June 2). The legal philosophy that produced Lani Guinier. *Wall Street Journal,* p. A15.

Bookman, A., & Morgen, S. (1988). *Women and the politics of empowerment.* Philadelphia: Temple University Press.

Bostdorff, D. M. (1991). Vice-presidential comedy and the traditional female role: An examination of the rhetorical characteristics of the vice presidency. *Western Journal of Speech Communication, 55,* 1–27.

Boxer, B. (with Nicole Boxer). (1994). *Strangers in the Senate: Politics and the new revolution of women in America.* Washington, DC: National Press Books.

Boyer, P. J. (1995, May 15). Children of Waco. *New Yorker,* pp. 38–45.

Branan, K. (1993, September/October). Lani Guinier: The anatomy of a betrayal. *Ms.,* pp. 51–57.

Brittan, A., & Maynard, M. (1984). *Sexism, racism, and oppression.* New York: Basil Blackwell.

Broughton, J. M. (1983). Women's rationality and men's virtues: A critique of gender dualism in Gilligan's theory of moral development. *Social Research, 50,* 597–642.

Browning-Cole, E., & Coultrap-McQuin, S. (Eds.). (1992). *Explorations in feminist ethics: Theory and practice*. Bloomington: Indiana University Press.
Bulkin, E., Pratt, M. B., & Smith, B. (1988). *Yours in struggle: Three feminist perspectives on anti-Semitism and racism*. Ithaca: Firebrand Books.
Bullough, V. L., Shelton, B., & Slavin, S. (1988). *The subordinated sex: A history of attitudes toward women*. Athens: University of Georgia Press.
Burros, M. (1995, January 10). Hillary Clinton seeking to soften a harsh image. *New York Times*, pp. A1, A15.
———. (1995, December 5). For Mrs. Clinton: Cookies, tea, and a dash of policy. *New York Times*, p. B10.
Buzzanell, P. M., & Murphy, B. O. (1993). Hillary Rodham Clinton: Managing her image. Paper presented at the annual convention for the Organization for the Study of Communication, Language, and Gender, Tempe, AZ (October).
Bystydzienski, J. M. (1987). Women in politics in Norway. Paper presented at the Third International Interdisciplinary Congress on Women, Dublin, Ireland (July).
———. (Ed.). (1992). *Women transforming politics: Worldwide strategies for empowerment*. Bloomington: Indiana University Press.
Campbell, K. K. (1973). The rhetoric of women's liberation: An oxymoron. *Quarterly Journal of Speech, 59*, 74–86.
———. (1980). Stanton's "The solitude of self": A rationale for feminism. *Quarterly Journal of Speech, 66*, 304–312.
———. (1989). *Man cannot speak for her: A critical study of early feminist rhetoric* (Vol. II). Westport, CT: Greenwood Press.
Campbell, K. K., & Jerry, E. C. (1988). Woman and speaker: A conflict in roles. In S. Brehm (Ed.), *Seeing female* (pp. 123–133). Westport, CT: Greenwood Press.
Canas, K. A. (1995). Subaltern positionality and representation: Shirley Chisholm constituting a rhetoric of agency. Paper presented at the annual conference of the Western States Communication Association, Portland, OR (February).
The candidates, unvarnished. (1992, October 17). *New York Times*, p. A24.
Caplan, L. (1994, May 15). Reverend Reno. *New York Times Magazine*, pp. 40–46, 51, 70.
Card, C. (1990). *Feminist ethics*. Lawrence: University of Kansas Press.
Carlson, M. (1992, September 14). All eyes on Hillary. *Time*, pp. 28–30.
———. (1995, January 16). Muzzle the b word. *Time*, p. 36.
Carroll, S. J. (1994). *Women as candidates in American politics*, 2nd ed. Bloomington: Indiana University Press.
Carroll, S. J., Dodson, D. L., & Mandel, R. B. (1991). *The impact of women in public office: An overview*. Rutgers: Center for the American Woman and Politics (CAWP), Eagleton Institute of Politics.
Chesler, P. (1989). *Women and madness*. New York: Harvest/HBJ. (Original work published 1972)
Christ, C. P. (1980). *Diving deep and surfacing: Women writers on spiritual quest*. Boston: Beacon.
Cirksena, K. (1987). Politics and difference: Radical feminist epistemological

premises for communication studies. *Journal of Communication Inquiry*, 11, 19–28.

Cirksena, K., & Cuklanz, L. (1992). Male is to female as ____ is to: A guided tour of five feminist frameworks for communication studies. In L. Rakow (Ed.), *Women making meaning: New feminist directions in communication* (pp. 18–44). New York: Routledge.

A civil rights struggle ahead. (1993, May 23). *New York Times*, p. E14.

Cixous, H. (1981). Castration or decapitation. A. Kuhn (Trans.). *Signs: Journal of Women in Culture & Society*, 7, 41–54.

Clarke, E. H. (1873). *Sex in education; or, a fair chance for girls*. Boston: J. R. Osgood.

Clinton, H. R. (1996). *It takes a village and other lessons children teach us*. New York: Simon & Schuster.

Clinton, W. J. (1993, February 1). Remarks on health care reform and an exchange with reporters. *Weekly Compilation of Presidential Documents*, pp. 96–98.

Cloud, S. W. (1993, May 10). Standing tall: The capital is all agog at the new attorney general's outspoken honesty. *Time*, pp. 46–47.

A club of her own (1993, August 28). *New York Times*, p. A1 [photo].

Clymer, A. C. (1993, July 23). Daughter of slavery hushes Senate. *New York Times*, p. B6.

Clymer, A. C. (1993, September 26). First Lady stars in spotlight on health. *New York Times*, p. A32.

Cohn, B. (1993, June 14). So long, Lani. *Newsweek*, pp. 26–28.

Coleman, W. T., Jr. (1993, June 4). Three's company: Guinier, Reagan, Bush. *New York Times*, p. A31.

Collins, P. H. (1991 [1990]). *Black feminist thought: Knowledge, consciousness, and the politics of empowerment*. New York: Routledge. (Original work published 1990)

Condit, C. M. (1993). Opposites in oppositional practice: Rhetorical criticism and feminism. In S. P. Bowen & N. Wyatt (Eds.), *Transforming visions: Feminist critiques in communication studies* (pp. 205–230). Creskill Hill, NJ: Hampton Press.

Conover, P. J. (1988). Feminists and the gender gap. *Journal of Politics*, 4, 985–1010.

Coontz, S. (1988). *The social origins of private life*. New York: Verso.

———. (1992). *The way we never were: American families and the nostalgia trap*. New York: Basic Books.

Cooper, M., Walsh, K. T., Dentzer, S. & Toch, T. (1993, February 8). Co-president Clinton? *U.S. News & World Report*, pp. 30–32.

Cott, N. (1987). *The grounding of modern feminism*. New Haven: Yale University Press.

Crawford, M. (1993, October 11). The Janet Reno collection. *New Yorker*, p. 81 [cartoon].

Crenshaw, K. (1992). Whose story is it, anyway: Feminist and antiracist appropriations of Anita Hill (pp. 402–440). In T. Morrison (Ed.), *Race-ing justice, en-gendering power*. New York: Pantheon Books.

Crossette, B. (1995, August 27). Worldwide study finds decline in election of women to office. *New York Times*, p. A10.

Daly, M. (1973). *Beyond God the father: Toward a philosophy of women's liberation.* Boston: Beacon Press.

———. (1974). Theology after the demise of God the father: A call for the castration of sexist religion. In A. Hageman (Ed.), *Sexist religion and women in the church* (pp. 125–142). New York: Associates Press.

———. (1975). God is a verb. In U. West (Ed.), *Women in a changing world* (pp. 153–170). New York: McGraw-Hill.

———. (1978). *Gyn/ecology: The metaethics of radical feminism.* Boston: Beacon Press.

de Lauretis, T. (1984). *Alice doesn't: Feminism, semiotics, and cinema.* Bloomington: Indiana University Press.

Dill, B. T. (1979). The dialectics of black womanhood. *Signs: Journal of Women in Culture and Society, 4,* 543–557.

Dodson, D. (Ed.). (1991a). *Gender and policymaking: Studies of women in office.* Rutgers: Center for the American Woman and Politics (CAWP), Eagleton Institute for Politics.

———. (1991b). *Reshaping the agenda: Women in state legislatures.* Rutgers: Center for the American Woman and Politics (CAWP), Eagleton Institute for Politics.

Dodson, D., Carroll, S. J., Mandel, R. B., Kleeman, K. E., Schreiber, R., & Liebowitz, D. (1995). *Voices, views, votes: The impact of women in the 103rd Congress.* Rutgers: Center for the American Woman and Politics (CAWP), Eagleton Institute for Politics.

Donovan, J. (1992). *Feminist theory.* New York: Frederick Ungar. (Original work published 1985)

Dow, B. J., & Tonn, M. B. (1993). "Feminine style" and political judgment in the rhetoric of Ann Richards. *Quarterly Journal of Speech, 79,* 286–302.

Dowd, M. (1992, October 17). A no-nonsense sort of talk show on issues, issues, issues. *New York Times,* p. A12.

———. (1993, September 29). Witness works Hill and ends an era. *New York Times,* p. A19.

———. (1994, April 23). Contrition as weapon against public doubts. *New York Times,* pp. A1, 10.

———. (1995, October 5). O.J. Simpson as metaphor. *New York Times,* p. A29.

Dreifus, C. (1994, January 30). Jocelyn Elders. *New York Times Magazine,* pp. 16–19.

———. (1996, February 4). And then there was Frank. *New York Times,* pp. 22–25.

Edson, B. (1985). Bias in social movement theory: A view from a female-systems perspective. *Women's Studies in Communication, 8,* 34–45.

Ehrenreich, B. (1992, November 16). What do women have to celebrate? *Time,* pp. 61–62.

Eisler, R. (1988). *The chalice and the blade.* San Francisco: Harper & Row.

Elshtain, J. B. (1981). *Public man, private woman: Women and social and political thought.* Princeton: Princeton University Press.

———. (1995). *Democracy on trial.* New York: Basic Books.

Entman, R. M. (1990). Modern racism and the images of blacks in local television news. *Critical Studies in Mass Communication, 7,* 332–345.

Estrich, S. (1987). *Real rape*. Cambridge: Harvard University Press.
Faison, S. (1995, September 10). First Lady in Mongolia: Mare's milk and politics. *New York Times*, p. A10.
Fausto-Sterling, A. (1985). *Myths of gender: Biological theories about women and men*. New York: Basic Books.
Ferraro, G. (1985). *Ferraro: My story* (with L. B. Francke). New York: Bantam.
Figes, E. (1970). *Patriarchal attitudes*. London: Faber & Faber.
Fine, M. G. (1988). What makes it feminist? *Women's Studies in Communication*, 11, 18–19.
First Lady's first job. (1993, February 8). *Time*, p. 16.
Fisher, B., & Tronto, J. C. (1991). Toward a feminist theory of care. In E. Abel & M. Nelson (Eds.), *Circles of care: Work and identity in women's lives* (pp. 35–62). Albany: State University of New York Press.
Fiske, J. (1994). *Media matters: Everyday culture and political change*. Minneapolis: University of Minnesota Press.
Flax, J. (1992). The end of innocence. In J. Butler & J. W. Scott (Eds.), *Feminists theorize the political* (pp. 445–463). New York: Routledge.
Foss, K. A., & Foss, S. K. (1983). The status of research on women and communication. *Communication Quarterly*, 31, 195–204.
———. (1989). Incorporating the feminist perspective in communication scholarship: A research commentary. In K. Carter & C. Spitzack (Eds.), *Doing research on women's communication: Perspectives on theory and method* (pp. 65–91). Norwood NJ: Ablex.
———. (1991). *Women speak: The eloquence of women's lives*. Prospect Heights, IL: Waveland Press.
———. (1994). Personal experience as evidence in feminist scholarship. *Western Journal of Communication*, 58, 39–43.
Foss, S. K., & Foss, K. A. (1988). What distinguishes feminist scholarship in communication studies. *Women's Studies in Communication*, 11, 195–203.
Foss, S. K., Foss, K. A., & Trapp, R. (1991). *Contemporary perspectives on rhetoric*, 2nd ed. Prospect Heights, IL: Waveland Press.
Foss, S. K., & Griffin, C. (1992). A feminist perspective on rhetorical theory: Toward a clarification of boundaries. *Western Journal of Communication*, 56, 330–349.
———. (1995). Beyond persuasion: A proposal for an invitational rhetoric. *Communication Monographs*, 62, 1–18.
Frantz, D. (1996, May 30). Elizabeth Dole: Her power as leader of Red Cross. *New York Times*, pp. A1, D20.
Friedan, B. (1963). *The feminine mystique*. New York: Norton.
Friedman, T. L. (1993, May 26). White House retreats on ouster at travel office, reinstating 5. *New York Times*, pp. A1, D20.
From Anita Hill to Capitol Hill. (1992, November 16). *Time*, p. 21.
Gates, H. L. (1993, October 18). Keep your eyes. *Newsweek*, p. 89.
———. (1996, February 26/March 4). Hating Hillary. *New Yorker*, pp. 116–133.
Gearhart, S. (1979). The womanization of rhetoric. *Women's Studies International Quarterly*, 2, 195–201.
Gibbs, N. (1993, February 1). Thumbs down: In the Zoë Baird case, it was Amer-

ican public opinion that forced Clinton to deliver on his repeated promise of a higher moral standard in government. *Time*, pp. 26–29.

———. (1993, July 12). Truth, justice and the Reno way. *Time*, pp. 20–27.

Gigot, P. (1993, May 7). Hillary's choice on civil rights: Back to the future. *Wall Street Journal*, p. A14.

Gilbert, S. M., & Gubar, S. (1979). *The madwoman in the attic: The woman writer and the nineteenth-century imagination*. New Haven: Yale University Press.

Gilligan, C. (1982). *In a different voice: Psychological theory and women's development*. Cambridge: Harvard University Press.

Gilman, S. (1985). *Difference and pathology: Stereotypes of sexuality, race, and madness*. Ithaca: Cornell University Press.

Ginzberg, L. D. (1990). *Women and the work of benevolence: Morality, politics, and class in the nineteenth-century United States*. New Haven: Yale University Press.

Goodman, E. (1995, August 29). Remembering those who hold women back. *Milwaukee Journal Sentinel*, p. A10.

———. (1996, January 21). Attacks on uppityness. *Times Herald Record*, p. 36.

Goodman, W. (1996, January 18). First lady as star of tv talk-show circuit. *New York Times*, p. C19.

Gould, S. J. (1981). *The mismeasure of man*. New York: Norton.

———. (1994, November 28). Curveball. *New Yorker*, pp. 139–150.

Gramsci, A. (1971). *The prison notebooks: Selections*. Ed. Q. Hoare and Geoffrey Nowell Smith (Trans.). New York: International Publishers.

Gray, P. (1992, October 5). Lies, lies, lies. *Time*, pp. 32–38.

Greenberg, D. S. (1993, January 30). Mrs. Clinton tackles health-care reform. *The Lancet*, pp. 295–296.

Griffin, C. L. (1993). Women as communicators: Mary Daly's hagiography as rhetoric. *Communication Monographs, 60*, 158–177.

Gross, T. (1995, January 15). Interview with Hillary Rodham Clinton. *Fresh Air* (National Public Radio).

Guinier, L. (1994, February 27). Who's afraid of Lani Guinier? *New York Times Magazine*, pp. 38–44, 54–55, 66.

———. (1994). *The Tyranny of the majority*. New York: Free Press.

Gurko, M. (1976). *The ladies of Seneca Falls: The birth of the women's rights movement*. New York: Schocken Books.

Haase, C. E. (1909). Ideal education for girls. Registrar of Milwaukee Downer College. Records 1852–1964. Milwaukee Manuscript Collection L. University Archives, Golda Meir Library, University of Wisconsin, Milwaukee. Research Center.

Habermas, J. (1989). *The structural transformation of the public sphere: An inquiry into a category of bourgeois society*. T. Burger (Trans.). Cambridge: MIT Press.

Harding, S. (1986). *The science question in feminism*. Ithaca: Cornell University Press.

Hardy-Short, D. C. (1993). The rhetoric of victimage: Women's movement leaders respond to the defeat of the ERA. In C. Berryman-Fink, D. Ballard-Reisch, & L. H. Newman (Eds.), *Communication and sex-role socialization* (pp. 209–231). New York: Garland Publishing, Inc.

Harrison, C. (1988). *On account of sex: The politics of women's issues, 1945–1968*. Berkeley: University of California Press.

Held, V. (1993). *Feminist morality: Transforming culture, society, and politics*. Chicago: University of Chicago Press.

Herrnstein, R. J., & Murray, C. A. (1994). *The bell curve: Intelligence and class structure in American life*. New York: Free Press.

Hill, A. F. (1995). Marriage and patronage in the empowerment and disempowerment of African American women. In A. F. Hill & E. C. Jordan (Eds.), *Race, gender, and power in America* (pp. 271–291). New York: Oxford University Press.

Hillary's big secret. (1995, October). *Spy* (cover).

hooks, b. (1981). *Ain't I a woman? Black women and feminism*. Boston: South End Press.

———. (1984). *Feminist theory: From margin to center*. Boston: South End Press.

———. (1992). *Black looks: Race and representation*. Boston: South End Press.

House Committee on Education and Labor. (1993, September 29). *Hearings on the president's health care reform proposal* (Vol. 1) (CIS No. 94–H341–11), pp. 4–57 (testimony of Hillary Rodham Clinton).

House Committee on Energy and Commerce. (1993, September 28). *Health care reform* (Part I) (CIS No. 94–H361–16), pp. 5–41 (testimony of Hillary Rodham Clinton).

House Committee on the Judiciary. (1993, April 28). *Events surrounding the Branch Davidian Cult standoff in Waco, Texas*, pp. 12–69.

House Committee on Ways and Means (1993, September 28). *President's health care reform proposals* (CIS No. 94–H781–20), pp. 11–62 (testimony of Hillary Rodham Clinton).

Houston, M. (1992). The politics of difference: Race, class, and women's communication. In L. Rakow (Ed.), *Women making meaning: New feminist directions in communication* (pp. 45–59). New York: Routledge.

Idea woman. (1993, July 14). *New Yorker*, pp. 4, 6.

Ifill, G. (1993, January 24). Clinton's blunt reminder of the mood that elected him. *New York Times*, p. E3.

———. (1993, September 22). Role in health expands Hillary Clinton's power. *New York Times*, p. A24.

In her own defense: Lani Guinier. (1993, June 2). *Nightline* transcript, pp. 1–12.

In her own words: Ruth Bader Ginsburg. (1993, June 15). *New York Times*, p. A24.

An interview with Janet Reno. (April 19, 1993). *Larry King Live*. CNN transcript, pp. 1–16.

Irigaray L. (1985). *This sex which is not one*. Ithaca: Cornell University Press.

———. (1991). *The Irigaray reader*. Cambridge: Basil Blackwell.

Jamieson, K. H. (1988). *Eloquence in an electronic age*. New York: Oxford University Press.

———. (1995). *Beyond the double bind: Women and leadership*. New York: Oxford University Press.

Jehl, D. (1994, December 10). Surgeon General forced to resign by White House. *New York Times*, pp. A1, B30.

Jewell, K. S. (1993). *From mammy to Miss America and beyond: Cultural images and the shaping of U. S. social policy*. New York: Routledge.

Johnston, D. (1993, January 14). Clinton's choice for Justice Dept. hired illegal aliens for household. *New York Times*, pp. A1, A20.

———. (1993, May 1). Reno's popularity rises from ashes of disaster. *New York Times*, p. A9.

———. (1994, January 29). Drift and turmoil in justice department. *New York Times*, p. A6.

Johnston, D., & Labaton, S. (1993, October 26). Doubts on Reno's competence rise in Justice Department. *New York Times*, pp. A1, 18.

Jong, E. (1993, February 10). The mother of all debates: Conspiracy of silence. *New York Times*, p. A23.

Jorgensen-Earp, C. R. (1990). The lady, the whore, and the spinster: The rhetorical use of Victorian images of women. *Western Journal of Speech Communication, 54*, 82–98.

Kahn, K. F. (1993). Gender differences in campaign messages: The political advertisements of men and women candidates for U.S. Senate. *Poltical Research Quarterly, 46*, 481–502.

Kahn, K. F., & Goldenberg, E. N. (1991). Women candidates in the news: An examination of gender differences in U.S. Senate campaign coverage. *Public Opinion Quarterly, 55*, 180–199.

Kaid, L. L., Myers, S. L., Pipps, V., & Hunter, J. (1984). Sex role perceptions and televised political advertising: Comparing male and female candidates. *Women and Politics, 4*, 41–52.

Kaminer, W. (1992, July). Crashing the locker room. *Atlantic Monthly*, pp. 59–70.

Keller, E. F. (1985). *Reflections on gender and science*. New Haven: Yale University Press.

Kelly, M. (1992, September 3). Days after "final" word on draft, Clinton faces renewed questions. *New York Times*, p. A20.

———. (1993, May 23). Saint Hillary. *New York Times Magazine*, pp. 22–25, 63–66.

Kerrison, R. (1993, July 14). Loony Lani is symbolic of Clinton's crazy reign. *New York Post*, p. A18.

Key, M. R. (1975). *Male/Female Language*. Mutuchen, NJ: The Scarecrow Press.

King, J. L. (1990). Justificatory rhetoric for a female political candidate: A case study of Wilma Mankiller. *Women's Studies in Communication, 13*, 21–38.

Klein, E. (1984). *Gender politics: From consciousness to mass politics*. Cambridge: Harvard University Press.

———. (1985). The gender gap: Different issues, different answers. *The Brookings Review, 3*, 33–37.

Kohlberg, L. (1969). State and sequence: The cognitive-developmental approach to socialization. In D. A. Goslin (Ed.), *Handbook of socialization theory and research* (pp. 347–480). Chicago: Rand McNally.

———. (1981). *The philosophy of moral development*. New York: Harper & Row.

———. (1984). *The psychology of moral development*. New York: Harper & Row.

Kramarae, C. (1981). *Women and men speaking: Frameworks for analysis*. Rowley, MA: Newbury House.

Kramarae, C., Schultz, M., & O'Barr, W. (Eds.). (1984). *Language and power*. Beverly Hills, CA: Sage.

Kramarae, C., Thorne, B., & Henley, N. (1978). Perspectives on language and communication. *Signs: Journal of Women in Culture and Society, 5,* 638–651.

Labaton, S. (1993, April 20). Reno sees error in move on cult: Fatigue of agents and failure of talks brought assault. *New York Times,* pp. A1, A21.

———. (1993, July 14). N.A.A.C.P. embraces a nominee abandoned. *New York Times,* p. A12.

———. (1994, January 26). Reno to take over inquiry in slaying in Crown Heights. *New York Times,* pp. A1, B2.

Lacayo, R. (1992, November 2). The outsiders. *Time,* pp. 44–46.

Lakoff, R. (1975). *Language and women's place.* New York: Harper & Row.

The Lani Guinier mess. (1993, June 5). *New York Times,* p. A20.

Larrabee, M. J. (Ed.). (1993). *An ethic of care: Feminist and interdisciplinary perspectives.* New York: Routledge.

Laslett, P. (1983). *The world we have lost,* 3rd ed. London: Methuen.

Laughlin, M. (1993, July). Growing up Reno. *Lear's,* pp. 48–51.

Leff, L. (1993, September/October). From legal scholar to quota queen. *Columbia Journalism Review,* pp. 36–40.

Lehigh, S. (1996, January 27). U.S. no longer needs a first lady. *Times Herald Record,* p. 6 (reprinted from the *Boston Globe*).

Leo, J. (1994, March 14). A second look at Lani Guinier. *U.S. News & World Report,* p. 19.

Lerner, G. (1967). *The Grimké sisters from South Carolina: Pioneers for woman's rights and abolition.* New York: Schocken Books.

———. (1986). *The creation of patriarchy.* New York: Oxford University Press.

Let's get real about feminism: The backlash, the myths, the movement. (1993, September/October). *Ms.,* pp. 34–43.

Letters to the Editor. (1993, January 27). Baird stands for all working mothers. *New York Times,* p. A22.

Lewin, T. (1993, October 3). A feminism that speaks for itself: Hillary Rodham Clinton's performance as promoter of the health care plan offers women an icon with mass-market appeal. *New York Times,* pp. E1, E3.

Lewis, A. (1993, January 25). If it were Mr. Baird. *New York Times,* p. A17.

———. (1993, February 8). It's gender stupid. *New York Times,* p. A17.

———. (1993, June 4). Anatomy of a smear. *New York Times,* p. A31.

———. (1993, September 27). Depriving the nation. *New York Times,* p. A17.

———. (1993, November 22). Where Is Janet Reno? *New York Times,* p. A11.

Lingren, J. R. & Taub, N. (1988). *The law of sex discrimination.* St. Paul, MN: West.

Lisle, L. (1996). *Without child.* New York: Ballantine.

Lont, C. M., & Friedley, S. (Eds.). (1989). *Beyond boundaries: Sex and gender diversity in communication.* Fairfax, VA: George Mason University Press.

Machiavelli, N. (1950). *The prince and other discourses.* New York: Modern Library.

Makeover candidate of the week. (1995, January 23). *Time,* p. 9 (illustration).

Manegold, C. S. (1995, August 19). Female cadet quits the Citadel, citing stress of her legal battle. *New York Times,* p. A1.

Mansbridge, J. J. (1977). *Why we lost the ERA.* Chicago: University of Chicago Press.

Margolies-Mezvinsky, M. (1994). *A woman's place: The freshman women who changed the face of Congress.* New York: Crown Publishers.

Martin, N. (1993, November/December). Clinton's compromises: Who is she? *Mother Jones*, pp. 34–38, 43.
Mayer, J. (1996, January 22). Blind trust. *New Yorker*, pp. 62–70.
McConnell-Ginet, S., Borker, R., & Furman, N. (1980). *Women and language in literature and society*. New York: Praeger.
McCormick, J. (1994, July 11). The year of the smear. *Newsweek*, pp. 18–19.
McCrary Boyd, B. (1995, September/October). Hillary the stealth feminist. *Ms.*, p. 17.
McFetters, D. (1995, October 24). Hillary's next career. *Chicago Tribune*, p. A17.
McMillan, J. R., Clifton, A. K., McGrath, D., & Gale, W. S. (1977). Women's language: Uncertainty or interpersonal sensitivity and emotionality? *Sex Roles*, *3*, 545–559.
McPhail, M. L. (1994). *The rhetoric of racism*. New York: University Press of America.
———. (1995). *Zen in the art of rhetoric: An inquiry into coherence*. Albany: State University of New York Press.
Miller, C., & Swift, K. (1977). *Words and women: New language in new times*. Garden City, NY: Anchor Books.
Millett, K. (1969). *Sexual politics*. New York: Ballantine Books.
Minow, M. (1990). *Making all the difference: Inclusion, exclusion, and American law*. Ithaca: Cornell University Press.
Mitchell, J. (1974). *Psychoanalysis and feminism: Freud, Reich, Laing and women*. New York: Random House.
Montrelay, M. (1977). *L'Ombre et le nom: Sur la feminite*. Paris: Minuit.
Moser, A. J. (1996, February 2). Full disclosure. *New York Times*, p. A13.
Ms. Moseley Braun's majestic moment. (1993, July 24). *New York Times*, p. A18.
Mulac, A., & Lundell, T. L. (1980). Differences in perceptions created by syntactic-semantic productions of male and female speakers. *Communication Monographs*, *47*, 111–118.
Mulac, A., Wiemann, J. M., & Gibson, T. W. (1988). Male/female language differences and effects in same-sex and mixed-sex dyads: The gender-linked language effect. *Communication Monographs*, *55*, 315–335.
My health care plan . . . it's just been watered down! (1994, June 7). *Chicago Tribune*, p. A18 (cartoon).
Neikirk, W. (1995, October 22). The politics of compassion. *Chicago Tribune*, pp. A1, A18.
Nepotism for the nineties. (1993, January 30). *The Economist*, p. 26.
Newman, M. (1994, June 2). Lani Guinier at Hunter: "Silence is not golden." *New York Times*, p. B5.
Nicholson, L. (1993). Women, morality, and history. In M. J. Larrabee (Ed.), *An ethic of care: Feminist and interdisciplinary perspectives* (pp. 87–101). New York: Routledge.
Noddings, N. (1984). *Caring: A feminist approach to ethics and moral education*. Berkeley: University of California Press.
———. (1989). *Women and evil*. Berkeley: University of California Press.
Norton, M. B. (Ed.). (1989). *Major problems in American women's history*. Lexington, MA: D.C. Heath.

Okin, S. M. (1979). *Women in western political thought*. Princeton: Princeton University Press.
Pagels, E. (1976). What becomes of God the mother? Conflicting images of God in early Christianity. *Signs: Journal of Women in Culture and Society, 2*, 293–303.
———. (1977). *The Gnostic gospels*. New York: Random House.
Painter, N. I. (1992). Hill, Thomas, and the use of racial stereotype. In T. Morrison (Ed.), *Race-ing justice, en-gendering power: Essays on Anita Hill, Clarence Thomas, and the construction of social reality* (pp. 200–214). New York: Pantheon Books.
Pateman, C. (1988). *The sexual contract*. Stanford, CA: Stanford University Press.
Pearson, J. C., West, R. L., & Turner, L. H. (1995). *Gender and communication*, 3d ed. Madison, WI: Brown & Benchmark.
Perry, W. G. (1970). *Forms of intellectual and ethical development in the college years*. New York: Holt, Rinehart, & Winston.
———. (1981). Cognitive and ethical growth: The making of meaning. In A. Chickering (Ed.), *The modern American college* (pp. 76–116). San Francisco: Jossey-Bass.
Phillips, J. A. (1984). *Eve: The history of an idea*. San Francisco: Harper & Row.
Piaget, J. (1951). *Plays, dreams, and imitation in children*. C. Gattegno & F. M. Hodgson (Trans.). New York: Norton.
———. (1952). *The language and thought of the child*. New York: Routledge & Kegan Paul. (Originally published in 1932)
———. (1965). *The moral judgment of the child*. Marjorie Gabain (Trans.). New York: Free Press. (Originally published in 1932)
———. (1973). *To understand is to invent*. George-Anne Roberts (Trans.). New York: Grossman.
Plaskow, J. (1990). *Standing against Sanai: Judaism from a feminist perspective*. San Francisco: Harper.
Polanyi, K. (1957). *The great transformation*. Boston: Beacon Press. (Originally published in 1944)
Pollitt, K. (December 28, 1992). Are women morally superior to men? *The Nation*, 799–807.
Porter, E. J. (1991). *Women and moral identity*. North Sydney, Australia: Allen & Unwin.
Press Conference on the Branch Davidians Crisis. (1993, April 19). United States Department of Justice. Miller Reporting Co., Inc.
Procter, D., Aden, R., & Japp, P. (1988). Gender/issue interaction in political identity making: Nebraska's woman vs. woman gubernatorial campaign. *Central States Speech Journal, 39*, 190–203.
Quindlen, A. (1993, January 20). The sins of Zoë Baird. *New York Times*, p. A23.
———. (1993, January 27). Welcome to the club. *New York Times*, p. A23.
———. (1993, February 10). Asking the questions. *New York Times*, p. A23.
———. (1993, June 6). Political illiteracy. *New York Times*, p. E19.
———. (1994, October 12). Hillary at midterm. *New York Times*, p. A23.
Rakow, L. F. (1986). Rethinking gender research in communication. *Journal of Communication, 36*, 11–26.

———. (1992). *Gender on the line: Women, the telephone, and communication life.* Urbana: University of Illinois Press.
Reno, J. (July 24, 1993). Speech before the National Press Club. Washington, DC: Alderson Reporting Co., pp. 1–38.
———. (January 8, 1994). Speech before Association of American Law Schools. Orlando: Zacco & Associates Reporting Service, pp. 1–35.
Resnik, J. (1993, February 10). The mother of all debates: Minor slips, big gains. *New York Times*, p. A23.
Reuther, R. R. (1983). *Sexism and god-talk: Toward a feminist theology.* Boston: Beacon Press.
———. (1985). *Womanguides: Readings toward a feminist theology.* Boston: Beacon Press.
Rhode, D. L. (1989). *Justice and gender: Sex discrimination and the law.* Cambridge: Harvard University Press.
———. (1990). *Theoretical perspectives on sexual difference.* New Haven: Yale University Press.
Rich, A. (1976). *Of woman born: Motherhood as experience and institution.* New York: Norton.
———. (1979). When we dead awaken: Writing as re-vision. In *On lies, secrets, and silence: Selected prose (1966–1978).* New York: Norton.
———. (1984). *The fact of a doorframe: Poems selected and new.* New York: Norton.
Rich, F. (1993, June 13). Whose Hillary? *New York Times Magazine*, p. 70.
———. (1995, January 15). Jo Rodham March. *New York Times*, p. E17.
Rimer, S. (1995, August 21). Nation analyzes and agonizes over Citadel dropout. *New York Times*, p. A8.
Robinson, K. (1993, March 3). Nannygate: The real reason Zoë Baird was nixed: She became the image of the dreaded anti-mother. *Seattle Weekly*, p. 7.
Rohter, L. (1993, February 12). Tough "front-line" warrior. *New York Times*, pp. A1, 22.
Rose, H. (1983). Hand, brain, and heart: A feminist epistemology for the natural sciences. *Signs: Journal of Women in Culture and Society, 9,* 73–90.
Rubin, A. J. (1993, October 2). *Congressional Quarterly Weekly Report*, pp. 2640–2643.
Ruddick, S. (1989). *Maternal thinking.* Boston: Beacon Press.
Rupp, L. J., & Taylor, V. (1987). *Survival in the doldrums: The American women's rights movement.* New York: Oxford University Press.
Russell, D. E. H. (1982). *Rape in marriage.* New York: MacMillan.
Russo, M. (1994). *The female grotesque.* New York: Routledge.
Sachs, A. (1993, June 14). Tailor-made to be used against her. *Time*, pp. 24–25.
Sachs, A., & Wilson, J. H. (1978). *Sexism and the law: A study of male beliefs and legal bias in Britain and the United States.* New York: Free Press.
Said, E. (1978). *Orientalism.* New York: Random House.
———. (1994). *Culture and imperialism.* New York: Vintage.
Saint or sinner? (1996, January 15). *Newsweek* (cover).
Sanday, P. R. (1981). *Female power and male dominance: On the origins of sexual inequality.* Cambridge, England: Cambridge University Press.

Sapir, E. (1970). *Culture, language, & personality: Selected essays*. David G. Mandelbaum (Ed). Berkeley: University of California Press.

Saxonhouse, A. W. (1985). *Women in the history of political thought: Ancient Greece to Machiavelli*. New York: Praeger.

Sayers, J. (1982). *Biological politics: Feminist and anti-feminist perspectives*. New York: Tavistock.

Schmitt, E. (1993, July 2). Congresswoman is target in Navy t-shirt episode. *New York Times*, p. A10.

Schroeder, P. (With A. Camp & R. Lipner). (1989). *Champion of the great American family: A personal and political book*. New York: Random House.

Schutz, A., & Luckmann, T. (1973). *The structures of the life-world*. R. M. Zaner & H. T. Engelhardt, Jr. (Trans.). Evanston, IL: Northwestern University Press.

Schutlz, K., Briere, J., & Sandler, L. (1984). The use and development of sex-typed language. *Psychology of Women Quarterly*, 8, 327–336.

Scott, A. F. (1970). *The southern lady: From pedestal to politics, 1830–1930*. Chicago: University of Chicago Press.

Seelye, K. Q. (1995, January 19). Gingrich's "piggies" poked. *New York Times*, p. A20.

———. (1996, January 16). Mrs. Dole to resume career even if she is the First Lady. *New York Times*, pp. A1, B7.

———. (1996, March 1). Republican debate reveals rift on abortion. *New York Times*, pp. A1, 22.

Senate Committee on Finance. (1993, September 30). *President's health care plan* (CIS No. 94–S361–14), pp. 3–46 (testimony of Hillary Rodham Clinton).

Senate Committee on Labor and Human Resources. (1993, September 29). *Health Security Act of 1993* (Part I) (CIS no. 94–S541–3), pp. 4–49 (testimony of Hillary Rodham Clinton).

Shah, H., & Thornton, M. C. (1994). Racial ideology in U.S. mainstream news magazine coverage of Black-Latino interaction, 1980–1992. *Critical Studies in Mass Communication*, 11, 141–161.

Shapiro, R. Y., & Mahajan, H. (1986). Gender differences in policy preferences: A summary of trends from the 1960s to the 1980s. *Public Opinion Quarterly*, 50, 42–61.

Shuter, R., & Turner, L. H. (1992, May). African American and European American women in the workplace: Perceptions of conflict communication. Paper presented at the International Communication Association Convention, Miami, FL.

Sjoo, M., & Mor, B. (1987). *The great cosmic mother: Re-discovering the religion of the earth*. New York: Harper & Row.

Smart, B. (1986). The politics of truth and the problem of hegemony. In C. C. Hoy (Ed.), *Foucault: A critical reader* (pp. 157–173). Oxford: Basil Blackwell.

Smolowe, J. (1992, May 4). Politics: The feminist machine. *Time*, p. 34.

Spelman, E. V. (1983). Aristotle and politization of the soul. In S. Harding & M. B. Hintikka (Eds.), *Discovering reality: Feminist perspectives on epistemology, metaphysics, methodology, and philosophy of science* (pp. 17–30). Boston: D. Reidel.

———. (1988). *Inessential woman: Problems of exclusion in feminist thought*. Boston: Beacon Press.

Spencer, H. (1852). A theory of population deduced from the general law of animal fertility. *Westminster Review, 57,* 468–501.
———. (1873). Psychology of the sexes. *Popular Science Monthly, 4,* 30–38.
———. (1876). *The principles of sociology.* New York: Appleton.
Spender, D. (1980). *Man made language.* Boston: Routledge & Kegan Paul.
———. (1989). *The writing or the sex? Or why you don't need to read women's writing to know it's no good.* Elmsford, NY: Pergamon Press.
Spitzack, C., & Carter, K. (1987). Women in communication studies: A typology for revision. *Quarterly Journal of Speech, 73,* 401–423.
Stanton, E. C., Anthony, S. B., & Gage, M. J. (1887). *History of woman suffrage,* I, 1848–1861. Rochester, NY: Charles Mann.
Sterk, H. M. (1995, November). The situation of rhetoric: Are women (and men) excluded from the frame? Paper presented at the Speech Communication Association Convention, San Antonio, TX.
Sterk, H. M., & Turner, L. H. (1994). Gender, community, and communication. In L. H. Turner & H. M. Sterk (Eds.), *Differences that make a difference: Examining the assumptions in gender research* (pp. 213–221). Westport, CT: Bergin & Garvey.
———. (forthcoming 1996). Anthony's silence: An examination of the intersection of gender and race in *Designing Women.* In P. Siegel (Ed.), *Outsiders looking in: A communication perspective on the Hill/Thomas hearings.* Cresskill, NJ: Hampton Press.
Stewart, S. (1984). *On longing: Narratives of the miniature, the gigantic, the souvenir, the collection.* Baltimore: Johns Hopkins University Press.
Stiehm, J. H. (1983). The unit of political analysis: Our Aristotelian hangover. In S. Harding & M. B. Hintikka (Eds.), *Discovering reality: Feminist perspectives on epistemology, metaphysics, methodology, and philosophy of science* (pp. 31–43). Boston: D. Reidel.
Sullivan, P. A. (1989). The 1984 vice-presidential debate: A case study of female and male framing in political campaigns. *Communication Quarterly, 37,* 329–343.
———. (1993). Women's discourse and political communication: A case study of Congressperson Patricia Schroeder. *Western Journal of Communication, 57,* 530–545.
Sullivan, P. A., & Goldzwig, S. R. (1995). A relational approach to moral decision-making: The majority opinion in *Planned Parenthood v. Casey. Quarterly Journal of Speech, 81,* 167–180.
———. (forthcoming 1996). Women's reality and the untold story: *Designing Women* and the revisioning of the Thomas/Hill hearings. In P. Siegel (Ed.), *Outsiders looking in: A communication perspective on the Hill/Thomas hearings.* Cresskill, NJ: Hampton Press.
Sullivan, P. A., & Levin, C. (1995). Women and political communication: From the margins to the center. In C. Levin & P. A. Sullivan (Eds.), *Political rhetoric, power, and Renaissance women* (pp. 275–282). Albany: State University of New York Press.
Swanson, D. L., & Nimmo, D. (Eds.). (1990). *New directions in political communication: A resource book.* Newbury Park, CA: Sage.

Terman, L. M., & Miles, C. C. (1936). *Sex and personality: Studies in masculinity and femininity.* New York: McGraw-Hill.
Toner, R. (1996, February 9). Candidates weigh cost of office to families. *New York Times*, p. A24.
Tonn, M. B. (1992). Effecting labor reform through stories: The narrative rhetorical style of Mary Harris "Mother Jones." In L. A. M. Perry, L. H. Turner, & H. M. Sterk (Eds.), *Constructing and reconstructing gender: Examining the links among communication, language, and gender* (pp. 283–293). Albany: State University of New York Press.
———. (1996). Militant motherhood: Labor's Mary Harris "Mother" Jones. *Quarterly Journal of Speech, 82,* 1–21.
Transcript of 2nd TV debate between Bush, Clinton, and Perot. (1992, October 17). *New York Times,* pp. A10–13.
Transcript of president's announcement of Ruth Bader Ginsburg's nomination and Justice Ginsburg's remarks. (1993, June 15). *New York Times,* p. A24.
Transcript of Philadelphia debate between Bush and Ferraro. (1984, October 12). *New York Times,* pp. B4–6.
Transcript of talk with Ruth Bader Ginsburg—life and the court. (1994, January 7). *New York Times,* p. A23.
Trent, J. S., & Sabourin, T. C. (1993). When the candidate is a woman: The content and form of televised negative advertising. In C. Berryman-Fink, D. Ballard-Reisch, & L. H. Newman (Eds.), *Communication and sex-role socialization* (pp. 233–268). New York: Garland Publishing, Inc.
Tronto, J. C. (1987). Beyond gender differences to a theory of care. *Signs, 12,* 644–663.
———. (1991). Changing goals and changing strategies: Varieties of women's political activities (Review Essay). *Feminist Studies, 17,* 85–104.
———. (1993). *Moral boundaries: A political argument for an ethic of care.* New York: Routledge.
Unger, R. (1975). *Knowledge and politics.* New York: Free Press.
U.S. Department of Justice. Media Conference on the Waco Report (October 8, 1993), pp. 1–51.
Vickers, J. (Ed.). (1987). *Getting things done: Women's views of their involvement in political life.* Ottawa, ON: Canadian Research Institute for the Advancement of Women.
A Vietnam Veterans Day (1992, November 11). *New York Times,* p. A24.
Waco: What went wrong. (April 19, 1993). *Nightline (with Ted Koppel).* ABC News transcript, pp. 1–16.
Walker, B. G. (1983). *The women's encyclopedia of myths and secrets.* San Francisco: Harper & Row.
Wallis, C. (1993, February 22). The lessons of Nannygate. *Time,* p. 76.
Walters, B. (1996, January 12). Interview with Hillary Rodham Clinton. *20/20.*
Watters, K. B. (1994). Visionary language: The voice of Mary Robinson. In L. H. Turner & H. M. Sterk (Eds.), *Differences that make a difference: Examining the assumptions in gender research* (pp. 195–202). Westport, CT: Bergin & Garvey.
Weaver, W. W., Jr. (1987, September 29). Speech: Pat Schroeder will not seek nomination. *New York Times,* p. 1A.

Welter, B. (1966). The cult of true womanhood: 1820–1860. *American Quarterly*, *18*, 151–74.

———. (1976). *Dimity convictions: The American woman in the nineteenth century*. Athens: Ohio University Press.

Whorf, B. L. (1976). *Language, thought, and reality: Selected writings of Benjamin Lee Whorf*. J. B. Carrol (Ed.). Cambridge: MIT Press.

Will, G. F. (1993, June 14). Sympathy for Guinier. *Newsweek*, p. 78.

Williams, L. (1993, November 4). Relatively few taxpayers are jolted by the nanny scandal. *New York Times*, p. C8.

Williams, P. J. (1991). *The alchemy of race and rights: The diary of a law professor*. Cambridge: Harvard University Press.

———. (1995). *The rooster's egg: On the persistence of prejudice*. Cambridge: Harvard University Press.

Wills, G. (1992, October 22). A doll's house? *New York Review of Books*, pp. 6–10.

Wilson, E. O. (1975). *On human nature*. Cambridge: Harvard University Press.

Wines, M. (1993, October 21). Reno chastises TV executives over violence. *New York Times*, pp. A1, B16.

Wirls, D. (1986). Reinterpreting the gender gap. *Public Opinion Quarterly, 50*, 316–330.

Wollstonecraft, M. (1978). *Vindication of the rights of woman*. M. Kramnick (Ed.). New York: Penguin. (Originally published in 1792)

Wood, J. T. (1992). Gender and moral voice: Moving from women's nature to standpoint epistemology. *Women's Studies in Communication, 15*, 1–24.

———. (1994). *Who cares? Women, care, and culture*. Carbondale: Southern Illinois University Press.

Word for word: A talk with Ginsburg on life and the court. (1994, January 7). *New York Times*, p. A23.

Zarefsky, D. (1995, November). The roots of American community. Transcript of a speech delivered as the Carroll C. Arnold Distinguished Lecture at the annual convention of the Speech Communication Association, San Antonio, TX.

Index

Addelson, Kathryn Pyne, 35, 37–38, 76, 107
Aden, Roger, 21
Albright, Madeleine, 96
Aldridge, Henry, 14
Alexander, Adele Logan, 64
Amos 'n' Andy, 60, 67n5
Androcentrism. *See* Bem, Sandra Lipsitz
Anita Hill–Clarence Thomas Hearings, 18, 38, 39, 42, 54–55, 59
Antistalking legislation, xviii
Anzaldúa, Gloria, 117
Aristotle, 1–2, 5, 31, 35, 50n5, 50–51n6
Armey, Dick, 78

Baird, Zoë, 18, 95–96, 110n1
Baker, Josephine, 59
Barton, Joe, 78
Bateson, Gregory, 11
Belenky, Mary Field, 40, 51–52n11, 79; and "separate knowing," 40, 51–52n11, 79, 91n6
The Bell Curve, 27n17
Bem, Sandra Lipsitz, xviii, xix, xxii; and ancient Greek philosophy, 5; biological essentialism, 12–16, 27 n16, 31, 32, 34, 57, 70, 73, 89, 98, 114, 117; and the connection between physiological and psychological attitudes, 7–8; and discrimination against African Americans, 12–13; and Enlightenment thought, 6; and gender schematicity, 8–9; and Judeo-Christian tradition, 4–5; lens of androcentrism, 3–7; lens of gender polarization, 7–12; lenses of gender, 2–3; and psychology, 6; and roots of biological essentialism, 13, 29
Bernstein, Richard, 88
Binary thinking, 115
Biographical articulations, 24–25n3
Biological essentialism. *See* Bem, Sandra Lipsitz
Blankenship, Jane, 23
Bleir, Ruth, 14, 16
Bolick, Clint, and critical race theory, 58, 59, 67n3
Bostdorff, Denise, 23
Boxer, Barbara, xviii
Boyd, Blanche McCrary, 71–72
Boyer, Peter, 98
Bradley, Bill, 79
Brake, Deborah L., 10
Brawley, Tawana, 59

Brown, Antoinette, 43
Browner, Carol, 18, 96
Buchanan, Patrick, 122
Burros, Marian, 70, 85
Bush, Barbara, 11
Bush, George W., 4, 10, 23, 47, 120–121
Buzzanell, Patrice, 75
Bystydzienski, Jill, 17, 18, 19

Campbell, Ben Nighthorse, 119, 126n2
Campbell, Karlyn Kohrs, 22, 23, 27n19, 42–43, 45, 47, 52nn12, 13, 14, 126n3
Care, xxi, 3, 30–31, 49–50, 92n10, 95, 117, 120, 121
Carlson, Margaret, 12
Carroll, Susan J., 19, 20
CAWP (Center for the American Woman and Politics), 19, 20
Cherokee culture, 48
Chesler, Phyllis, 82
Christ, Carol P., 40
Cixous, Hélène, 6
Clarke, Edward, 13
Clinchy, Blythe McVicker, and "separate knowing," 40, 79, 91
Clinton, Chelsea, 85
Clinton, Hillary Rodham, xx, 11, 12, 96, 107, 108, 114, 115, 116, 118, 120, 123, 125; accommodating and confronting, 74–87; case study, 69–93; dangers of superwoman myth, 85; dual rhetorical approaches, 75; hair styles and appearance, 69, 84, 123; "Hillary's Hair" web site, 123; *It Takes a Village and Other Lessons Children Teach Us*, 81, 88, 92n7; liberal feminism, 69, 72, 76, 92n7; limitations of accommodating and confronting rhetoric, 82–87; media coverage, 70–74, 81–87, 89–90; and power, 74, 92; responses to as chair of task force to reform health care, 73–74; rhetorical stunting, 86–87, 88, 116; as saint/sinner, 72, 85, 86, 87; smiling and laughing, 81, 82, 92n9; *Spy* magazine cover, 15, 16; testimony before Congress on health care reform, 74–81; Whitewater, 15, 48, 81; Whitewater Press Conference, 84–85, 124; "woman's touch," 80–81; use of familial tropes, 91n3
Clinton, William Jefferson, xx, 18, 19, 23; and health care task force, 73; and Jocelyn Elders, 46–47; and Lani Guinier, 53, 56, 58, 61, 64, 65–66; and nomination of Janet Reno, 95–96; press reactions to lack of military service, 26; relationship with Hillary Rodham Clinton, 120; and response to fire at Branch Davidian complex in Waco, Texas, 99; re-visioning politics (town meeting debate, 1992), 120–121
Coleman, William, 62, 67n6
Coles, Robert, 39
Collins, Patricia Hill, 64
Conover, Pamela Johnston, 21
Contextual moral theories, 31
Conyers, John, 102, 110
Coontz, Stephanie, 32, 107
Crenshaw, Kimberle, 38, 39

Daly, Mary: confronter, 47, 76; "methodolatry," 39–40, 63; reclaiming the term "spinster," 111n4
Darwin, Charles, 13
Davis, Angela, 47, 76
de Lauretis, Teresa, 117
Designing Women, 67n1
Discrimination against women, xix, 2, 91–92n7
Discursive struggles, 123–124. *See also* Fiske, John
Dodson, Deborah, 20
Dole, Elizabeth Hanford, 93n13
Donovan, Josephine, and liberal feminist thought, 90
Double binds, 10, 11–12, 27n15, 42, 47, 48, 69, 72, 87
Dow, Bonnie, 23, 52n15
Dowd, Maureen, 39, 75, 79, 80, 82, 84, 85, 121
Dworkin, Andrea, 47

Earhart, Amelia, 86
Ehrenreich, Barbara, 113
Eisler, Riane, xvii, xviii, 5
Elders, Dr. Jocelyn, 18, 46–47
Ellerbee, Linda, 85
Elshtain, Jean Bethke, 2, 35–36, 40–41, 51nn7, 8
Empowerment, 17–18, 19, 24n2
en choque, 117, 118
English, Karan, 4
Enlightenment, 6, 25n7, 33, 38, 79, 90n1, 92n7, 107, 115; Scottish, 50n5, 51n10. *See also* Tronto, Joan C.
Entman, Robert, 122
Eve, 4, 43, 64

Family, changing definitions of, 32, 107
Faulkner, Shannon, 9, 10, 11, 26n12
Fawell, Harris W., 78
Feinstein, Dianne, xviii, 23
Feminism, 2–3, 14, 24n1, 30, 38; essentialism, 50n3; liberal feminism, 69, 90n1, 92n7, 93n13. *See also* Donovan, Josephine
Ferraro, Geraldine, vice-presidential candidacy of, 4, 10, 11, 23, 24, 47
Fish, Hamilton, 100
Fisher, Berenice, 49–50
Fiske, John, 122–124
Flax, Jane, 38, 65, 79; innocent knowledge, 38, 51n10, 65, 79, 82, 92n7, 107, 115
Foley, Thomas, 125
Foss, Karen A., xxii
Foss, Sonja K., xxii, 17, 30
Frank, Barney, 88–89
Freaks, 86, 92–93n12, 108, 115

Gates, Henry Louis, 69, 86
Gender gap, 20, 21
Gender polarization. *See* Bem, Sandra Lipsitz
Gender schematicity. *See* Bem, Sandra Lipsitz
Gigot, Paul, 58
Gilbert, Sandra, *The Madwoman in the Attic*, 91n5

Gilligan, Carol, 26n10, 31
Gilman, Sander, 27n16
Gingrich, Newt, 15, 16
Ginsburg, Ruth Bader, 49, 122
Ginzberg, Lori D., 36, 51n9
Goldberger, Nancy Rule, and "separate knowing," 40, 79, 91
Goldzwig, Steven R., 30
Goodman, Ellen, 15, 89–90, 92n9
Gould, Stephen Jay, 14, 27n17, 29
Gramsci, Antonio, and civil society, 56, 67n2
Greenberg, Stan, 80
Griffin, Cindy, 3, 17, 30
Grimké, Angelina, 43
Grimké, Sarah, 43
Gross, Terry, 81–82
Gubar, Susan, *The Madwoman in the Attic*, 91n5
Guinier, Lani, xx, 18, 46, 97, 108, 114, 115, 116, 118, 123, 124, 125; case study, 53–68; and denial, 65–66; Hunter College Commencement Address, 63; and intersectionality, 54; and media misrepresentations, 53–55, 58–60, 62–63; moral point of view boundary, 61–63; morality and politics boundary, 57–61; N.A.A.C.P. conference speech, 55; *Nightline* appearance, 62, 63, 65; public and private boundary, 63–64; stereotypical images of African American women, 55, 59–61, 64; *Tyranny of the Majority*, 57, 63, 65, 66

Haase, Clara, 9, 34, 42
Heflin, Howell, 119
Heidegger, Martin, 50
Held, Virginia, 35, 37, 41, 80
Helms, Jesse, 119
Hesiod, 5
Hobbes, Thomas, 41
Hollingworth, Leta Stetter, 8
hooks, bell, 24n1, 47, 68n7
Houston, Marsha, 60
Hume, David, 50n5
Hunter, Jan, 21

Hutcheson, Frances, 50n5
Hutchinson, Anne, 44
Hysteria/hysterics, 44, 115

Images of African American women. *See* Jewell, K. Sue
Intersectionality, 60, 63, 67n1, 115, 118
It Takes a Village and Other Lessons Children Teach Us, 81, 88, 92n9

Jackson, Jesse, 97
Jamieson, Kathleen Hall, 11, 12, 20, 27n15, 42, 44, 69, 126n3
Japp, Phyllis, 21
Jerry, E. Claire, 27n19, 42–43, 45, 47, 52nn12, 13, 14
Jewell, K. Sue: cultural depictions of African American women (Mammy, Aunt Jemima, Sapphire, Jezebel), 60–61; and media depictions of African American women in the 1980s, 60–61
Jezebel, 64
Johnson, Samuel, 77
Jones, Mary Harris ("Mother"), 22

Kahn, Kim Fridkin, 22
Kaid, Lynda Lee, 21
Kang, Jong Guen, 23
Kant, Immanuel, 32, 37, 50n5
Kassebaum, Nancy, 19, 27n19, 47
Keller, Evelyn Fox, 14
Kennedy, Jacqueline, 53
Kerrison, Ray, 59
Kevorkian, Dr. Jack, 78
King, Janis L., 48
King, Larry, 96, 103
Kohlberg, Lawrence, 7–8, 26n10, 40
Koop, Dr. C. Everett, 77, 78
Koppel, Ted, 62, 65, 101
Koresh, David, 99, 100

Landers, Ann, 85
Language intensity, 92n8
Laszlo, Erwin, xvii
Leff, Laurel, 58, 67n3
Leo, John, 59

Lewin, Tamar, 82, 89, 91
Lewis, Anthony, 58, 59
Lilith, 64
Limbaugh, Rush, 16
Lisle, Laurie, 111
Little Women, 83
Locke, John, 41
Lott, Trent, 15, 16
Luckmann, Thomas, 24–25n3

Macbeth, Lady, 115
Machiavelli, Niccolò, and theory of politics, 35–36, 41, 46, 48, 51nn7, 8, 76, 78, 90n1, 101, 116
Mandel, Ruth, 20, 75, 93n13
Mankiller, Wilma, 48
Margolies-Mezvinsky, Marjorie, xvii, 4
Marshall, Thurgood, 62
McPhail, Mark Lawrence, and rhetoric of coherence (*Zen in the Art of Rhetoric*), 118, 125–126n1
Media coverage of political women, 22; Hillary Rodham Clinton, 70–72, 73, 84; Lani Guinier, 55; Janet Reno, 107
Medicare/medicaid, 47
la mestiza, 117
Miles, Catharine Cox, 8
Mill, John Stuart, 41
Miller, Casey, 6
Millett, Kate, 4
Minow, Martha, and detached legal reasoning, 38, 39
Monroe, Marilyn, 15
Moral boundaries, xix, 34, 86; Guinier and moral point of view, 61–63; Guinier and morality and politics, 57–61; Guinier and public/private, 63–64; moral point of view, 37–40; morality and politics, 34–36; morality first, 34–35; politics first, 35–36; public/private, 40–45; Reno and moral point of view, 102–103; Reno and morality and politics, 100–102; Reno and public/private, 103–106; re-visioning of, 98, 106. *See also*

Guinier, Lani; Reno, Janet; Tronto, Joan C.
Morrison, Toni, 64
Moseley-Braun, Carol, xviii; Senate speech opposing patent renewal for United Daughters of Confederacy, 118–120, 121
Moser, Anthony, 87
Murphy, Bren Ortega, 75
Myers, Sandra, 21

Nicholson, Linda, 41–42
Nimmo, Dan, 16
Noddings, Nel, 17
NOW (National Organization for Women), 90n1, 91n7

O'Connor, Sandra Day, 89–90
Okin, Susan Moller, androcentrism and ancient Greek thought, 1, 5, 35, 51n6
"Old Maid," 110, 111
"Old symbolic mold" of gender roles, 9, 26n11
O'Leary, Hazel, 18, 96
Orr, Kay, 21

Packard, Mrs. E. P. W., 44
Packwood, Robert, 77
Pagels, Elaine, 7
Pandora, 5, 64
Perot, Ross, 120–121
Phillips, John, 4; androcentrism and the Judeo-Christian tradition (the story of Eve), 4–5
Philosophical standpoint, 52n15
Piaget, Jean, 40
Pipps, Val, 21
Plato, 5, 33
Political advertisements, 21
Political communication, definition of, 16, 17
Political women: definition of, 17, 18; rationale for selection of women for study, 18
Procter, David, 21
Public and private spheres, xviii, xix, 17, 32–34; and bifurcation of sentiments and reason, 32; and engendering of capacities to reason and feel, 32; nineteenth-century U.S. women's benevolence movement, 36; the public and private boundary, 40–45; women and public speaking, 42–45
Public speaking and women. *See* Public and private spheres

Quindlen, Anna, 59, 71–72, 90n2; and bully pulpit, 72, 90–91n2
Quota queen, 55, 58

Rakow, Lana, 17
Rationalist paradigm, 69, 72; and practical wisdom, 78
Reno, Janet, xx, 18, 114, 115, 116, 118, 123, 125; Association of American Law Schools Speech, 101, 104–105; caricatures in *New Yorker*, 108–109, 124; challenge to the moral point of view boundary, 102–103; challenge to the public/private boundary, 103–106; challenges to morality and politics boundary, 100–102; defense of Lani Guinier, 97; ethics, 99; family relationships, 107, 111n3; fire at Branch Davidian complex in Waco, Texas, 96–107, 116; gendered media coverage, 107–110; House Judiciary Committee hearing on the Waco incident, 100–103, 110, 116; media responses to, 96–99; National Press Club Speech, 104, 105–106; press conference on the Branch Davidian crisis, 100, 101, 102, 105; press relationships, 105–106; re-visioning moral boundaries case study, 95–112; U.S. Justice Department media conference on the Waco report, 102, 103, 104
Restak, Richard, 100–101
Reuther, Rosemary Radford: androcentrism and the Judeo-Christian tradition, 5; misogynistic interpretations of sacred texts, 25nn5, 6; stories of Pandora and Eve, 5

Re-visioning political structures, 118–125; role of media, 122–124; role of rhetorical critical approaches, 124–126. *See also* Clinton, William, re-visioning politics; Moseley-Braun, Carol, Senate speech; Reno, Janet, re-visioning moral boundaries
Rich, Adrienne, 1, 4, 49
Rich, Frank, 11, 83, 85
Richards, Ann, 23, 52n15
Riegle, Donald, 80
Roberts, Cokie, 62
Robson, Deborah C., 23
Rose, Hillary, 14
Rose law firm, 81, 87
Rousseau, Jean Jacques, 25n7, 33, 35
Rubin, Alissa J., 74
Ruddick, Sara, 17
Russo, Mary, and the female grotesque and rhetorical stunting, 86–87, 89, 92–93n12, 108, 110, 116

Sabourin, Teresa Chandler, 21
Said, Edward: and democratic ideals, 65, 67n2; sanctioned narratives, 57, 59, 60, 63
Saints/sinners, 114
Sapir, Edward, 6
Schroeder, Patricia, 11, 15, 22, 27n14, 45–46, 113, 114
Schutz, Alfred, 24–25n3
Shah, Hemant, 122
Shalala, Donna, 96
Silence, 64, 115
Simpson, Carole, 120
Simpson, O. J., 39
Smeal, Eleanor, 89
Smith, Adam, 50n5
Social construction, 24n3
Sociobiology, 13–14; critique of, 14
Solarz, Stephen, 124
Spelman, Elizabeth V., 1, 50–51n6
Spencer, Herbert, 13
Spender, Dale, 5, 6, 7, 18
"Spinster," 111
Spy magazine, 15, 16. *See also* Clinton, Hillary Rodham
Stanford-Binet IQ test, 8

Stanton, Elizabeth Cady, *The Women's Bible*, 44
Stearns, Clifford, 77
Steinem, Gloria, 24n1
Sterilization and immigration laws (United States), 12, 13
Sterk, Helen M., xxi, 3, 30
Stewart, Susan, 86
Stiehm, Judith Hicks, 1
Stone, Lucy, 43
Strategies for political women, xix, xx; confronting and accommodating, 47–48; denying, 46–47; re-visioning, 48–50. *See also* Clinton, Hillary Rodham; Guinier, Lani; Reno, Janet
Swanson, David, 16
Swift, Kate, 6

Tailhook, 114
Tarule, Jill Mattuck, and "separate knowing," 40, 79
Thornton, Michael C., 122
Tonn, Mary Boor, 22, 23, 52n15
Trent, Judith S., 21
Tronto, Joan C., xviii, xix, xx, xxii, 20, 48, 49–50, 56, 57, 69, 73, 75, 88, 98, 99, 106, 114, 117, 118, 121; and Kantian and utilitarian philosophies, 37; moral boundaries and Western conceptions of morality, 29–34; moral point of view boundary, 37–40; morality and care, 30, 31; morality and politics boundary, 34–37; morality first, 34–35; politics first, 35–36; public and private boundary, 40–45; re-visioning moral decision-making, 31; social and political transformations in eighteenth and nineteenth centuries, 31–32; women's morality, 30

Unger, Roberto, 41–42
United Daughters of the Confederacy, 119
Universalistic moral theories: categorical imperative, 31, 37, 40; utilitarian, 37

Vaid, Urvashi, 24n1
Velazquez, Nydia, 27n18, 124–125
Virginia Military Institute, 3–4, 10
Virginia Women's Institute, 9–10
Voting Rights Act, 68n6

Walker, Barbara, 25n5, 81
Walters, Barbara, 81
Whorf, Benjamin, 6
Will, George, 63
Williams, Patricia J., 14–15, 41, 47, 53, 58, 59, 64, 66, 76
Williams, Vanessa, 61
Wilson, Edward O., 13–14
Witches, 44, 71, 72; and assaultive speech, 44, 115
Wolf, Naomi, 24n1
Wollstonecraft, Mary (*Vindication of the Rights of Woman*), 33, 90n1
Women: as characters in media coverage, 108–110, 123; in the legal profession, 91n7
Women's benevolence movement, 36, 51n9. *See also* Ginzberg, Lori D.; Public/private spheres
Women's morality, 30
Women's rhetorical style, 22–24, 126; characteristics of, 23
Wood, Julia T., xxi, 3, 17, 30, 31, 50n3, 95
Wood, Kimba, 18, 95, 101n1
Woolley, Helen Thompson, 8

Year of the smear (Campaign 1994), 113, 114
Year of the woman (Campaign 1992), 18, 19, 113, 114, 118

Zarefsky, David, xxi

About the Authors

PATRICIA A. SULLIVAN is Associate Professor of Communication at the State University of New York at New Paltz. She is coeditor of *Political Rhetoric, Power, and Renaissance Women* (1995).

LYNN H. TURNER is Associate Professor of Communication at Marquette University in Milwaukee. She is coeditor of *Differences That Make a Difference* (Bergin & Garvey, 1994).

HQ 1391.U5 S85 1996